ALGERIA

PROFILES • NATIONS OF THE
CONTEMPORARY MIDDLE EAST
Bernard Reich and David E. Long,
Series Editors

Algeria: The Revolution Institutionalized, John P. Entelis

Israel: Land of Tradition and Conflict, Bernard Reich

The Republic of Lebanon: Nation in Jeopardy, David C. Gordon

Jordan: Crossroads of Middle Eastern Events, Peter Gubser

South Yemen: A Marxist Republic in Arabia, Robert W. Stookey

Syria: Modern State in an Ancient Land, John F. Devlin

Turkey: Coping with Crisis, George S. Harris

The Sudan: Unity and Diversity in a Multicultural State,
John Obert Voll and Sarah Potts Voll

Libya: Qadhafi and the Green Revolution, Lillian Craig Harris

The United Arab Emirates: A Venture in Unity,
Malcolm C. Peck

Iran: At War with History, John W. Limbert

Afghanistan: Marx, Mullah, and Mujahid, Ralph H. Magnus

Bahrain: The Modernization of Autocracy, Fred Lawson

Oman, Calvin H. Allen, Jr.

Tunisia, Kenneth J. Perkins

North Yemen, Manfred W. Wenner

ABOUT THE BOOK AND AUTHOR

After 124 years of intensive colonial rule and nearly 8 years of revolutionary warfare, Algeria emerged in a state of total economic decrepitude and political backwardness. Yet in the two decades since regaining its national independence in 1962, the country has achieved a remarkable degree of political stability and economic growth. Fueled by extensive gas and oil reserves, Algeria embarked on a massive industrialization program that has enabled it to reach a level of development placing it among the more advanced of the newly industrializing states of the Southern Hemisphere. Political life has been institutionalized under a presidential system rooted in a single party organization, the armed forces, and a burgeoning technocratic class. This book traces the shape of Algeria's revolutionary experience through an analysis of the country's culture, history, economy, politics, and foreign policy.

In foreign affairs, Algeria continues to maintain a militant diplomatic posture on most issues affecting North-South relations, espousing an ideology of revolutionary socialism and giving moral and material support to Third World movements for national liberation. In its bilateral relations with the Western industrialized world, Algeria pursues pragmatic, businesslike exchanges that give balance and perspective to its otherwise heady ideological pronouncements on a wide range of global issues. Despite increasing domestic problems related to high inflation, unemployment, corruption, and political authoritarianism, Algeria has achieved a level of development that, in combination with its avant-garde stature in world affairs, makes the country one of the most significant actors in international diplomacy, oil politics, North-South and South-South relations, revolutionary social transformation, and global efforts toward the creation of a new international economic order.

John P. Entelis is professor of political science and codirector of the Middle East Studies Program at Fordham University. He has been a senior Fulbright professor at the University of Algiers and the University of Tunis.

A France,
mon amour

ALGERIA

The Revolution
Institutionalized

John P. Entelis

Westview Press • Boulder, Colorado

Croom Helm • London and Sydney

All photographs not otherwise attributed are by Françoise Draux Entelis.
Jacket Photo: A street scene in the Casbah, the old quarter of Algiers (Françoise Draux Entelis)

Published in 1986 in the United States of America by Westview Press, Inc.; Frederick A. Praeger, Publisher; 5500 Central Avenue, Boulder, Colorado 80301

Published in 1986 in Great Britain by Croom Helm Ltd., Provident House, Burrell Row, Beckenham, Kent, BR3 1AT

Library of Congress Cataloging in Publication Data
Entelis, John P. (John Pierre), 1941–
    Algeria: the revolution institutionalized.
    (Profiles. Nations of the contemporary Middle East)
    Bibliography: p.
    Includes index.
    1. Algeria—History—1962–   . I. Title.
II. Series.
DT295.5.E58   1986   965'.05   85-20234
ISBN 0-86531-470-5

British Library Cataloguing in Publication Data
Entelis, John P.
    Algeria: the revolution institutionalized.—
    (Profiles: nations of the contemporary Middle
    East)
    1. Algeria—History—1962–
    I. Title   II. Series
    965'.05   DT295.5
    ISBN 0-7099-0973-X

Printed and bound in the United States of America

10   9   8   7   6   5   4   3   2   1

Contents

Tables and Figures

Illustrations

Algeria

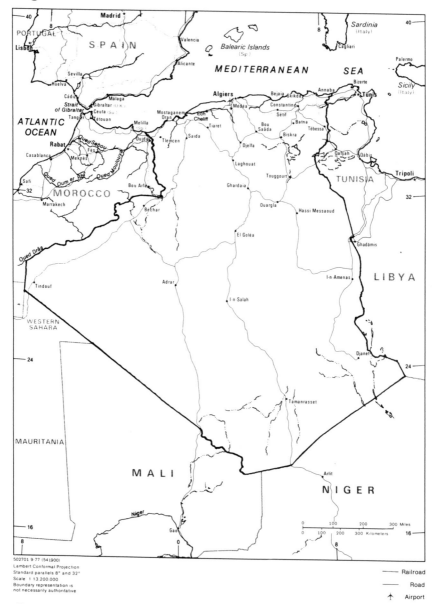

502701 9-77 (541900)
Lambert Conformal Projection
Standard parallels 8° and 32°
Scale 1:13,200,000
Boundary representation is
not necessarily authoritative

———— Railroad

———— Road

↑ Airport

(From John P. Entelis, "Democratic and Popular Republic of Algeria," in David E. Long and Bernard Reich, eds., *The Government and Politics of the Middle East and North Africa* [Boulder, Colo.: Westview Press, 1980]. Used by permission of Westview Press.)

1

Introduction

On November 1, 1984, Algeria celebrated the thirtieth anniversary of the beginning of its revolutionary war of independence against France with a brilliant display of military and economic might that would have amazed observers three decades earlier. When a motley assortment of guerrilla fighters had launched their "revolution," few people in Algiers or Paris even noticed. Yet, by the time the struggle was over, the world had witnessed one of the twentieth century's major military, political, and social events. A hapless array of disorganized rebels were eventually to "defeat" one of the world's major powers and, in so doing, to establish the legitimacy of wars of national liberation for colonial peoples.

When independence was achieved, critics still remained doubtful as to Algeria's ability to run its own ship of state—and with justification. After 124 years of intensive colonial rule and nearly 8 years of revolutionary warfare, Algeria emerged in a state of total economic decrepitude and political backwardness. Yet, in the more than two decades since regaining its national independence in 1962, the country has achieved a remarkable degree of political stability and economic growth. Aided by extensive hydrocarbon reserves, Algeria has embarked on a massive industrialization program that has enabled it to achieve, by the middle 1980s, a level of development that places the country among the more advanced of the newly industrializing states of the Southern sphere. Political life has been institutionalized under a presidential system of government that finds its principal support from the single party organization, the armed forces, and the burgeoning technocratic class.

In foreign affairs Algeria continues to maintain a militant diplomatic posture on most issues affecting North-South relations, espousing an ideology of revolutionary socialism and giving moral and material support to numerous Third World movements of national liberation, including the Palestine Liberation Organization (PLO), the

1

Popular Front for the Liberation of Saguiat el Hamra and Rio de Oro (the POLISARIO guerrilla movement), and its government in exile, the Sahrawi Arab Democratic Republic (SADR), situated in Algiers. In bilateral relations with the Western industrialized world, Algeria pursues pragmatic and businesslike exchanges that give balance and perspective to its otherwise heady ideological pronouncements on a wide range of global issues.

On balance—and despite increasing domestic ills related to high inflation, unemployment, corruption, and political authoritarianism—Algeria has achieved a respectable level of development. In combination with its avant garde stature in world affairs, this achievement makes the country one of the most significant actors in the multiple worlds of Afro-Asian and inter-Arab affairs, international diplomacy, oil politics, North-South and South-South relations, revolutionary social transformation, and the global efforts at creating a new international economic order.

This book traces the institutionalization of Algeria's revolutionary experience through an analysis of the country's history, culture, society, economy, politics, and foreign policy. I hope to capture, both in its broad scope and empirical details, the profundity of the revolutionary struggle as it has had an impact on the Algerian identity and the complexity of the bold experiment at political and social engineering initiated by the country's postindependence leadership. More than most nation-states of the Third World, Algeria has demonstrated a remarkable ability to adjust and adapt, in a relatively nonviolent manner, to changing circumstances both at home and abroad. That it has still managed to maintain a sense of historic purpose consistent with the revolutionary principles articulated thirty years ago is testimony to the authenticity and durability of the Algerian experience.

GEOGRAPHICAL FEATURES AND THEIR EFFECTS

The tenth-largest country in the world, the largest in Africa after the Sudan and Zaire, Algeria extends over almost 2.4 million square kilometers, more than four-fifths of which is desert—part of the immense and arid Sahara. Enormous sand dunes, vast areas of barren rock and gravel plains, and distinctive moonlike plateaus associated with the Hoggar Massif cover virtually the entire southeast portion of the country. Until recent years this expanse of sand desert and arid steppe effectively separated the Arab north from the rest of the African continent. The building of the trans-Saharan highway, which today links Algiers by road to Lagos, Nigeria—asphalted 100 kilometers beyond Tamanrasset, deep in the Algerian Sahara, and awaiting connections to Mali and Niger—and the rapid development of air and other communication systems have effectively bridged what was once viewed as a barrier, a vast sea to be traversed. In addition, petrodollars and the Islamic revival are contributing to the formation of a new, single geopolitical unit known as Trans-Sahara Africa, incorporating the Maghreb, Sahara, Sahel, and the coastal belt from Guinea to Nigeria.

Although much of the country's extensive mineral and hydro-carbon wealth is located in Algeria's desert territories, only about 10 percent of its population is found there. The majority of Algeria's 22 million people live in the northern portion of the country, which constitutes about 12 percent of the total land surface. Mediterranean in climate and vegetation, the lengthy yet narrow coastal area extends more than 1,000 kilometers and is characterized by a varied terrain and fragmented topography. The Atlas Mountain chain stretches across the whole of northwestern Africa (the Maghreb), with the Algerian portion made up of three broad natural regions that run parallel to the Mediterranean coast: the Tell Atlas, the High Plateaus, and the Saharan Atlas. Most of the country's arable land is concentrated in the northern part of the country, between the Mediterranean Sea and the southern slope of the Saharan Atlas Mountains.

Generally speaking, the average annual rainfall on the coast is about 500 millimeters. The amount increases as one moves east from Oran (360 mm.) to Algiers (700 mm.) and Constantine (550 mm.). In the high plateau, the average is about 300 millimeters per year and decreases sharply as one moves farther south. The rains are concentrated in the late fall and winter and are highly variable from one year to another.

In many ways Algeria's distinctive geographical features—lengthy coastline, rugged mountain chains, vast desert areas—have created isolated pockets of self-enclosed topographical and economic units that have not always been easy to overcome, as demonstrated by the distinctive life-styles that have been maintained by such diverse Berber tribes as the Kabyles in Greater and Little Kabylia and the Mozabites located in the Ghardaia region of the Saharan desert. Paradoxically it has been "easier" to "unify" the trans-Saharan zone than to integrate fully the varied regions of internal Algeria. Yet what the roads, transportation networks, and communication systems have failed to achieve completely, large-scale migration to the country's overpopulated northern cities is accomplishing with a vengeance. Each year Algiers, Oran, and Constantine—the country's largest urban centers—become the homes of thousands of former mountain herds-men, desert nomads, and agricultural laborers who arrive in search

Ben Mehidi Larbi Street, a major thoroughfare in downtown Algiers.

of a better life that more often than not eludes them. The urbanization process has accelerated so rapidly in recent years that today Algeria is one of the most urbanized societies in the Arab world (approaching 60 percent), with all the problems that this has created with regard to housing, schooling, health, jobs, and transportation.

POPULATION

Urban Algeria also serves to overcome whatever regional, ethnic, or linguistic differences still exist in the society. In this regard Algeria has been fortunate: Unlike most Third World societies, it is devoid of any serious ethnic or regional cleavages. Virtually all Algerians are Sunni Muslims of the Malikite sect, and almost all are Arabic speaking. Since both Arabs and Berbers are descendants of the same tribal peoples, it is a mistake to think of these two groups as representing rigid and exclusive ethnic blocs. The Berbers, an indigenous population that predates the Islamic conquest of North Africa, number around 4 million or 20 percent of the total Algerian population. Algerian Berbers do not constitute a single group, however. The several distinctive Berber subcultures that exist in the country have little in common with each other, except that their dialects are derived from a common root. The Kabyles are the largest and most important of the four major Berber-speaking groups; they originated in the mountainous area east of Algiers. The other groups are the Shawiyas (in eastern Algeria), the Mozabites, and the Tuareg nomads of the south, deep in the Algerian Sahara. A "Berberist" cultural revival, centered mainly in Kabylia, has developed as a challenge to the Arabization policies currently being pursued by the regime. The disturbances and violence associated with Berberist demands, however, have not been allowed to fractionalize society along ethnic lines.

*   *   *

The book is organized into eight chapters. Chapters 2 and 3 provide a historical review of Algeria from ancient times to the present. Emphasis is placed on the colonial experience, the subsequent decolonization process, and political developments since independence. Chapter 4 concentrates on the way culture and society in contemporary Algeria have been undergoing fundamental change and the disruptive consequences that this is having on the growth of a uniform sense of cultural and personal identity. Particular focus is placed on the multiple roles—maraboutic, official, and populist—that Islam is playing in Algeria today. Chapter 5 analyzes Algeria's political economy of development by looking at two crucial economic sectors: an expanding heavy industry based on hydrocarbon reserves and a failing agriculture that is placing Algeria into serious food deficit in the 1980s. How one sector has been advantaged to the detriment of the other will be examined in some detail. Chapter 6 looks at Algeria's internal politics by analyzing four interrelated components: political culture, political structures, political processes, and political power. Chapter 7 focuses on the three roles of identification, mediation, and leadership that Algeria has assigned for itself as part of its globally oriented diplomacy and foreign-policy behavior. Finally, the conclusion (Chapter 8) provides a summary assessment of Algeria's political and economic performances under the current leader, Chadli Benjedid.

2

The Imprint of History: Antiquity to 1919

Algeria as a distinct political entity is a relatively recent creation, emerging as it has within the last 400 years. The history of its Berber and Arab peoples, however, is of considerably greater antiquity. The original Berber population was subject to different waves of foreign conquest over the centuries. The first external influence was that of Phoenicia and Carthage. Carthaginian power began to dominate the Mediterranean coastline of North Africa, including Algeria, around 1200 B.C.; it lasted nearly 1,000 years. The Romans assumed dominance following the defeat and destruction of Carthage in 146 B.C. The area was controlled by the Roman Empire for more than 500 years before the Romans succumbed to the Vandals. They in turn remained more than a century—from A.D. 429 to 533. Christian power was reasserted for over a hundred years—after the Byzantines ousted the Vandals and took control of North Africa. The Byzantines' defeat came at the hands of the first wave of Arab invaders, who arrived in the region in the mid-seventh century (647) carrying a new and powerful faith—Islam.

What is remarkable about the lengthy pre-Islamic domination of Algeria (and the whole of North Africa, whose early history is inseparable from that of Algeria) is the relatively minor impact it had upon native Berber society. Arab-Muslim influence, however, was to prove expansive and permanent. In the several centuries following Islam's arrival in the Maghreb, practically all the Berbers of Algeria became Muslims, although not all became Arabized. The 132 years of French colonial rule beginning in 1830, despite the intensity and destructiveness of the experience, in no way altered—indeed, in many instances reaffirmed—the profundity of the Islamic-Arab identity.

My discussion of Algeria's past, therefore, will be broken down into seven historical phases: (1) the pre-Islamic era from antiquity to

6

the seventh century A.D.; (2) the arrival of Islam; (3) Ottoman rule and the regency of Algiers, 1518–1830; (4) French conquest and colonization, 1830–1919; (5) nationalist awakening, 1919–1954; (6) the war of national liberation and political independence, 1954–1962; and (7) the postindependence period of Ben Bella, Boumediene, and Benjedid, 1962 to the present.

THE PRE-ISLAMIC ERA: FROM ANTIQUITY TO THE SEVENTH CENTURY A.D.

In historic times the inhabitants of Algeria have lived along the Mediterranean shore, the settled area seldom reaching more than 250 kilometers inland. In the prehistoric era, however, the Sahara was much wetter than now, permitting settlement ten times farther from the sea. In fact, south of the Atlas range dividing the country's coastal zone from today's desert interior, nomadic hunters and herders roamed a vast area of subtropical grassland containing scattered trees and drought-resistant undergrowth, well watered and abounding in game. We have a relatively accurate picture of Algeria's Neolithic culture (from about 6430 B.C.) from the cave drawings and paintings discovered in the Hoggar and Tassili N'Ajjar regions located over 1,500 kilometers south of Algiers. These gracefully drawn cave paintings provide a rich record of a prehistoric African culture that flourished until the region began to dry up as a result of climatic changes after 2000 B.C.

Fragmentary historical evidence suggests that sailors from the island of Crete in the Aegean Sea may have established depots on the Algerian littoral sometime before 2000 B.C. However, Algeria and the Maghreb as a whole enter recorded history only after, and as a result of, the arrival of seafaring tradesmen from Phoenicia (today's Lebanon), who established colonies along the southern shores of the Mediterranean before the twelfth century B.C. Originally intending their colonies as stopping points along the way to the Iberian Peninsula, the Phoenician traders gradually established commercial relations with the native Berber population of the interior and paid them tribute to guarantee their cooperation in the exploitation of raw materials. The Phoenician trading posts set up along Algeria's coast in places such as Cherchell and Hippo (Annaba) and elsewhere along the Maghreb constituted one of the earliest known cases of merchant empire building; the colonization set a pattern for North Africa, which was from then on to be the meeting ground of Asian and European currents contesting its soil.

The city of Carthage, founded in 814 B.C. and located several kilometers northeast of Tunis, the Tunisian capital, emerged as the most important center of this Punic trading empire (Punic refers to the Phoenician dialect of ancient Carthage and is used synonymously with Carthage and the Carthaginians), which had extended its hegemony across much of North Africa by the fifth century B.C. The Carthaginian state included the northern portions of modern Tunisia but extended westward to include the region from Annaba to Constantine in Algeria and eastward to include the Tripolitanian coast of today's Libya. Outside this area Carthage was satisfied to cultivate friendly relations with the Berber chiefs, which included intermarriage between them and the Punic aristocracy. As was fitting for a mercantile state, the political structure of Carthage was an oligarchy of the rich. Public life was controlled by a senate, whose members were drawn from the patrician families and held office for life, and vacancies in it were filled by cooptation.

In the area to the west and south of the Carthaginian territory, several kingdoms of Berber tribes emerged by about the third century B.C., two of which (the Maesulian and the Masaeslian) were located in Numidia, constituting regions of northcentral and northeastern present-day Algeria. The Numidian monarchs, like their counterparts in the neighboring Berber kingdom of Mauritania (in ancient times, an area that is now mostly Morocco rather than contemporary Mauritania), ruled in the shadow of Carthage and later Rome when the latter vanquished the Punic empire.

Probably the most famous Numidian king was Masinissa (ca. 240–148 B.C.), who is considered by classical historians such as Polybius and Cicero as the strongest personality that native North Africa produced in ancient times. He served with the Carthaginians in Spain but later shifted his support to Rome when it defeated Carthage. As a Roman ally, Masinissa was able to unite Numidia under his authority; he established his capital in Cirta, today's Constantine—Algeria's third largest city. Besides being a conqueror, Masinissa was also an agronomist, economist, linguist, religious reformer, and philosopher. His estates, forerunners of Roman latifundia (usually defined as great landed estates with primitive agriculture and labor often in a state of partial servitude), were vast enough to enable him to leave each of his forty-four children 875 hectares of land. To his Berber heritage he added a Punic education and an openness to Greek culture and commerce. Between 200 and 170 B.C. he supplied vast and increasing amounts of grain to the Roman army in Macedonia, while at his Hellenistic palace in Cirta he installed Greek tutors and Greek court musicians. The lasting peace his reign provided did much for Numidia's agricultural prosperity.

After Masinissa's death and the destruction of Carthage in 146 B.C., Masinissa's son Micipsa was able to maintain the kingdom's unity for another three decades. There was dissension, however, among Micipsa's heirs, and Numidia was transformed into a Roman vassal-state. Masinissa's grandson Jugurtha, an outstanding chieftain, in order to revive his grandfather's Berber kingdom, tried to extend his hegemony to his eastern neighbors. This action provoked Roman intervention and a long and exasperating war involving guerrilla tactics, scorched earth, poisoned wells, cattle rustling, ambushes, raids, treachery, and murder. Jugurtha was finally subdued when a rival chieftain, King Bocchus I of Mauritania, betrayed him and received the western third of Numidia as reward. Jugurtha was taken to Rome's dank prison, the Tullianum, and strangled in 105 B.C.

Although Jugurtha was devious and treacherous, he proved himself a match for all but Rome's best generals. In fact, among some Algerians of today this "resistance fighter" is considered the first authentic nationalist hero of their country. Clearly a certain nationalist sentiment lay behind the activities of both Masinissa and Jugurtha, yet the historical evidence is neither sufficiently comprehensive nor objective enough to justify the appellation of Algerian *nationalism* to the second century B.C. Berber kingdom of Numidia.

Rome entrusted Numidian territory to satellite kings until Julius Caesar deposed Juba I, great-great-great-grandson of Masinissa, when Juba, chafing at being a puppet king, tried to annex Roman Africa by allying with Pompey against Caesar in the civil wars in 46 B.C. Caesar joined Juba's kingdom to Proconsular Africa (Tunisia of today), which had become a Roman province after the destruction of Carthage in 146 B.C. Ultimately Numidia and the rest of North Africa were annexed to the Roman Empire, which sought to control only those areas that were economically useful or could be defended without additional manpower. Berber chieftains recruited by Rome acted as frontier policemen, keeping unruly mountain tribes from the farms and towns.

As the breadbasket of the empire, the provinces of the Maghreb were valued for their agricultural exports. Agriculture and forestry, already highly developed by the Carthaginians, were maintained and extended under Rome. In addition, Roman rule left great material monuments (in Algeria, Timgad and Djemila, for example, remain impressive and popular Roman ruins), cities, roads, dams, and country houses. Yet the scope and intensity of Roman influence on native Berber society was uneven. To be sure, the Romans' remarkable

Arch of Lambeze in Roman ruins at Timgad (ancient Thamugadi founded by the Emperor Trajan in A.D. 100) southeast of Batna.

tolerance of Berber religious cults and the Romans' lack of display of racial exclusiveness helped to explain Berber receptivity to Roman civilization. Within the vast, ill-defined territory of Roman North Africa, particularly in the coastal centers of trade and culture, a certain degree of assimilation to Roman ways took place, but in the mountains and deserts of the interior the Berber tribes maintained their independence by frequent revolt.

The Roman toleration of pagan cults and other beliefs of the indigenous people did not extend to Christianity, which was viewed as a serious threat to Roman rule. Rome strove to stem the tide of Christianity through persecution, but this proved ineffective in checking Christianity's progress in Roman Africa—which began in 180 A.D. By the early part of the fourth century Christianity had been adopted as the official religion of the Roman Empire, with North Africa constituting one of the most heavily Christian areas.

Yet schismatic and heretical movements also developed, often as forms of political protest, with the Donatist heresy, which swept through North Africa in the fourth century, exemplifying many of the peculiarities of Maghrebin Christianity. Indeed, the central fact of North African history in the late empire is the rise and fall of the Donatist schism. The split arose out of persecutions between 303 and 305 under Diocletian. Donatus and his followers held, puritanically, that those who had lapsed and handed over the Scriptures to imperial officials had forfeited the right to call themselves Christians. Refusing to recognize the new Catholic bishop of Carthage, they elected Donatus as his rival (in 313). Their adherents centered in southern Numidia. The sense of the movement being native to North Africa gave it strong social, economic, and political-nationalist overtones. Donatism's puritanism was combined with a strong, even morbid attachment to martyrdom; Donatist literature betrayed the attachment to violent abuse, indifference to reason, and the smug self-righteousness of the social revolutionary.

It was against the threat of Donatism to the African church that Saint Augustine (354–430), bishop of Hippo (today's Annaba, Algeria's fourth largest city), directed the sermons and books, including his autobiographical *Confessions*, that merited him recognition as one of the Latin Fathers of the Church. He was born in Thagaste, present-day Souk Ahras (on the frontier with Tunisia), of Romanized Berber parentage. Originally he started to work toward bringing the Donatists under the authority of the Roman church by holding debates with their leaders, but he gradually came to accept coercion as an instrument for leading Donatists into the Catholic faith. Ultimately most North African Christians returned to the fold, although Donatism was finally extirpated only by the Vandal invasion a year before St. Augustine's death. However, the Vandals brought a parallel heresy, Arianism, into ascendancy in Africa.

A nomadic people of Germanic origin, the Vandals crossed the Mediterranean from Spain in 429, seized power, and established a kingdom centered in Carthage. They built a number of coastal garrisons as they moved from west to east with almost no resistance from the peasants. As an isolated warrior caste wishing to exploit the land, the Vandals confined their rule to the most economically profitable areas. Their rule lasted a century and although life went on in Vandal Africa less bleakly than is commonly portrayed (for example, historians now agree that the acts of wanton destruction attributed to the Vandals, which went by the name of "vandalism," were much exaggerated), the alliance of Berber mountaineers and Sahara nomads that the Vandals permitted was destined in the end to doom Roman civilization in North Africa. In the end, and for all their efficient conquest, the Vandals made less impression on the Maghreb than any other foreign conquerors.

In the first half of the sixth century (533) the Vandals, having lost much of their warlike spirit, succumbed to the Byzantines as part of Emperor Justinian's scheme of restoring the unity of the Roman Empire. The Byzantine reconquest included the provinces of Proconsular Africa (Tunisia) and Numidia and established a tenuous hold on the coast as far west as the region of modern Algiers. The rest of Algeria was left under the control of Berber tribes whose traditional independence made them resistant to reassimilation into the imperial system. Although the Byzantines left a legacy of extensive building for both defensive and religious purposes, the century of revived Latin civilization was not one of great prosperity. The feeble Roman renaissance in North Africa flickered out with the arrival of the first Arab raiders from the East in 647.

Both pagan and Christian Roman rule over the Berbers of the Maghreb lasted for nearly eight centuries. During this era the Berbers seemed willing to adopt Roman civilization and the Latin language. As we have seen, Roman North Africa produced an important religious schismatic sect (Donatism) but also became a main center of Catholic orthodoxy. Yet despite the institutions, customs, and language that the Romans had brought with them they left few traces, apart from the ruins of their cities. The last surviving native Christian communities in North Africa disappeared from Bejaia in eastern Algeria and Tlemcen in the country's far west in the eleventh century. When Christianity reappeared in the nineteenth century, it was as an alien religion introduced by Europeans; its impact and durability were insignificant.

THE ARRIVAL OF ISLAM

Islam arrived in the Maghreb within two decades of the death of the prophet Muhammad in 632. Operating from their stronghold in Mecca in the Arabian Peninsula, Arab armies swiftly took over Egypt in 642 and from there struck out across the Western Desert, reaching the outskirts of Tunisia in 647. In 670 they established a permanent base for their operations in Kairouan, on the steppes of central Tunisia. They took Carthage in 698, and by 710 the whole of North Africa had been brought under the rule of the Arabs.

Arab expansion had been undertaken as a means of gaining greater military prestige and booty for the armies. Inspired with zeal for extending the domain of Islam, the Arab armies proved insurmountable to the Byzantine forces who had remained in the area and to the native Berber tribesmen who, nonetheless, put up a fierce resistance. Indeed, it took the Arab invaders over half a century to overcome the stubborn opposition of the Berbers and to complete the conquest of the Maghreb. Initial Berber resistance appeared in the Tlemcen region of western Algeria as well as in the eastern part near Biskra, where the semi-legendary female chieftain, al-Kahina, was killed in fighting. In the rugged surroundings of Algeria's Aurès mountains, Berbers, under the leadership of al-Kahina, had held off Arab invaders for several years before succumbing to their superior military force. (Not surprisingly it was in the same Aurès range that the Algerian revolt against the French began in November 1954.)

Once defeated, however, the Berbers accepted Islam fully and, as history was to show, permanently. Many Islamicized Berbers swelled the ranks of the Arab armies, enabling the latter to cross the Strait of Gibraltar, invade and conquer Spain, and reach wide areas of southern France—until halted by Charles Martel in the famous Battle of Tours, near Poitiers, in 732.

What explains this seeming paradox of a resistant people, so difficult to overcome but who, once suppressed, so readily adopted and adapted the Islamic faith to themselves? The Maghreb's Carthaginian heritage is an important factor. However Hellenic its outward features, the Punic state had been essentially oriental, and many of its customs had taken root in North Africa. Arabic is related to the Hamitic tongue spoken by the Berbers. The invading Arabs were close to the Berbers in other ways as well. Both groups, for example, possessed life-styles based on movement, plunder, and pastoral nomadism. Finally, the Berber tendency to heresy must have made Islam appealing—for so many who had only superficially adopted Christianity the new belief from Arabia must have appeared as a variant of the Catholic faith. In all of this one must not underestimate the ardor with which Islam was communicated and the prestige that attracting new adherents to the Islamic fold brought to its proselytizers.

A common religious bond, however, was unable to maintain the unity of Berbers and Arabs. For the most part Arab rule was dictatorial, with the conquerors setting themselves apart in an urban clique that refused to admit the newly converted to the equality guaranteed by Islam. As a way of breaking away from Arab control, the Berbers, with their characteristic love of independence and impassioned religious temperament, embraced schismatic Muslim sects as enthusiastically as their forefathers had accepted Christian heresies. This explains Berber conversion to Kharijism, an esoteric radical Muslim sect that stressed the equality of all Muslims and taught that the only hierarchy among them was that of the intensity of their faith and the rectitude of their conduct. Believing that authority came only from God, who alone was the lawgiver, Kharijites made the legitimacy of the caliphate dependent on the strict application of the religious law. The heretical beliefs of Kharijism with special appeal to the Berbers were the doctrines that non-Arabs could become caliphs (that is, successors to the Prophet Muhammad as leader of the Islamic community) and that Muslims had the right to depose an unjust imam (in this context, the political and religious head of the Muslim community).

Armed with a new puritanical belief, Berbers across the Maghreb—first in Morocco in 739 and reaching Kairouan in Tunisia in 776—rose in revolt against Arab domination. This insurrection threatened Arab control of the entire area and ushered in nearly half a century of anarchy and civil war. In the wake of this revolt small, unstable, anarchic Berber states based upon Islam or one of its heretical manifestations were established. Most of these theocratic tribal kingdoms had short, troubled histories. Some of them, however, like Tlemcen, which prospered because it straddled the principal trade routes, proved more viable.

In the middle of the eighth century the focal point of Berber Kharijism was transferred from Tlemcen several hundred kilometers due east to Tiaret. This Kharijite state was founded by a group of Persian immigrants called the Rustamids, after their leader Abdul Rahman Ben Rustam. The Rustamid principality was a theocracy built on the native population's support (in the name of Islamic principle) of a foreign religious figure. The Rustamid dynasty extended its rule over most of the central Maghreb and developed a cosmopolitan reputation in which Christians, non-Kharijite Muslims, and adherents of different subsects of Kharijism lived. Ultimately the Rustamids were overrun and massacred by the Fatimids who captured Tahirt, the dynasty's capital situated several miles west of Tiaret, in 909.

Those who managed to escape fled to Ouargla, a Saharan oasis, eventually creating what was to become the center of Ibadite Kharijism in the Mzab region of Saharan Algeria. What has survived of the Rustamid state today is the Ibadites living in the Mzab and a smaller group on the Tunisian island of Djerba, an original center of Ibadite concentration. The 100,000 or so Mozabites of today are clustered around the oasis community of Ghardaia and constitute a fascinating self-enclosed and exclusive community, organized along tribal lines and governed by elders who endorse and enforce a rigorously strict moral code. As a community once active in the trans-Saharan trade, today's Mozabites have become enterprising merchants who dominate, for example, much of the butcher and grocery business in the capital city of Algiers.

The Fatimids or Ismailis were themselves an extremist religious group that had split off from the main body of the Shiites—Islam's

Mozabite holy village of Beni Isguen, located several kilometers southeast of Ghardaia, the principal city of the Mozabites in the northern Sahara.

second principal branch, the Sunnites being the first—and that had arrived in the Maghreb at the end of the ninth century, having fled persecution in their native Syria. The center of Fatimid rule became the Algerian region of Little Kabylia where the Berbers had been converted and from which attacks against the neighboring Sunni Aghlabid dynasty in Tunisia and eastern Algeria were undertaken. With the conquest of Kairouan in 909 the Fatimid dynasty gained control of the central Maghreb, which it ruled in an uneven and disputed manner for more than fifty years. Eventually the Fatamids turned their attention eastward toward Egypt, conquering it in 969 and founding Cairo as their new capital. This departure toward the east led to the gradual disappearance of the Shia doctrine among the Berbers who, as restive and defiant as usual, challenged indirect Fatimid rule. This challenge led to the return of orthodox Sunnism to the region.

In the three hundred years following the initial conquest of the Maghreb by the forces of the Arab-Islamic world, a confused pattern of political rule, social forms, and religious movements emerged. Of lasting importance in this period, however, was the slow but permanent assimilation of Islam by Berber nomads, tribesmen, and city dwellers as they sought to adjust the new faith's various tendencies to the solution of their local problems. What emerged, despite the foreign leadership and the Islamic causes and slogans that were articulated, were the social organization of the Maghreb and a distinct North African personality.

The eleventh century was marked by two important events in the Maghreb. The first occurred around 1050 when the Banu Hilal, a confederation of nomadic Arab tribes that had been dislodged from Egypt, invaded North Africa in large numbers (around 200,000, including families), dramatically altering the face and culture of the region. Not since the original Arab conquest of the area had such a large Arab immigration into the Maghreb taken place. Described by the gifted North African historian, Ibn Khaldun, writing three hundred years later, as an "army of locusts who destroyed everything in their path," the Hilalian nomads severely damaged North Africa's economy. They destroyed towns and impoverished the land, turning once productive farmland into steppes. Politically, bedouin domination created anarchy and confusion throughout much of the greater Maghreb.

Although this invasion, like the first, failed to turn the Berbers of present-day Algeria into Arabs ethnically, it did effectively spread the Arabic language into the countryside, which hitherto had remained profoundly Berber in speech and custom. What was once an urban-centered linguistic and cultural socialization process now extended to the rural and desert areas. In relatively rapid fashion the Berbers of the villages, mountains, and nomadic camps became linguistically Arabized as comprehensively as they had become Islamicized. (Pockets of Berber dialectical insularity remained immune to Arabization influences, however, well into the present century.) Thus the inhabitants of Algeria today, as of the rest of the Maghreb, are more or less Arabized Berbers.

The other consequential event of the eleventh century was the creation of the first of three indigenous empires that during the next four hundred years gave modern Maghrebin history its distinct character and established the groundwork for the formation of what were to become the national states of Morocco, Tunisia, and, less so, Algeria.

The Almoravid Empire (1042–1147) was established by Berber-speaking nomads from the western Sahara and Mauritania. The Almoravids were the first dynasty to unify Morocco, and at one time their rule extended as far as Algiers. They established the historic link between the Maghreb and Muslim Spain that was to last two-and-a-half centuries, bringing enormous benefits to North Africa and extending the life of Muslim Spain. It was also during this period that the Almoravids eliminated all heretical sects and imposed, with a permanent imprint, the Malikite school, a strict, orthodox sect of Islam named after an eighth century religious leader of Medina, Malik Ibn Anas.

The second major indigenous empire to be established was the Almohads (1147–1269), who were the direct successors to the Almoravids. They were sedentary Berber mountaineers of the High Atlas (Morocco) who in the fashion of their predecessors had been impelled by the visionary leadership of a puritanical religious teacher, Ibn Tumart (1076–1130). Probably the most significant political contribution of the Almohads was that they unified the Maghreb under a single home rule from Agadir (on Morocco's southern Atlantic shore) to Tripoli (on Libya's western Mediterranean coast) for the first and only time in history. In the areas of literature and philosophy they had a lasting impact, as attested to by the intellectual originality of such Muslim thinkers as Ibn Tufail and Ibn Rushd (or Averroës, as he is more commonly known in the West).

The capture of Marrakesh (Morocco) in 1269 by Merinid leader Abu Yusuf marked the end of the Almohad Empire and the subsequent emergence of three separate Berber kingdoms: the Hafsids, a branch of the Almohad dynasty founded by one of their lieutenants, in the east (Tunis); the Zayanids or Banu Abdul Wadides in the center (Tlemcen); and the Merinids in the west (Fez). The Zayanids ruled over a society that was essentially tribal, yet urban and civilized life developed in their realm as well. The Zayanid state, like the Merinid and, to a lesser extent, the Hafsid, profited from the skills of Andalusian refugees (Muslims from Spain) in creating the rudiments of an administration and embellishing the capital, Tlemcen, with mosques and schools. During the Zayanid period Tlemcen, the "pearl of the Maghreb," became for the first and only time the capital of an independent state.

The progressive initiative characterizing these separate Berber empires was virtually exhausted by 1500, when things had changed greatly. With the Christian reconquest of Spain complete, it was the Iberian powers that began to intervene in North Africa and to establish coastal enclaves, some founded as early as 1415 when the Portuguese got a foothold in Ceuta (today a Spanish enclave along Morocco's Mediterranean coastline). The Spanish objective was the creation of garrison posts on strategic points on the coast, leaving the interior to be held by indigenous rulers. During the first decade of the sixteenth century the Spaniards occupied most of the posts they coveted on the Maghrebin coast. In Algeria, Mers al-Kebir was captured in 1505,

Veiled women in the traditional city of Tlemcen in western Algeria. Once the capital of the Zayanids, this historic city retains much of the charm, architectural elegance, and cultural traditions that reflect its Moorish heritage.

Oran in 1509, and Bougie (Bejaia) in 1510; Algiers, at that time a small port of little importance except as a center for piracy, was reduced to submission in the same year. Other Algerian ports, notably Tenès, Dellys, Cherchell, and Mostaganem, agreed to pay tribute to Spain and to abandon corsair activity in order to avoid a similar fate.

Eventually Spanish attention was turned elsewhere, but the European offensive in central North Africa was not reversed until the middle of the sixteenth century. At that time the Ottomans (the successors of the Muslim empire centered in Istanbul, Turkey) established their rule in North Africa as a result of the activities of Maghrebi pirates in the Mediterranean and the increasing religious fervor among the Muslims caused by the Spanish presence.

OTTOMAN RULE AND THE REGENCY OF ALGIERS, 1518–1830

Ottoman intervention in North Africa came about indirectly but was to last for three hundred years. In the process it provided Algeria with its recognizable political configuration, which subsequent European colonialism was to catalyze into the Algerian national idea.

The architects of Ottoman rule in Algeria were two searoving Muslim corsairs originally from the eastern Mediterranean, Aruj and Khair al-Din Barbarossa. These brothers had been invited by the maritime principality of Algiers to dislodge the Spaniards who were exacting a severe annual tribute on the city and interfering with its commerce. Aruj took control of Algiers, which became both a base of operations for the piracy that was to become the principal occupation of this port city and the takeoff point for conquests into the country's interior. The subsequent capture of other places on the littoral and Tlemcen in the hinterland led to Aruj's being proclaimed sultan. Through ruthless subjugation of the Algerine municipal oligarchy Aruj became master of Algiers. In the process he established the pattern whereby the Turks ruled and the rest of the population accepted their superiority without overt challenge or question.

Following the death of his older brother in 1518, Khair al-Din assumed command of Algiers. In order to consolidate his position still threatened by the Spaniards and the restless and fickle citizenry of Algiers, the younger Barbarossa offered to become a vassal of the Ottoman state by placing all the territories that he controlled under the protection of the Ottoman sultan, Selim I. Pointing out the advantages of Algiers as a Muslim forward base for the struggle against the infidel, Khair al-Din's emissary to the Sublime Port (Istanbul) asked Selim for direct assistance. In response the sultan conferred on Barbarossa the title of *pasha beylerbey* ("prince of princes," but referring specifically to him) and provided him with artillery as well as an army of 6,000 men with which to fight the Spaniards.

Thus strengthened, Khair al-Din gradually conquered northeastern Algeria, subdued the coastal region between Constantine and Oran, and captured the Spanish fortress outside Algiers in 1529, after which he constructed an earth platform to connect the town with the four rocky isles facing it. In this strategically situated port, he built an imposing and formidable naval fleet. Although regarded by the Ottoman government in Istanbul as the official western division of its naval forces, Khair al-Din's fleet was used mostly for piracy and corsair activity against Christian shipping in the western Mediterranean. Algiers came to monopolize Muslim privateering along the Algerian coast (Oran and Bougie remained in Spanish hands until the end of the eighteenth century), from which Algiers obtained most of its basic revenues.

By the time Barbarossa left Algiers in 1533 to serve as the captain-pasha of the sultan's Ottoman fleet, the political and military foundation of Algiers as a regency had been established. With the extension of his control into parts of the Algerian hinterland, Khair al-Din's rule brought under one jurisdiction an area that was to constitute the beginning of Algiers as a political concept.

Following Khair al-Din's departure, a more regular administration was established in Algiers under a succession of *beylerbeys* responsible directly to the sultan in Istanbul. After 1587 the regencies of Algiers, Tripoli, and Tunis were set up, each governed by a separate *beylerbey*. But of the three it was Algiers—the center of pirate activity—that captured the imagination of Europe as a fearsome and vicious enemy.

From the beginning of Ottoman rule adventurers and renegades were to play an important part in the political and military life of the regency. It is estimated that by 1600 perhaps a third of the 100,000 Algerines were renegades from Sicily, Corsica, Malta, and other poorer parts of the Mediterranean area. These converted captives manned the Algerine pirate ships that preyed upon maritime activities in the western Mediterranean, seizing merchant ships and enslaving sailors. The Barbary corsairs attacked the European coasts and captured hostages whom they held for ransom or as human merchandise for the prosperous slave markets that flourished in North Africa in the seventeenth century.

Although plunder and the sale of Christian captives were indeed profitable, they were not the only occupations of the regency. Algiers was also an important center of legitimate commerce. Yet according to most historians, this period is best remembered for the notorious activities of the Barbary pirates. Indeed one of the many reasons put forth by the French for their direct intervention into Algeria was to put a stop to the slavery, piracy, and tribal anarchy that came to symbolize the Ottoman regency in the minds of Europeans.

Two aspects of the regency's internal political and social development merit special attention. First, since the mid-sixteenth century actual Ottoman supervision of Algerian domestic affairs had been reduced to a minimum. In all matters of substance, for example, the dey of Algiers was an independent monarch ruling directly over the province of Algiers (Dar al-Sultan) and indirectly through appointed beys in the three other administrative districts—Oran in the west, Titteri in the center, and Constantine in the east—which in combination constituted the government of Algeria from 1671 to 1830.

Although political power resided in the virtually autonomous pasha, the more crucial military and economic power was concentrated in two main bodies. The first was the foreign army that had been sent from Istanbul at the time of Khair al-Din and that had evolved into the cornerstone of Ottoman administration in Algiers. This Turkish

Mosquée de la Pêcherie, also known as Djamaa El Djedid ("the new mosque"), built in 1660 by the Turks. Located in the old quarter of Algiers.

military colony, collectively known as the *ojaq*, was recruited from elsewhere in the Ottoman Empire, mainly among the peasants of Anatolia, in Turkey's central heartland. Assigned to the territory on a virtually permanent basis, the *ojaq* developed into a self-governing military guild, set apart by vocation and status from the rest of the Algerine population and subject to its own laws, administered by a separate court.

The other major group influencing the state was the guild of corsair captains who were the main financial source of support for the state. Rivalries and tensions often characterized the uneasy relationship between the janissaries (that is, the foreign Turkish army) and the sea captains.

The second important and striking aspect of Turkish rule in Algeria was its complete lack of interest in and neglect of the Arab-Berber population in the country's interior. Throughout the whole of the regency period the countryside was little affected by the Turkish administration. To be sure, garrisons were stationed in the towns, but in many places the Turks had no authority or power and were content to draw a salary and let a local administration take its course.

This situation was especially true among the Berber tribes of the Aurès and the Kabyle, who maintained their independence. In other areas the Turks' use of tribal chiefs to keep their respective areas under control contributed to the entrenchment of the tribalism that continued to be the most important feature of social organization.

All in all, the regency was isolated from the population and was a self-contained society, with its history of internal intrigues and assassinations having little effect on the overall development of Algeria proper. The Turkish government operated as an extractive machine that functioned essentially to promote piracy and to collect the taxes that supported the *ojaq*. In fact Turkish relations with the indigenous Algerians were based solely on two things: obtaining the largest possible amount in taxes and other payments, and maintaining sufficient law and order to assure the undisturbed collection of these taxes. As a result the country developed into a veritable mosaic of fiefs, autonomous towns, and independent tribes, subjected to periodic taxation but not to direct political control.

By the eighteenth century, which saw the growth of European seapower in the Mediterranean, a period of decline set in for Algiers. Yet as important as this self-enclosed maritime city-state was to Mediterranean affairs, the history of Algiers was not the history of Algeria of that time. Having no roots in its own country from which it was spiritually and physically cut off, Algiers could have little effect on the relatively changeless course of life in many of the smaller towns of the countryside. Yet, in a tragic twist of fate, the fundamental reordering of traditional life and social organization in the Algerian interior came about via the destructive experience of European settler colonialism that arrived in Algeria under the pretext, among others, of halting Algerine corsair activities.

As long as the regency possessed military and economic might, it could effectively forestall a European takeover. However, with the shifting of the balance of power in the Mediterranean in favor of the Europeans, Algiers became a tempting target, offering an opportunity to settle old scores and past grievances. In a more positive light Ottoman rule did manage to create the territorial and administrative base upon which European political structures were grafted and through which the Algerian political idea was animated and the country's nationalist identity catalyzed. In retrospect this process of political delineation constituted an important intermediate step in the creation of the Algerian nation-state as we know it today.

FRENCH CONQUEST AND COLONIZATION, 1830–1919

A seemingly trivial incident that transpired in Algiers in 1827 was to initiate 132 years of French colonial rule—a period in which

Algeria's territory and society were devastatingly violated and its disparate tribal parts destroyed and reconstituted under the bureaucratic authority of the colonial state. Yet it was out of this profoundly disruptive process that a sense of national identity, hitherto feeble or nonexistent, was forged. Indeed, intensive French colonization provided in the political and nationalistic realms what the Arab-Islamic invasions of the seventh and eleventh centuries and the three hundred years of Turkish domination accomplished in the religious-linguistic and territorial-administrative areas respectively—namely, a sense of Algerian nationhood.

A meeting in Algiers on April 29, 1827, between the dey of the regency, Hussein, and the French consul, Pierre Deval, to resolve a series of complex and tangled trade deals involving French merchants led to a heated exchange. French indifference to the Turks' repeated attempts to resolve a debt problem between the two countries led to the dey's using intemperate language. He supposedly called Deval "a wicked, faithless, idol-worshipping rascal." In any case, Hussein tapped the consul's shoulder with his embroidered fly whisk to indicate that their interview was over. This gesture was interpreted as an insult to the person of the consul and the honor of France. In response the king of France, Charles X, sent the commander of the French naval squadron to the Turkish ruler in Algiers with an ultimatum that read, in part, as follows: "His Majesty angered at the horrible and scandalous outrage committed against Himself demands an immediate reparation and public satisfaction prescribed as follows— a public apology . . . the flag of France will be flown above the forts of Algiers and the Palace of the Dey and shall receive a one-hundred-gun salute."[1]

When the dey refused to comply, the French government ordered a blockade of Algerian ports, but this failed to bring the dey to submission. It was not until three years later that the French avenged the insult. On June 14, 1830, 37,607 French soldiers landed at Sidi Ferruch, a coastal town some 21 kilometers west of Algiers. Encountering little resistance, French troops marched toward Algiers and captured the city three weeks later on July 5, 1830—the historic date marking the beginning of the French occupation of Algeria. Although there were other factors that could explain the French military expedition—French claims to a privileged bastion on the coast in eastern Algeria to suppress piracy and slavery in the regency, the need for an insecure Bourbon government to enhance its domestic standing with a stirring and patriotic external diversion (nonetheless, it failed to prevent the regime's overthrow within a month after the conquest), revenge for past effrontery of Algiers, a vague desire for prestige, and ill-defined sentiments stirred by the post-Napoleonic imperialism—none were compelling enough to justify invasion and occupation. Rather than being motivated by explicit strategic and economic interests, the French came to Algeria almost "accidentally" with no premeditation for a thoroughgoing annexation.

My subsequent discussion of the colonization and decolonization processes is organized according to five historical phases based on the impact of and response to French domination of Algerian society. The conquest phase (from 1830 to 1847) represented the period of initial French takeover and the first xenophobic resistance by nativistic forces to this foreign incursion. The 1848–1871 period represented the phase of colonial intensification and secondary resistance when the last feeble pockets of tribal opposition were suppressed and indigenous society was restructured to serve settler needs. The third phase from 1871 to 1919 constituted the period of total European colonization. During this period many segments of the native elite attempted to imitate their colonial masters in order to be more accepted by them. Meanwhile, the mass of ordinary Algerians fatalistically acquiesced to the colonial status quo. French unwillingness to respond positively to the moderate reformist demands made by the acclimated Algerian elite led to a fourth stage: nationalist agitation for self-rule from 1919 to 1954. It was during this phase that Algerian nationalism emerged as a concrete historic reality embodied in specific political movements. The last and decisive phase (from 1954 to 1962) led to political independence through a war of national liberation and revolutionary struggle. (The last two phases are discussed in Chapter 3.)

Conquest and Primary Resistance, 1830–1847

The ease with which Algiers was conquered greatly surprised the French. Having come with no long-range plan of occupation, French authorities debated whether to limit the occupation to Algiers, expand into the country's interior, or abandon Algeria altogether. The overthrow of the Bourbon dynasty—replaced by the July Monarchy less than a month after the initial victory in Africa—added to the general confusion and uncertainty. Out of this political disarray a compromise of sorts was reached between those who argued for expansion into Algeria proper and those who favored abandoning the country completely. The resulting policy of "limited occupation" meant that the French would occupy the main towns of the Algerian coast and exercise sovereignty over the rest of the country through native or Turkish rulers. Thus within two years of the original takeover, France could only show modest results. The areas under its control, for example, included Algiers and its surroundings, Oran and its port in the west, and Bône in the eastern province. Out of a total population of nearly 3 million, there were only about 5,000 Europeans in 1832.

Yet this policy of limited occupation could not long endure, partly because of the implacable hostility of Algerian Muslims to Christian rule but also because of the uncontrollable ambitions of the still small but vocal colon (European settler or colonist) community. Consequently by 1834, following a report of a special French commission on Africa appointed by Louis Philippe the year before, the occupied areas were annexed as a colony of France. The position of governor-general was created for the territory, and in 1839 it was officially named "Algeria." The governor-general, a high-ranking military officer, was under the responsibility of the minister of war in Paris, and had civil and military jurisdiction over the newly annexed territories. With this structure in place, the legal-administrative and military foundation for settler colonialism was now firmly entrenched along the coast and was soon to expand inland.

However, unlike the relative ease with which the Algerian littoral was conquered and colonized, French incursions into the interior met with fierce and sustained native resistance that took nearly two decades to overcome. (Tribal dissidence was not completely eliminated until 1871.) The head of the earliest and most stubborn opposition was Abd el-Kader, a dynamic Muslim leader from western Algeria who rallied tribal resistance against the French by invoking simultaneously the mystical appeal of Sufism (ascetic Islamic mysticism) and orthodox Islamic belief. The appearance of Abd el-Kader as resistance leader indicated the extension of the conflict with the French. Now it involved the tribal pastoral communities; previously, it had been limited for the most part to the urban areas.

Through consensus, coercion, and conquest Abd el-Kader successfully united the many warring tribes under his command, and he succeeded in creating a Muslim state in the interior, a kind of Berber confederacy, with Tlemcen as its headquarters. Superceding the moribund structure of the Ottomans, Abd el-Kader's state was modern in organization and administration, yet dedicated to Islamic purity and opposition to contacts with Christians. His state, however, did not hesitate to borrow selective Western military innovation to improve the fighting capability of its army. This indigenous state was to reach its zenith between 1837 and 1839, following the signing of the Treaty of Tafna (May 20, 1837), which defined the boundaries between the territory held by the amir (commander, in this case Abd el-Kader) and the localities under French control.

The bargain struck at Tafna did not prove to be the basis for a lasting relationship between Abd el-Kader's state and the French army. In the two-and-a-half years following the treaty's signing, the Muslim ruler penetrated the province of Constantine and enforced his authority over the tribes in the west and south of Algeria who still rejected it. This increased power and prestige could only be regarded as a threat by the French. Moreover, the rapid growth of a viable territorial state that barred the extension of European settlement was cause for concern by expansionist-minded French military bureaucrats. As a result armed conflict between the amir and the French forces, including the foreign legion (which had been created in 1831 for service in Algeria), took place across the whole of the country. In one battle Muslim forces reached the outskirts of Algiers. Early in 1840, the amir's troops were besieging Mostaganem and attacking the suburbs of Oran. No area of French control seemed secure as French-occupied coastal towns came under constant military harassment.

By March 1840, Abd el-Kader, followed by virtually all the tribes of the interior of western and central Algeria, was at the height of his power. Yet it was the magnitude and scope of the amir's successes that led the French to undertake a determined and systematic campaign against him and to institute a policy of total occupation. Gradually, with superior French resources and manpower and numerous tribal defections taking place, Abd el-Kader's forces were put on the defensive. When the fighting seemed to stall, the French brought in General Thomas Robert Bugeaud to pursue the battle more vigorously. With superior and better trained forces Bugeaud—according to many, the real architect of French rule in Algeria—initiated against Abd el-Kader a policy of total war, using the tribal method of *razzia* (literally, "raid," but more generally referred to as "scorched earth"). This involved the destruction of villages and encampments, the burning of crops, the killing of herds, and the imposition of collective responsibility on tribes whose leaders continued to support the amir.

These ruthless tactics proved effective in demoralizing the Algerian Muslims. One by one the amir's strongholds in the cities and the countryside fell to the French. Realizing the futility of fighting any further, Abd el-Kader surrendered to the French in December 1847. After imprisonment in France from 1848 to 1852, he was released and allowed to settle in Damascus, where he remained until his death at the age of seventy-five in May 1883. He had spent fifteen years of his life in battle and thirty-six in prison and exile.

Considered as the first authentic nationalist hero of Algeria, Abd el-Kader's green-and-white standard became the banner of the revolution in the 1950s and was adopted after independence as the country's official national flag. In July 1966 Abd el-Kader's remains were brought back from Damascus to Algiers, where he was given a hero's burial. Abd el-Kader was a pragmatic Islamic resistance leader and state builder who fought a heroic, but ultimately hopeless, struggle against the French. With his defeat the Algerians lost not only their freedom but also their land.

Almost from the outset the French took possession of large tracts of former Ottoman lands and religiously endowed properties for settlement and cultivation. French military officers, for example, were encouraged to purchase land in the Mitidja plain, an area extending about 100 kilometers westward from Algiers. This plain had been converted from a malarial swamp into a fertile agricultural zone. Its alluvial soil permitted the French eventually to establish magnificent vineyards and citrus groves. Later, the French confiscated private holdings and communal or tribal properties. Thus, by the 1840s, the French had sequestered outright or through legal chicanery the most productive lands around the coastal cities, leaving the Muslims with the less-fruitful areas farther inland. Additionally, laws were passed creating state domains from lands whose proprietors could not justify previous title. At the same time the theory of cantonment of the tribes was developed (according to which each tribe's title was restricted to the amount of territory considered necessary to support it). Later ordinances went as far as to prescribe confiscation in situations where "hostility to the French presence" was demonstrated. It was during this first phase of colonial domination that the country's best lands began to be confiscated; this process was greatly accelerated in the second and third phases.

Along with land transfers came officially encouraged and supported settlement by Europeans from France, Corsica, Spain, Italy, and Malta. Compared to the total 5,000 European civilians living in Algeria at the end of 1832 there were nearly five times that number seven years later. By 1847 more than 100,000 had settled in the country, most having a peasant or working class background. The colons, who became known as *pieds-noirs* ("black feet") broke down into two major socioeconomic groups: *grands colons*, constituting the class of wealthy businessmen and prosperous landowners and the *petits blancs* ("little whites"), people of modest standing in lower-level occupations who, nonetheless, were better off than the overwhelming majority of their native Algerian Muslim counterparts.

Both groups of settlers were politically united in their intense hostility toward the indigenous Muslims. They were also opposed to French military rule; they felt it purposely obstructed their opportunity for unrestricted land acquisition and settlement. Under Bugeaud's direction the French army had created *bureaux arabes* ("Arab departments") in 1832 to take care of Muslim affairs—including the defense of Arab land rights against civilian settlers. Assuming a paternalistic role in their government of the Muslims, military officers of the *bureaux arabes* hindered the appropriation by the settlers of lands they coveted. For Bugeaud the kind of colonization he envisioned for Algeria was one composed of ex-servicemen who as farmers would remain under the control of the army. In any case, for the native Muslim inhabitants it made no difference to whom they lost their land—military officers, ex-servicemen, *grands colons, petits blancs*— because the result was the same: destitution, deprivation, and dependency status within their own country.

This process of widespread confiscation of land and its transfer to settler groups recalls the similar settler-Indian conflict in the U.S. West: "There is the same story of treaties made and broken, the frontier pushed continually back; outposts built to protect the homesteaders; friendlies and hostiles, and sporadic surprise raids of frustration and vengeance by the natives as they are gradually tracked down and cornered."[2]

In less than twenty years what had begun as a mere accident had evolved into a massive French military presence throughout Algeria. European settlers had multiplied by a factor of twenty, and French colonization had made deep incursions into the country's interior. The destruction of Abd el-Kader's indigenous Muslim state, constituting the bulk of Algerian resistance to further French expansion, facilitated the country's pacification and structural reordering, which the second phase of colonialism was to witness.

Colonial Intensification and Secondary Resistance, 1848–1871

In the quarter century following Abd el-Kader's surrender the number of land acquisitions, tribal displacements, and settlers all increased while sporadic, secondary resistance in the interior continued. The resistance culminated in 1871 in a serious tribal rebellion that ended in defeat for the Algerians and opened the way for the subjugation of Kabylia, the last stronghold of native opposition in the nineteenth century.

Among the initial acts of the French Second Republic government, which came to power following the 1848 revolution, was to declare Algeria as an integral part of France. In the first move toward assimilation three *départements* (French administrative units) were organized under a civilian government for the Algiers, Oran, and Constantine territorial areas. Other constitutional and administrative arrangements that effectively divided the Algerian population into a privileged European and a suppressed Muslim community followed. Differences in political and civil rights, social outlook and organization, and economic opportunities separated the communities. Fusion seemed impossible and coexistence impractical, as experience soon demonstrated.

Napoleon III had assumed power following the establishment of the Second Empire in 1852. After visiting Algeria in 1860 and 1863, he pursued a policy of meaningful coexistence within the framework of French sovereignty. Sensitive to Algerian aspirations and concerns, he promulgated decrees affecting tribal structure, land tenure, and the legal status of Muslims in French Algeria. These decrees protected tribal lands against settler encroachments; he also secured for Muslims the right to acquire French nationality. In the aggregate, however, these measures did more harm than good—they failed to prevent, for example, over 1.2 million hectares of land being set aside for colonization. Napoleon III, who had an idealized noble warrior image of the Muslims, failed to understand the basic incompatibility between continuing colonization and the welfare of the Arabs whom he wanted to protect.

Of the many edicts and administrative laws put into effect during this period, the decrees of 1863 and 1865 were of particular significance in terms of the essentially negative impact they had on the status of native Algerians. Originally intended as a measure to guarantee to each tribe inalienable title to the lands it held, the 1863 statute, which applied European concepts of private property in land to Muslim holdings, made land a freely circulating commodity and thereby facilitated its sale by individuals to settlers. In personalizing and privatizing communally held property, the decree destroyed the authority of the chief and tribal cohesion; it eliminated the entire pyramid of rights and privileges that had guaranteed a livelihood for the poor cultivator; in effect, the decree destroyed the economy on which tribal life was based. The broad social consequences of this and other land use measures on Algerian society was summarized by one keen observer of North African life:

Such land policies [reached] for the heart of society because they [contributed] to the dislocation of a whole series of relations and practices of production and property rights that [were] the basis of social life. As one instrument among many of a new colonial social order, they [combined] to transform life in different ways and different rates and rhythms, sometimes with brutal suddenness, sometimes in modes that [were] not immediately directly perceived but, as it were, [crept] up on a society, setting in train processes whose nature and outcome neither colonizer nor colonized [could] grasp.[3]

For their part colon settlers hailed the 1863 edict, as reflected, for example, in one of their newspapers published in Constantine.

> Thanks to the constitution of property which proceeds from this [decree], the greater part of Algerian territory passes immediately from the condition of dead value to the state of real value; millions spring from nothing. . . . The countryside will become populated and the cities will witness in their midst the flowering of all aspects of commerce and industry.[4]

The imposition of French norms of private property in land went hand in hand with a program for the dismemberment of the great tribes. This was accomplished by settling the tribal population in *douars*, or distinct settlement clusters, and assigning rights to land in terms of membership in the *douar* rather than by virtue of tribal membership. Because many of these settlement clusters contained sections from quite different tribes, the latter were fragmented and their chieftains' power reduced. The collective impact of this and earlier land measures was that the Algerian Muslims were increasingly deprived of land and pushed back by the advancing colonists upon ever more unproductive terrain. Traditional mechanisms of ensuring economic security were abrogated, tribes were scattered, and the familiar political structure dismantled.

An 1865 decree ostensibly aimed at giving Muslims an equal legal position with the *pieds-noirs* was another example of a well-intentioned, but ultimately counterproductive, measure put forth by Napoleon III. Essentially this document made Algerian Muslims legally French subjects—they could enter the French civil service, enlist in the army, migrate to metropolitan France—but not French citizens. To become full citizens of France they had to renounce their personal status, a move that implied abandoning allegiance to Islamic law. Given the unitary nature of Islamic belief, which makes no distinction between the secular and the sectarian, one had to commit apostasy in order to qualify for French citizenship—a totally unacceptable and deeply resented act. No wonder that this legal twilight zone elicited few responses; only several thousand Muslims ever accepted such a condition for political equality with the French during the whole of the colonial period. (Insult was added to injury when native Algerian Jews were made full French citizens by a simple decree in 1870.) The conditions for French citizenship offered to the Muslims further alienated an already disenfranchised community and provided the legal basis for much of the subsequent civil and political problems of Algeria.

In the meantime colonization continued at an accelerated rate. In the 1851–1857 period, for example, the immigrant population grew by almost 40 percent: from 131,000 to 181,000. Toward 1870 the number of colons approached 250,000.

In the countryside, Muslims, feeling the full burden of French taxation and resenting the loss of their lands, carried out sporadic but ineffective uprisings from 1848 onward. Rebellions, often led by marabout religious figures (believed to be holders of divine, mystical powers), took place both in oasis settlements, such as Biskra, Laghouat, and Touggert, as well as in the rugged mountainous area of Greater Kabylia. In every case through the use of *razzia* tactics and the systematic destruction of villages, the French were able to achieve the upper hand. These native uprisings reflected the deep hostility felt by the Muslims toward the French that would come out into the open whenever political or economic grievances provided the spark and the French military control seemed in doubt.

The last and most serious such revolt prior to the war of independence occurred in 1871 in Kabylia under conditions of general economic misery and hopelessness resulting from the years of famine and epidemics preceding the Franco-Prussian War. The circumstances of that war, which saw the defeat of Napoleon III and the elimination of the Second Empire, and the governmental changes that followed, also added to the general state of uncertainty and confusion in Algeria. The agitation of the Muslims under such conditions was exploited by one tribal leader, Mohamed Mokrani, for his own purposes.

What had begun as an attempt to achieve personal aims by starting a limited uprising sparked off a general rebellion instead. The fighting was bitter on both sides as rebels devastated farms and destroyed and pillaged villages. The savage conflict ended in defeat and in the death of Mokrani and was followed by French sequestration of the rebels' lands, which they had to buy back at ruinous prices. It is estimated that over 500,000 hectares of tribal land were confiscated. In addition, the Kabylia region was placed under extraordinary rule in which due process guarantees were denied. Mokrani's desperate uprising was the last revolt of a native feudal state. With his defeat all of Algeria lay prostrate. The Muslim population had been reduced from 3 million in 1830 to just over 2 million forty years later. Algeria was pacified, but its population had been figuratively drawn and quartered. For the next half century the country was to be a "land of silence" for the Muslims—politically, economically, and socially.

Total Colonization and Native Acquiescence, 1871–1919

The third phase of the colonial process in Algeria was marked by the fatalistic acquiescence of the Muslims to an expanding settler society. The political and economic structures of this society were intended to serve the interests of the colon community in its building of *l'Algérie française* (French Algeria). Moreover, the size of that community continued to enlarge dramatically during the next fifty years, when Algeria was thrown wide open to European immigration and settlement. French, Italian, and other European emigrants settled in rural districts, thereby expanding the civil territories whose control came under colon rather than military authorities. In the 1870s alone, European-owned land and the number of settlers doubled. Economically a feature of this period was the growth of large-scale agricultural and industrial enterprises, which concentrated still more power in the hands of the *grands colons*, the most powerful members of the *pied-noir* community.

By the turn of the century Algeria had gained administrative and financial autonomy, exercised through a sort of Algerian parliament—the so-called Financial Delegations—composed of two-thirds European and one-third Muslim members. With their ability to withhold consent for the budget, the settlers had the key to power.

As custodians of this new society, the settlers exacted a harsh price from their Muslim countrymen, levying higher taxes on the Arabs than those collected from the Europeans and using these revenues for further colonization; keeping the native Algerians subdued through a penal system meant only for the Arabs; weakening the existing Muslim educational system without, at the same time, providing Arabs an opportunity for access to French schools; and replacing the Muslim system of justice with one based on French legal precepts and principles.

Perhaps the most effective and onerous device for governing the Muslim population was the *Code de l'Indigénat* (a law applying only to native Algerians), which was promulgated in 1881 and remained in force virtually unchanged until after World War II. In essence, it was a statutory mechanism by which to control and contain the Muslims. Its forty-one unconscionable provisions included: an Algerian Muslim was forbidden to speak against France and its government; Algerians were prohibited from keeping stray animals for more than twenty-four hours; natives were not allowed to become schoolteachers without proper authorization nor were they permitted to travel from one place to another within Algeria without a visaed permit, a kind of internal passport. Punishment for these crimes or others such as delay in paying taxes, giving shelter to strangers without permission, or holding gatherings of more than twenty people ranged from payment of fines, to confiscation of property, to indefinite administrative internment.

Muslims suffered greatly in the field of education as well. The expansion of schools for Muslims was limited by the settlers' opposition to Muslim education, which they regarded as potentially subversive and by the natural reluctance of Muslim parents to send their children to non-Muslim schools. What schooling did exist for the Algerians was limited, mediocre, or both.

By the late 1800s the government sought to educate small numbers of Algerian Muslims in the European-populated French school system where the curriculum was entirely in French. Believing it had a *mission civilisatrice* ("civilizing mission"), the French sought to bring the benefits of French culture, language, history, and society to highly selected groups of indigenous Algerians. Ultimately this group was to form part of a stratum of gallicized Muslims, or *évolués* (that is, those who had "evolved" sufficiently toward French civilization) that would be the core of the country's native intellectual elite. (Ironically, it was from this group that nationalist ideologues and political activists eventually emerged.) Nowhere in this curriculum was Arabic studies taught, and indeed the whole of the educational system was designed to submerge the Arab-Muslim identity.

Probably the most politically destructive long-term impact of French educational policies in Algeria was the failure to create a sizable, qualified, and credible native elite who could effectively represent their people in contacts with French colons and administrators. Having destroyed the power and stature of traditional tribal leaders and prevented the formation of an authentic Arab-Muslim Algerian bureaucratic class, the French, confident in their overwhelming superiority, limited their communication with Muslims to the unrepresentative *évolués* or coopted traditional elite who, in many instances, were reduced to condescending yes-men, or, as they were derisively known locally, *beni-oui-ouis* (sons of yes-men). When the political situation began to change in the period between the two world wars, the French found that they had no *interlocuteurs valables* (authoritative go-betweens) who could represent the bulk of the Muslim masses in their dealings with the French. With no credible spokespersons having the trust or confidence of either settlers or Algerians, communication between the two communities became extremely difficult if not impossible.

Under such conditions it was no surprise that in the five decades prior to World War I French colonial policies and settler practices reinforced the severe polarization of Algerian society and made any meaningful fusion impossible. The Muslims, restricted, deprived, and humiliated, suffered in submissive silence while the colons, possessing advanced technology, efficient organization, and a strong army enjoyed all the advantages of prosperity. Yet in a relatively brief time following the events of the war in Europe, new forces emerged, turning Muslim frustrations into hopes that were to shape the history of Algeria in the twentieth century.

NOTES

1. William Spencer, *Algiers in the Age of the Corsairs* (Norman: University of Oklahoma Press, 1976), pp. 149–150.

2. Charles F. Gallagher, *The United States and North Africa: Morocco, Algeria, and Tunisia* (Cambridge: Harvard University Press, 1963), p. 64.

3. Michael Gilsenan, *Recognizing Islam: Religion and Society in the Modern Arab World* (New York: Pantheon Books, 1982), p. 145.

4. André Nouschi, *Enquête sur le Niveau de Vie des Populations Rurales Constantinoises de la Conquête Jusqu'en 1919* (Paris: Presses Universitaires de France, 1961), p. 282.

3

The Imprint of History: 1919 to the Present

NATIONALIST AWAKENING, 1919–1954

Several factors coalesced around the interwar period to create the conditions from which Algerian nationalism was to emerge. First was the call by a small, but influential, group of highly educated and thoroughly gallicized *évolués* for greater equality between the Muslims and the French in Algeria. Their purpose was not to separate Algeria from France but to give real meaning to assimilation by reforming or abolishing discriminatory laws that treated Muslims as a colonized people. Although moderate in purpose and tone and distinctly removed from the experiences of most of the Muslim masses, this "equal status" appeal of the *évolués* could be considered the beginning of the Algerian nationalist awakening. Among their objectives, for example, was the conscription of Algerian Muslims into the French army on the same basis as their European counterparts. For its part the colon community reacted violently to any attempts at altering its privileged status vis-à-vis the Muslims. From the beginning it was settler intransigence that made peaceful change virtually impossible. The defeat of one reformist measure after another paved the way for the increasing radicalization of native nationalist forces.

A second factor contributing to the political awakening of indigenous Algerians was World War I—which forced Paris to conscript all able-bodied men, including Muslims from Algeria and other overseas colonies. Nearly 200,000 Algerian Muslims served France loyally during the war and about 25,000 lost their lives. The war experience exposed Algerians to new ideas and expectations. As reward for their contribution to the war effort the French government offered a limited right of citizenship to certain categories of Muslims,

35

enlarged local government bodies to include more indigenous representatives, and increased the number of Muslims who could participate in municipal elections. In practice, however, many of these benefits were undermined by settler manipulation and coercion, creating frustration and bitterness among the newly conscious ex-servicemen.

Another group of Algerians voicing nationalist aspirations were industrial and other workers residing in France. A high birthrate and the French colonization of the Algerian countryside that reduced into smaller and smaller holdings the amount of land available to support the Muslim population impelled large numbers of unemployed young men to flock to the cities in Algeria and, during and after World War I, France. By 1923, for example, there were about 70,000 Algerian workers employed in France's major cities. Many of these laborers experienced severe hardships common to poorly paid workers in industrial countries. The workers' economic and social grievances quickly gave way to political demands.

There were also some Algerians, both at home and in France, who were exposed during the interwar period to the ideas of Arab nationalism that were widespread in the Middle East at that time. Finally, the powerful appeal of Islam, which throughout the centuries had provided individual Algerians with a sense of collective identity, was mobilized anew in the 1920s and 1930s as an instrument for cultural assertiveness and nationalist self-worth. In combination all these factors created a favorable environment for the emergence of an Algerian nationalist spirit.

However, because settler society had both destroyed traditional native institutions and prevented new ones from developing, when indigenous responses to colonial domination arose they were not synchronized or allowed to form a united front. Instead, three different responses were articulated simultaneously in the 1930s by distinct strata. Political competition among these movements served to divide further rather than to unite their followers. The three nationalist streams were those of liberal assimilationism as represented in the thinking of Ferhat Abbas, Islamic reformism, as embodied in Abdelhamid Ben Badis and his Association of Algerian Ulema (Islamic religious scholars or clergy), and radical anticolonial nationalism as expressed in the ideas of Messali Hadj. These three strands in the diverse fabric of Algerian nationalism raised the political consciousness of Muslim Algeria but failed to provide the cohesive organizational structure and ideological direction necessary to gain complete independence. Given the timing of the respective responses and the environments in which they operated, it was not surprising that this should be the case.

Liberal Assimilationists and Ferhat Abbas

The ideas and objectives of the liberal assimilationists are best represented in the political career of Ferhat Abbas, in many ways the essence of the westernized, middle-class Arab *évolué*. Yet politically he went through successive disillusions: from thorough integrationism in the middle 1930s to advocacy of total independence a decade later. The evolution of his position was symptomatic of how French insensitivity to Algerian nationalistic aspirations forced liberal moderates to give up on France. The moderates were superceded by revolutionary extremists who found assimilationist appeals irrelevant and Abbas's delayed conversion beside the point.

Given the time in which they lived and the objective conditions facing them, it is understandable that Abbas and his contemporaries made no demand for independence but instead sought to achieve equal rights with Frenchmen. Although articulate and intelligent, these assimilationists were too removed, because of their social background and French education, from the mass of Algerian Muslims to be considered authentic spokesmen of the nationalist movement. Yet at a certain stage in the evolution of the Algerian political identity, assimilationist nationalism represented one important albeit inadequate, component.

Abbas originated from the Constantine area, where his father had risen to the status of a local Arab governor in the service of the French. Born in 1899 and raised in a francophile household, the young Ferhat went to a French lycée (high school) in Constantine and then on to the University of Algiers following his military service in the French army during World War I. With a degree in pharmacy, Abbas went to Sétif where he set up a pharmacy. At about the same time he divorced his Muslim wife, whom he had married by family arrangement, and married a *pied-noir* divorcée, thus completing the gallicization of Ferhat Abbas.

More comfortable in French than Arabic, which he spoke haltingly, Abbas was enamored with French society and its bourgeois values. When he became politically active during his university days, his purpose was to secure equality for Muslims, thereby giving them a better chance to participate in all aspects of French metropolitan society. In this sense Abbas's ambitions lay in France, but the obstacles to their achievement were rooted in the colonial system existing in Algeria.

The earliest organizational manifestation of this assimilationist tendency was found in the Movement of Young Algerians that brought together, in the early 1900s, a small group of well-educated, middle-class *évolués*, working toward Franco-Algerian equality. This orientation took more concrete form in 1934 when *évolué* representatives in elected Algerian bodies, including Abbas, formed the *Fédération des Elus* (Federation of Elected Muslims). This group argued for Muslim integration into French society—including full citizenship without having to renunciate one's personal status as a Muslim. Among other objectives were representation in the French parliament, administrative equality in which Muslims could exercise real power, equality in military and civil service, and the suppression of discriminatory legislation directed against Muslims.

In making these demands Abbas used conciliatory methods of persuasion and petition. Although a skillful debater, Abbas had a pacific temperament and was willing to bargain and compromise. He was tolerant of diversity and deeply committed to modernization, yet he and his colleagues often adopted a paternalistic view of their responsibilities for guiding Algeria's backward peoples to a better life. Until after World War II, Abbas was a passionate protagonist of assimilation with metropolitan France. He did not believe Algeria possessed a separate national identity and denied that an Algerian nation had ever existed. He made his position clear on this matter in an article he published in 1936 in his periodical, *Entente*, in which he declared:

> Had I discovered the Algerian nation, I would be a nationalist and I would not blush as if I had committed a crime. . . . However, I will not die for the Algerian nation, because it does not exist. I have not found it. I have examined History, I questioned the living and the dead, I visited cemeteries; nobody spoke to me about it. I then turned to the Koran and I sought for one solitary verse forbidding a Muslim from integrating himself with a non-Muslim nation. I did not find that either. One cannot build on the wind.[1]

The victory of the left-wing Popular Front government of the French Socialist premier, Léon Blum, in 1936 gave rise to the hopes of Abbas and his federation members that some of the changes they proposed could now be peaceably achieved through constitutional means. The Blum-Viollette Plan, for example, which would have granted French citizenship with full political equality to a certain limited class of Muslims, including university graduates, elected officials, army officers, and professionals, was dropped by the French government in the face of fierce opposition from the settler community and the Algerian civil service.

This outcome was a bitter disappointment to Abbas and other *évolués* who would have gained much from this legislation but who also saw the French government's action as an opportunity to broaden Algerian support for their integrationist objectives. The federation had succeeded in July 1938 in bringing together Islamic, Communist, and other nationalist groups to form the First Muslim Congress as a means of promoting its goal of Franco-Algerian equality. Yet the demands made by the congress were rejected outright by French authorities. Only small portions had found their way into the Blum-Viollette Plan. As a result neither the maximalist nor the minimalist demands of the assimilationists were ever satisfied. Disaffection with the Popular Front government and internecine quarrels among Muslim congress participants quickly followed.

Thus by the late 1930s assimilation had become a dead concept. Moreover, the aborting of the Blum-Viollette bill marked a vital turning point for the Algerian nationalist movement. Henceforth the slogan, "assimilation with equality," no longer figured in the political pronouncements of Ferhat Abbas. As a viable alternative to self-determination it had been abandoned and replaced by the notion of an autonomous Algeria in loose federation with France.

The World War II period temporarily froze Algerian nationalist activities, but they were quickly resumed following Allied landings in Algeria in late 1942. More by default than design Abbas became the sole spokesman for native political demands, which included the establishment of a postwar Algerian constituent assembly within the existing French framework. Finding no positive response from French authorities, Abbas, along with other *évolués*, put forth in early 1943 a declaration known as the Manifesto of the Algerian People, which included demands for legal equality, agricultural reform, free compulsory education, and creation of an Algerian state associated with France. Both the tone and the content of these demands were more militant than anything that had come before.

As a veritable charter for a new political movement this manifesto represented an important step in the disengagement of Algerian Muslims from France. It took organizational form in March 1944 in Sétif with the creation of the Friends of the Manifesto and Liberty (AML), which brought together the principal components of nationalism, including Islamic reformers and radical anticolonial nationalists along with secular *évolués*. In the most precise terms yet the AML insisted on the creation of an Algerian nation with its own republican constitution but politically federated with France. This newfound

unity, which did not last long, carried immense political and propaganda importance for the Algerians. For his part Abbas had now
come from assimilation to the idea of a Franco-Algerian community,
but he still did not go so far as the more militant nationalists who
were ultimately to outflank and overtake him.

It is uncertain how far this political path toward national self-
determination could have gone had the unexpected and brutal massacres of the Sétif uprising in May 1945 not taken place. What began
as a public demonstration in celebration of V-E day by pro-AML and
other pronationalist Algerians in Sétif, a predominantly Muslim town
in the Constantine region, quickly turned into a mass display of anti-
French, pro-Algerian sentiment. People began raising placards demanding the release of the popular leftist leader, Messali Hadj, and
immediate independence for Algeria. For the first time during the
twentieth century the green-and-white banner that had been the
standard of the legendary Abd el-Kader was unfolded, an act that
provoked local police to move against demonstrators.

Given the long years of political subordination and socioeconomic
subjugation, it was not surprising that a slight provocation was
sufficient to transform a demonstration into a bloody riot throughout
the city and its environs. Dozens of helpless European men, women,
and children were slaughtered indiscriminately. In retaliation government forces acted even more brutally: The army was joined by
police and settler vigilante squads in the mass murder of thousands
of mostly innocent Algerian Muslims by means of systematic *ratissage*
(raking over), including summary executions. When the bloodletting
was over, 103 Europeans and more than 6,000 Muslims had been
killed in a few days of savagery.

In the aftermath of the Sétif uprising the AML was banned and
Abbas imprisoned, along with thousands of others, although he was
never directly implicated in any of the developments prior to and
following the riots. In retrospect it is clear why so many who were
later to join the Algerian revolution date their espousal of the nationalist
cause from the shock and horror of Sétif. One liberal Algerian poet
accurately summarized the feelings of most Algerian nationalists when
he wrote that it was at Sétif "that my sense of humanity was affronted
for the first time by the most atrocious sights. I was sixteen years
old. The shock which I felt at the pitiless butchery that caused the
deaths of thousands of Muslims, I have never forgotten. From that
moment my nationalism took definite form."[2]

After 1945 the two communities of Algeria—settler and native—
were separated by an abyss of mutual misunderstanding, hatred, and

fear that fed on itself right down to the end of the revolution and all its bloody horrors.

Once the repressions were over, the French government sought to preclude any future disturbances by granting to Muslims certain social and economic benefits, along with a token opportunity for Algerian political participation in the French assembly. Abbas, released from prison in March 1946 following a general amnesty, subsequently organized a successor to his AML called the Democratic Union of the Algerian Manifesto (UDMA). This new organization, abandoning the AML's alliance with the Islamic reformers and Messali's left-wing militants, sought to create an autonomous, secular Algerian state within the French empire. Although his tone had become subdued since the Sétif riots, Abbas still clung to the hope of an alliance of equality between France and Algeria.

Despite his party's electoral victories in the French National Assembly, the UDMA failed to achieve any of its objectives. It withdrew from the assembly in September 1946 and refused to participate in the next elections. When other more extremist groups that emerged challenged the leadership of the nationalist movement, Abbas and his UDMA declined in strength and influence. What had been in 1946 perhaps the strongest Algerian Muslim party was reduced to a mere 3,000 members by 1951. Clearly, assimilationist nationalism had become inadequate and all attempts at reform within the legal French framework had failed. During the war of independence, Abbas, the ideal moderate spokesman in Western eyes, was brought in by the National Liberation Front (FLN) to act as the symbolic head of its Provisional Government of the Algerian Republic (GPRA). He never actually held power and was quickly shunted aside after independence in 1962—permanently removed from active political life despite a brief reappearance as an opposition figure in the public debates preceding the promulgation of the Algerian National Charter in 1976. In late 1985 he died of natural causes at 86.

The tragic political career of Ferhat Abbas shows how colonial intransigency made liberal reformism impossible as a means by which a peaceful decolonization process could take place. The assimilationists learned through bitter experience that, no matter how moderate or compromising they were, France would never grant the Algerians a status of equal partners with equal opportunities and legal rights. Thus Abbas gradually moved away from assimilation to a position seeking autonomy and inevitably to calling for complete independence from France.

The transformation of the assimilationists meant more than simply the elimination of an integrationist formula; more significantly, it effectively eliminated the possibility of a secular nationalist movement emerging, free of the pressures of the conservative clergy and Muslim factions. Instead, Algerian independence was ultimately achieved through the instrumental use of religious and Islamic symbols that became the unifying force of the revolution. The discrediting of indigenous secular movements by the colonial power allowed Islam to arise as the only legitimate and popular ideological rallying cry around which all Algerians could unify. Islam would thus prove to be one of the roots of Algerian nationalism. Despite its disavowal of any explicit political purpose, the Islamic body that Ben Badis was to lead constituted the second major strand in the Algerian nationalist movement.

Islamic Reformism and Abdelhamid Ben Badis

A specific Islamic revivalist trend emerged in Algeria as part of the broader awakening of Arab-Muslim consciousness that was taking place among the peoples of the Middle East and North Africa during the interwar period. There were both locally derived forces and external influences involved in this revival. Most important among the internal factors was the psychological impact of World War I on the Algerian masses. Although the majority of the population remained indifferent to the social and economic appeals of évolué assimilationists, this was not the case with Islam—with which all Algerians could identify as a religious-psychocultural as well as a political symbol. More important perhaps was the influence of the pan-Islamic salafiyya (salaf means "forefather") reform movement on the thinking of certain Algerian religious figures. Calling for a return to the puritanical ways of the Muslim past to confront better the challenge of European technological and organizational superiority, the salafiyya movement was aimed at reasserting the Islamic identity and Arab-Muslim heritage of individual Arabs. The leading Algerian Muslim figure of this Islamic reformism was Sheik Abdelhamid Ben Badis. Along with other Muslim reformers, Ben Badis created in 1931 the Association of Algerian Ulema, whose motto was to be Islam is my Religion, Arabic is my Language, Algeria is my Country, reflecting the group's nationalist character and its emphasis on the dual Arab and Islamic nature of Algeria.

Ben Badis (1889–1940), who was to fuse Algerian religious tradition with the innovating influence of the Islamic reform movement, was born in Constantine of Berber parentage although his cultural formation was entirely Arab. He came from a prosperous pro-French family and was brought up in comfortable urban surroundings as were his leading Muslim collaborators in the association, Bashir al-

Ibrahimi and Tayeb al-Okbi. He received a thoroughly Arabic, religious, and traditional education. Later he studied at the famous Zitouna mosque university in Tunis from which he received a religious degree in 1912. Returning in the same year to Constantine, he began programs of Islamic and Arabic education and reform for adults at night and for boys during the day. Ben Badis later left Algeria to travel and study in the Middle East where his ideas on Islamic reformism were refined and advanced. After World War I he returned home and took up a minor teaching post at the Green Mosque in Constantine. From this base he along with other reformist-minded ulema launched a large number of free religious schools.

The Association of Algerian Ulema aimed at religious, social, and political reform, although the last was not openly stated. Ben Badis fulminated against the religious brotherhoods, Sufi orders, and marabouts. He accused these groups both of corrupting the faith by their espousal of mysticism and of collaborating with France in its administration of Algeria. Sunni or orthodox Islam as laid down by the prophet Muhammad in the Koran knows no saints or brotherhoods intermediate between people and God: all Muslims are theoretically equal members of the *umma* (Community of the Faithful). But nearly everywhere in North Africa and especially in Algeria religious practice, as opposed to religious dogma, has centered on local shrines and local holy men. This popular practice of religion borders on

> superstition and magic, where local saints provide a warmer religious experience than is to be found in an austere mosque, a world where divine, or supernatural power reaches down to the people through faith-healers, midwives, and sellers of charms so that people respond by worshipping, meditating, or just dancing round tombs, shrines, relics, or rocks.[3]

Such a segmented localized form of Islam served to connect points in the hinterland—with their local rural tradition—to the body of Islam in general. Yet this connection was accomplished at the expense of great religious differentiation, with each lodge and each holy man espousing a variant form of the universal religion. These popular religious brotherhoods had acted strongly in support of Abd el-Kader in his resistance to the French. They remained anti-French until the turn of the century when they came into accommodation with the French authorities who supported them consciously as convenient means for keeping the body social of Algeria as divided as possible. It was this collaborationist aspect of maraboutism that earned it the pejorative label of "domestic animal of colonialism." It was to counter these inequities and the autonomous power of the traditional holy men that the ulema directed their attack. The Sufi leaders, on the one hand, were denounced for their political cooperation with the French, and on the other, they were attacked more bitterly as the embodiment of Islamic doctrinal corruption.

In their struggle against maraboutism and the wayward practices in the faith, the ulema established Koranic schools, free of French control, as a means of reforming Islam and reviving an interest in Arabic language and culture. They also used the sermons in the mosques as a way of propagating their religious and social message that was often laced with specific political meaning. In addition Ben Badis and his associates utilized the press as an important feature of their drive for reform with *Al Shihab* (*The Meteor*) constituting one of the most influential Algerian reviews of the period. Equally important was the establishment of clubs and intellectual circles that became gathering places of the Algerian-educated class as well as foreign visitors. Through this chain of schools, newspapers, and intellectual circles, and by preaching in mosques, the ulema sought to restore the Islamic community of Algeria to its unity and strength. Sunnis and schismatics, Arabs and Berbers were to forget their differences in a return to the purity of the faith.

Despite the ulema's disavowal of specific political ambitions, their rekindling of a sense of religious and nationalist consciousness among Algerians helped to delineate the Algerian identity as something different and distinct from France. When Ferhat Abbas, for example, declared that he could find no such entity as the Algerian "nation," Ben Badis was quick to reply in *Al Shihab*:

> History had taught us that the Muslim people of Algeria were created like all the others. They have their history, illustrated by noble deeds; they have their religious unity and their language; they have their culture, their customs, their habits with all that is good and bad in them. This Muslim population is not France; it cannot be France, it does not want to be France. It is a population very far from France in its language, its life and its religion; it does not seek to incorporate itself in France. It possesses its fatherland whose frontiers are fixed, and this is the Algerian fatherland.[4]

This statement of 1936 constituted an unequivocal rejection of assimilation and the idea of integrating Algeria into France. Yet a definitional description of the Algerian nation did not imply a commitment to rapid change or a complete break with France. In all their political dealings the ulema were cautious and moderate, more concerned with education and culture than with immediate political independence. They argued for political equality and improved economic conditions for Muslims and even cooperated in the AML and the First Muslim congress with Abbas's assimilationists for gradual rather than radical change.

Tied up in their own theological coils, the ulema failed to find pragmatic applications of their doctrines. Yet in the absence of any other distinctly Algerian bases of identity, the ulema's affirmation of Islamic religion and Arabic language had greater impact upon other Algerian nationalists than any other group. Although Ben Badis was concerned with the problems of Islam—which offered an immunity from French civilization—his contribution to the development of nationalist opposition increased the importance of Islam as part of Algerian identity.

Radical Anticolonial Nationalism and Messali Hadj

If reformist Islam provided one of the sources of Algerian nationalism, another, more radical source lay in the increasing development of an Algerian semiproletariat. This, in turn, was the product of two major causes: the change in the traditional pattern of Algerian sharecropping, coupled with the need—especially strong in central Algeria, among the Kabyles—to supplement a meager agriculture with some other form of employment. An additional factor, one that has been an ineradicable cause of Algeria's economic woes, has been the net Muslim birthrate, one of the highest in the world.

New French legal codes, intended to eliminate traditional forms of bondage, allowed sharecroppers to abandon their landlords. As a result sharecropping, which had standardized economic relations between farmer and peasant, thus providing a reasonable measure of labor security on the land, gave way to day labor, which created a surplus of men looking for work. To the swelling ranks of an already large floating semiproletariat was now added the group that could find only unstable and unpredictable employment. Added to this was the pressure of population growth on food resources in many areas—but especially in the mountains of Kabylia. Forced by colonization to settle on the barren hinterland, Muslims crowded into compact and dense settlements on terrain that could not support their increasing numbers. Military pacification and the spread of modern health care further curtailed natural checks on the population growth. The result of all this was that many Kabyles were forced to seek alternative sources of livelihood outside the mountains, often in the country's coastal cities, but also in the urban centers of the metropolis.

For example, between 1915 and 1918, 56,000 Algerians, mostly Berber-speaking Kabyles, left their mountain villages to work in factories in France to replace laborers serving in the army during the war. By 1923 another 15,000 Muslims were added to the labor force in France. This trend continued steadily over the years—more than 1,000,000 were there in the early 1970s—until economic stagnation throughout Europe forced a reduction to the estimated 700,000 of today.

It was within this alien, industrial environment that there developed a fully fledged Algerian proletariat with strong and enduring ties to the rural Algerian hinterland. And in the midst of this working-class milieu was born the first organized Algerian movement in the twentieth century advocating the complete separation of Algeria from France. This was the North African Star or ENA (*Etoile Nord Africaine*).

Originating in Paris in 1926, the ENA was intended as a means of organizing and defending "the material, moral, and social interests" of North African Muslim workers. Under the charismatic Messali Hadj (1898–1974), who assumed the leadership of the movement in 1927, the ENA quickly came under the control of Algerians and became the most left-wing and radical of all Algerian nationalist tendencies. Superimposing a proletarian character over its nationalist and religious doctrines, the ENA demanded, almost from the outset, complete independence for Algeria and its North African neighbors, Morocco and Tunisia, confiscation of all colon-acquired property, creation of a national army, and withdrawal of all French troops from Algeria.

Messali was born in Tlemcen, an old Islamic town of the interior that was once the seat of active and well-to-do Islamic traders and entrepreneurs but that had receded into the background under the impact of French colonization and economic competition. His origin in a family of "obscure religious personages," his youth influenced by saintly worship and religious discipline of a Sufi brotherhood, and his tendency toward the "mystical" attest to the effect of an environment in which Islamic belief served as the language of protest and protection for the faithful. Messali's education was rudimentary; he received a certificate from French colonial authorities for the completion of his primary school studies. Drafted into the French army, he joined thousands of his fellow Muslim countrymen who were to fight for France in World War I. Once abroad he was to spend the better part of his adult life outside Algeria, organizing and mobilizing support for the independence of his homeland.

Like Ferhat Abbas, Messali married a Frenchwoman, whose Marxist ideas were to influence his own association with the French

Communist party. Yet Messali's "mystical" Arab-Islamic roots, his flamboyant personal style, oratorical excesses, and organizational energies could not be contained within the narrow ideological confines of the Communist party which, in any case, seemed antithetical to Algerian political aspirations. From the start, Messali was a nationalist whose ideology "was a hybrid, combining a nostalgic and sentimental attachment to Algeria with Muslim loyalties under a Marxist facade."[5]

Through the ENA Messali urged Muslim workers to adopt the working-class virtues and militant class consciousness that he observed among French workers and to which he felt communist organizational techniques were ideally suited. Indeed it was left-wing and trade-union activity associated with the working-class experience in urban France that provided the migrant workers both with the models of organization and with fragments of socialist ideology that they would find useful in interpreting the condition of their homeland. When the workers returned to Algeria, the colon-dominated socialist and communist unions and parties of the metropole could give little meaning or substance to their aspirations. From the first, the logic of the colonial situation forced the Algerian semiproletariat to give its support to nationalist parties like the ENA and later to its more militant successors.

His radical ambitions and activist style led French authorities to imprison Messali and dissolve his organization, which nonetheless merely resurrected itself under different names. Released from prison in 1935, Messali went into self-imposed exile in Switzerland where he came into contact with the well-known pan-Arabist intellectual, Shakib Arslan, whose extensive writings on Arab nationalism influenced Messali's own thinking on the subject. These intellectual exchanges caused him to abandon much of his Marxism and to adopt a more revolutionary nationalist position without, however, diluting the populist strain in his program.

Allowed to return to Algeria by the Socialist Blum government, in 1937 Messali formed a successor to the ENA called the Algerian People's party or PPA (*Parti du Peuple Algérien*), a truly mass-based nationalist party that fused socialist and Islamic values. It differed from Ben Badis's ulema, for example, both in its more modernistic interpretation of Islamic dogma and in its radical social demands that included the redistribution of land among the Algerian peasants. Yet the PPA was concerned with Islam not only for itself but also as a means of mobilizing the proletariat and other traditional strata in the collective struggle for an independent Algeria.

Like its predecessor, the PPA was severely repressed by the French government; yet it still managed, by the eve of World War

II, to have 3,000 members. Sentenced to prison once again in 1941, Messali was not to reappear until after the war when his PPA was reconstituted in 1946 as the Movement for the Triumph of Democratic Liberties (MTLD). This latter organization sought to work within the colonial system to achieve its goals. It thus contested elections, participated in the various deliberative assemblies, and, in general, operated according to the established legal order. Despite the fact that by the late 1940s the MTLD had outdistanced Abbas's rival party as the leading nationalist organization both inside and outside of the country, it lacked a clear-cut ideology or political program with which to inspire membership adhesion and maintain enthusiasm. Instead it gave much time to rhetoric, exploiting the evocative principles of independence, Islam, and class interest.

Messali's authoritarian governing style and his insistence on absolute obedience to him found less and less favor among a new generation of more action-oriented revolutionary types who were emerging after World War II. These activists were becoming impatient with interminable political dialogues, meaningless manifestos, and unfulfilled promises. It was among these activists that divisions within the MTLD arose—with "centralists" (those working within the party's Central Committee) opposing Messali's intransigent, one-man rule.

Earlier a clandestine body called the Special Organization or OS (*Organisation Spéciale*) had been created to undertake violent and other terrorist operations when legal political protest was suppressed by the French. Yet having parallel overt (MTLD) and clandestine (OS) structures blurred the lines of party hierarchy, making it difficult to develop internal institutions for resolving conflicts.

The combination of all these factors—an inarticulate ideology, a cult of personality leadership, organizational splits between overt and covert operations, political divisions involving Messali and the centralists, and the growing impatience of a revolutionary generation more predisposed to using force and violence—made conventional political discourse within the French constitutional framework outdated and irrelevant. Messali and the centralists' unwillingness to compromise, the hostility of both to any external alliances with either the ulema or Ferhat Abbas, and the continued French repression virtually assured that all would be outflanked and superceded by more violence-prone elements.

When the OS was uncovered in March 1950 by the French secret service, the organization was broken up and Messali arrested. He was deported to France, where he remained throughout the most violent stage of the Algerian independence struggle and eventually died in 1974. With his arrest the MTLD foundered in factionalism as members became divided over tactical questions. A spate of internecine killings between the two rival groups within the MTLD followed.

Disgusted by these divisions and all the sterile disputes around them, a third group that was convinced that only through armed revolt could a change in French policy be brought about gradually developed. A former OS leader who had been arrested when that organization was uncovered but who managed to escape incarceration gathered a group of former OS members, dissidents from the MTLD, ex-French army men who had gained much combat experience in the Indochina campaign, and a miscellaneous category of dedicated and desperate men to form a new body called the Revolutionary Committee for Unity and Action (CRUA) in early 1954.

Ahmed Ben Bella and eight others came to be known as the nine "historic chiefs" of the Algerian revolution. They renounced past nationalist rivalries and dedicated themselves in the CRUA to the violent overthrow of the French colonial system. Unlike the educated, *évolué* leadership heading the assimilationist, Islamic, and radical nationalist movements of the 1930s, these revolutionaries were of modest semiproletarian origin. None had university training and only two had even a secondary school education. Only one of the nine had experience in French and Algerian politics, and none had risen to be officers in the French army. Their average age was thirty-two, and the youngest was only twenty-seven. What linked these men together was their experience in clandestine activities and their absolute commitment to direct, violent, and revolutionary action. One CRUA leader, Mohamed Khider, summarized the difference between his group and reformist nationalists like Ferhat Abbas: "What separated us . . . from Ferhat Abbas and his friends [was] the refusal to believe in persuasion. There [was] a logic to violence, and it [was] necessary to carry this logic to its conclusion."[6] Abbas himself was to admit as much when in 1956, in tones of grim disillusion, he said:

> My party and I have thrown our entire support into the cause defended by the [nine historic chiefs]. My role, today, is to stand aside for the chiefs of the armed resistance. The methods that I have upheld for the last fifteen years—cooperation, discussion, persuasion—have shown themselves to be ineffective; this I recognize. . . .[7]

Organizationally the CRUA split up into a group of "internals" involved in organizing Algeria into six separate military regions and "externals" headquartered in Cairo from which they worked to gain foreign support for the rebellion. Once a date for the insurrection was set, the National Liberation Front (FLN) was proclaimed. On November 1, 1954, All Saints Day, the revolution began, and a proclamation was issued by the FLN calling on all Algerians "to rise and fight for their freedom."

Summary

As we have seen, Algerian nationalism evolved following World War I and reached a critical stage in the 1930s. It was in this period that certain liberal assimilationists and other moderate nationalists were willing to accept some of the reforms in the status of Algerian Muslims vis-à-vis their colon counterparts that Paris was proposing. But in almost every instance settler intransigence managed to undermine even the mildest of liberal measures, the most noteworthy being the Blum-Viollette Plan of 1936. The realization that no effective change could take place so long as the colon community defiantly held on to its privileged position forced assimilationists to abandon integrationist schemes and move quickly toward the notion of autonomy and, ultimately, complete independence. French inability and unwillingness to grant concessions in time, under the pressure of the settlers, spelled the end of the assimilationist cause.

The Sétif massacres of 1945 further catalyzed the process of disengagement and radicalization. For his part, Messali, although rightly considered "the first twentieth century Algerian separatist, the most constant and intransigent nationalist, and perhaps even the father of the idea that Algeria should be an independent nation, not an autonomous state within the French system, and not a colony,"[8] failed to overcome the many personality, organizational, and ideological divisions besetting the MTLD. It was within this political vacuum that a new generation of revolutionary upstarts emerged to organize and lead the FLN in its revolution against French rule. Unlike their more sophisticated predecessors, however, these people were not ideologically motivated. Instead,

> their decision to act was based on a common agreement that the legal nationalist movement had failed and was disintegrating, that national independence was the primary condition for Muslim Algerians both to regain their honor and to advance socially and economically, and that violence was the only way that the French colonial system could be destroyed in Algeria. Beyond these simple perceptions there was little agreement.[9]

THE WAR OF NATIONAL LIBERATION AND POLITICAL INDEPENDENCE, 1954-1962

Anxious to "do something," the revolutionaries undertook, on that November day, several scores of coordinated attacks throughout the whole of the country north of the desert. Nevertheless, despite preparations going back as early as 1945, the revolt failed to arouse a mass uprising and achieved little in material terms. The poorly equipped and barely organized guerrillas numbered only between 1,000 and 3,000 *moudjahidines* ("fighters for the faith").

Initial French reaction was one of annoyance and disdain mixed with certain incoherence but was soon followed by swift and effective action against the *maquisards* (guerrillas) of the National Liberation Army, or ALN (the FLN's military organization). French *paras* (crack paratroop units) from France who were brought in to quell the insurrection in the Aurès—the area where FLN strength was concentrated—managed in relatively short order to reduce the *maquisards* to several hundred active fighters.

Despite these initial setbacks the revolt continued to spread slowly from the Aurès and southeastern Algeria to the wooded, mountainous regions around Constantine. Gradually those early "heroic years" galvanized the uncommitted Muslims into supporting the rebellion despite (or because of) the *moudjahidines'* terrorist tactics that involved mass murders of Europeans, French soldiers, and uncooperative Muslim civilians alike. A year after the uprising began, the FLN had consolidated its position and acquired new recruits, creating a unified military front against the French, who by now realized that the revolt had become a revolution. The serious and numerous political divisions that racked the FLN leadership throughout the war notwithstanding, its guerrilla activities managed to disrupt profoundly the internal life of both Algeria and France while tying down thousands of increasingly demoralized French soldiers.

The fighting itself was particularly savage and involved the brutal slaughter of thousands of civilians.

> Kidnapping was commonplace, as were the ritual murder and mutilation of captured French military, colon of both genders and of every age, suspected collaborators or traitors, and Muslims who had been recalcitrant in their support of the FLN. A favored method of killing was the application of a "Kabyle smile," a euphemism for a slit throat.[10]

Ultimately, however, the guerrilla fighters in the country were no match against superior French forces who were mobilized in large

numbers for combat in Algeria. What the war did accomplish, however,
was to politicize on a broad scale the conflict not only within Algeria
and France but also across the globe. This politicization led eventually
to diplomatic and political pressures for complete French withdrawal—
not unlike the similar experience of the United States in Vietnam.
Indeed, the French military elite in Algeria, like its U.S. counterpart
in South Vietnam, was almost neurotically obsessed with the idea
that it could solve the Algerian problem through the simultaneous
application of force, persuasion, and propaganda if only the civilian
authorities would cease their interference.

In strictly military terms the battle began to turn in France's
favor as early as mid-1956 when the addition of French units from
Europe and French West Africa, brought to Algeria to augment existing
troops, created a total French force of nearly half-a-million men under
arms. These large numbers enabled the French to shift tactics: They
replaced the use of occasional flying columns with a grid system in
which towns and communication centers were held in strength while
mobile units of paratroopers, volunteers, and foreign legionnaires
probed the countryside. With this tactic the French were able to check
many but not all ALN military activities. In response the Algerians,
toward the end of 1956, instituted a strategy of urban terrorism as
a means of regaining the military initiative and attracting public
support. Random and ruthless acts of terrorism that were undertaken
in Algiers and elsewhere inspired fear and uncertainty among the
colon, but admiration and support within the Muslim community,
especially its urban underclass.

French tactical planning was adjusted accordingly, leading to
the eventual destruction of the urban terrorist organization in Algiers'
impoverished, Muslim-populated Casbah section of the city. The Battle
of Algiers was brutal but decisive in eliminating all hopes of using
urban warfare as an effective instrument of revolution. From this
point on, the guerrillas abandoned large-scale terrorism in the cities
as a military tactic. Instead the defeat in Algiers in late 1957 led to
a recognition that nowhere in Algeria was the ALN strong enough
to face any major armed confrontation with the French army. Therefore,
the war could really no longer be won inside Algeria.

Checked within the country itself, the ALN was thus forced to
seek alternative sources of support, which it found in neighboring
Tunisia and Morocco, both of which had become independent of
France in March 1956. Large recruitment and training centers were
established in these territories from which an army of 25,000 men
was created. This number exceeded by 10,000 the number of *moudjahidine* fighters who remained within the country to continue their

guerrilla struggle. The external army was to play a decisive role in the political control and organization of postindependence Algeria although its military contribution during the war was relatively insignificant. This impotence was due in great part to the French army's construction of lengthy and elaborate barriers of electrified wire, alarm systems, barbed wire, strongholds, mine fields, and observation posts along both the Moroccan and the Tunisian frontiers— thus effectively sealing off the external army from the internal zone of operations.

With the borders effectively sealed, the French army turned its attention to the military situation in Algeria itself. Starting in 1958, it began to isolate ALN bases by surrounding them with so-called pacified zones. In addition, each of the *wilayas* (Algerian military districts) was targeted separately for attack, thereby destroying communications between the zones and weakening the ALN's capacity to mount large-scale operations against the French. Reduced to small-group tactics once again, the rebels were kept continuously off balance and limited to "pinprick" attacks that, although appropriate during the early part of the insurrection, seemed insufficient and ineffective now. More significant perhaps was the massive civilian population relocation that the French undertook in order to separate the guerrillas from their potential source of support. By 1961, for example, nearly two million people had been moved from their houses, mostly in the mountainous areas, and resettled in the plains, where many found it impossible to reestablish their accustomed economic or social situations. Thousands of others escaped to the already overcrowded cities in order to avoid the various zones of combat.

Along with military operations, forcible relocations, and population regroupments, the French employed psychological warfare, ranging from mass persuasion and the provision of social services by army personnel to forcible indoctrination and torture. In combination these French efforts seriously hampered Algerian nationalist operations. It became increasingly difficult for them to communicate and coordinate their armed struggle. Military districts were split up, supply lines interrupted, and the command structure divided between the FLN leadership operating abroad and the military chieftains actually in the field. Standing in the wings in ever larger numbers, well-equipped, organized, and trained, was the external army. It saw little action and therefore suffered few serious setbacks, but in the end it was the only organized body to emerge from the war in a position to bargain in the final negotiations for peace.

Not all the problems besetting the Algerian war effort, however, were due to French military efforts. More important was the highly fragmented nature of the nationalist movement itself. Lacking political organization, an incontestable leader, and an articulated ideology, the FLN remained loosely unified only under the imperatives of war. Indeed the intensely divisive character of Algerian intra-elite behavior during the revolution tells us more about how postindependence Algeria evolved politically than does the actual conduct of the war or the impact it had on native society and economy.

Almost from the outset of the war divisions occurred within the Algerian nationalist movement. Although all "purely Algerian parties and movements" were invited to join the FLN, the best known and most popular figure at the time, Messali Hadj, refused the invitation. Instead he created a competing nationalist organization called the Algerian National Movement (MNA), whose base of support came essentially from the many Algerian workers living in France. Like the FLN it too was dedicated to a policy of violent revolution and total independence. As it did in Algeria, the FLN established a significant presence in France. One of its earliest and most enduring tasks was the destruction of the MNA and its influence among the Algerian laborers. Indeed many of the atrocities that characterized the war of independence grew out of the internecine MNA-FLN battle and the merciless "café wars" that were waged on French sidewalks and in back streets and that cost several thousand lives.

In Algeria a national congress of the FLN was held in August 1956 in the Soummam valley in lower Kabylia in an attempt to provide organizational cohesion and policy direction for the party's steadily expanding membership. The FLN membership encompassed virtually the full spectrum of elite orientations from the Communists on the left to the ulema on the right, with the liberal nationalists of Abbas's ilk in the middle. The congress confirmed three principles: "the priority of the interior over the exterior, the political over the military organization, and collegial decision-making."[11]

The absence of the external delegation headed by Ben Bella from the congress undermined the surface harmony achieved following approval of the Soummam platform. The fundamental personality differences between Ben Bella and the principal organizer of the congress, Abane Ramdane, added to the divisions. These probably would have had more serious implications if it were not for the arrest of Ben Bella and three other historic chiefs by the French following a midair kidnapping. Ben Bella's arrest effectively eliminated him as a factor in the day-to-day conduct of the war although his popularity and prestige among many Algerians probably increased during the period of his incarceration. That many of the congress organizers were Berbers and the majority of the externals Arab, may have also fueled the difference; one must be cautious, however, about attributing too much importance to Arab-Berber ethnic cleavages.

Despite these open and latent conflicts it was expected that by including virtually all groups within the authoritative structures of the FLN the prerevolutionary differences would be eliminated. Instead, the Algerian struggle demonstrated that violence directed at a common enemy was insufficient as a base of political cohesion among former competitors. Throughout the war divisions that had pervaded the nationalist movement before 1954 were perpetuated and intensified within the expanded FLN decisionmaking structures. In an attempt to incorporate into the overall FLN structure so many diverse elements already in place or newly formed, the party sacrificed the ideological coherence necessary to give the revolution its political and social meaning in the postwar period.

The establishment in 1958 of a provisional government (GPRA) along with other trappings of political institutionalization could not hide the fundamental heterogeneity of the political elite and the many personality, structural, and logistical differences that had developed in the last five years of the war. Given all these shortcomings, it remains remarkable that the FLN was still able to maintain control over the war effort, gain the support of a large proportion of the Algerian Muslim population, and ultimately achieve independence from the French on terms that nearly met all of the FLN's demands.

Yet the revolution's ultimate success came less at the hands of a victorious guerrilla army than as a consequence of the intensive political, economic, and worldwide diplomatic strains that the conflict had inflicted on the foundations of the French polity. More often than not French military efforts in a contrary way produced the forces of their own undoing. Internally, for example, the more the French proved victorious on the battlefield, the more the nationalist cause grew in the hearts and minds of the Algerian people.

It could not be otherwise, given the experience of forcible relocation, flight of refugees to the overcrowded cities, the destruction of agricultural resources, and the annihilation of nomadic groups that could no longer carry out their migrations—"all these pulverized the social relations of traditional society and produced a fearsome ideological vacuum."[12]

The already massive chasm separating the colon community and Algerian Muslims was further widened by the conflict, and French efforts at psychological warfare deepened this chasm. Within France itself the war was taking a frightful toll and was pushing the country to the brink of moral, economic, and political disintegration. Tearing the country apart was the battle going on between the large segments of liberal France and the alliance of the intransigent colon with a professional army that was determined that the country would not suffer another defeat in a guerrilla struggle in the manner of the French experience in Indochina. Eventually these and other conflicts between and within France proper and its troublesome overseas department led to several abortive insurrections against the established government. These included the May 1958 threatened coup d'état in Algiers that brought Charles de Gaulle to power, an unsuccessful army-colon rebellion against de Gaulle in January 1960, and the revolt of army leaders in Algiers in April 1961 that was effectively put down by forces loyal to the French president.

On the international level as early as 1955, at the first conference of nonaligned nations in Bandung, Indonesia, the FLN was accorded observer status, thereby significantly enhancing its prestige in world forums. The disastrous Suez war of 1956 (involving a publicly unacknowledged tripartite military alliance of Israel, England, and France against Egypt) further discredited French colonial claims, including those to Algeria. The establishment of the GPRA in 1958 and the extension by many Arab, Third World, and Communist countries of full diplomatic recognition to Algeria's provisional government allowed the latter to establish a more formal presence in many parts of the world where it advanced its cause through publicity and propaganda. In the United States itself in mid-1957 John F. Kennedy, then a young junior senator, spoke out publicly in favor of Algerian independence on the Senate floor—thus breaking with the United States' official support for France's North African policy.

The combination of external and internal pressures ultimately had a decisive impact on France's Algerian policy and revealed the basic paradox of the conflict that had been developing since 1956: "France was strong, militarily, in Algeria, but weak, politically at home; the FLN was weak, militarily, at home, but strong, politically, abroad."[13]

De Gaulle finally led a war-weary and isolated France to the negotiating table. In March 1962 in Evian, France, a cease-fire was agreed upon by both sides. Several months later, on July 5, 1962, Algeria became independent—on the 132d anniversary of the French entry into Algeria. But independence did not arrive before diehard individual French officers and some deserters, in cooperation with activist groups of settlers, formed the Secret Army Organization (OAS), which began a systematic campaign of terror in Algeria's cities. Those last days of colonialism witnessed blind rages of senseless violence and ultimately mass flight by virtually all Europeans to France. The last, apocalyptic days of Oran symbolized the close of the European era in Algeria: "the city engulfed in a great pall of smoke from the exploded oil tanks in the port and empty of everything save death and hatred. The only fitting epitaph for this ending was that the colonial period died as it had lived, in violence and incomprehension."[14] Years later one observer was to comment: "Despite the Timgad-like bricks and stones left by the pieds noirs, were they ever really here at all?"[15] This recalls the earlier observation about the fleeting impact that Rome had on Algeria during its eight-hundred-year "sojourn" in the country.

That Algeria finally achieved independence, however, could not hide a central fact: Algeria's revolution was more "war" than social or political "revolution"; the battle was fought by men united in hardly anything except the common object of their hatred—the European settlers. The war, of hideous and singularly intimate brutality, served to avenge the trauma of colonization. As one French scholar has written: "The insurrection was not . . . the expression of a uniform political apparatus, nor was it tied to a commonly held underlying revolutionary theory. November was an act of rejection of the French colonial system; what it aimed at was Independence."[16]

It was thus not surprising that although it was able to oust the French, the FLN was unable to survive the fragmentation inherent in guerrilla warfare. Its failure to develop ideology into an effective system of political communication to enhance the cohesion of the cadres was to cause the postindependence government's near disintegration, bordering on civil war. Indeed, it can be said that the deep ideological divisions in the body politic that had been widened during the war were not to be completely eliminated until the government of the country's first president, Ahmed Ben Bella, was overthrown by the military in mid-1965.

THE POSTINDEPENDENCE PERIOD OF BEN BELLA, BOUMEDIENE, AND BENJEDID, 1962 TO THE PRESENT

The superficial unity that marked the FLN's military and diplomatic efforts broke down immediately after independence, and a vicious struggle for power among contending groups began. The three major contestants for power were the Algerian provisional government, the *wilaya* commands, and the army of the frontier or external army (ALN), based in Morocco and Tunisia during the revolution. At issue were wartime misdemeanors, ideology, ethnic and clan ties, loyalties to specific individuals, and competing perspectives on the nature of postindependence Algerian society. At stake was political predominance in the state.

The first round in the postwar struggle was fought at the Tripoli (Libya) congress of the FLN national council in May 1962. Factionalism and deep-seated antagonism among all the principal nationalist leaders quickly surfaced. The purposes of the Tripoli meeting were to elect a political bureau to assume control of the FLN and to devise a political and economic program, which later became the official policy of independent Algeria.

When the competing factions returned to Algeria, Ben Bella, with the military support of the ALN chief of staff, Colonel Houari Boumediene, was able to gain the initiative and establish his authority over party and nation. On September 20, 1962, elections for the Algerian National Assembly were held. All powers of the GRPA were transferred to the new assembly and formal proclamation of the Democratic and Popular Republic of Algeria was made. Six days later, the assembly elected Ben Bella premier and empowered him to form a government. He immediately formed a cabinet that included Boumediene as defense minister. Others were chosen from the Algerian army (Armée Nationale Populaire—ANP) and from among Ben Bella's personal and political associates.

Once the new government had consolidated its position, it set about addressing the severe economic plight of the country, caused in great part by the sudden and massive exodus of the Europeans. The latter included virtually all the entrepreneurs, technicians, administrators, teachers, doctors, and skilled workers in the country. After factories and shops closed and farms ceased operations, over 70 percent of the population was left unemployed. In March 1963, overwhelmed by the catastrophic economic situation and unguided by any particular socialist ideology, Ben Bella signed into law several decrees (the March Decrees) that legalized the takeover of extensive agricultural and industrial properties abandoned in the colon exodus and instituted the system of *autogestion*, or workers' self-management.

Autogestion was conceived as an economic system based on workers' management of their own affairs. The workers would elect officials and cooperate with the state through a director and national agencies. The state's function was to guide, counsel, and coordinate their activities within the evolving national plan. *Autogestion* was considered necessary for the transformation from a colonial to a socialist economy. The severe shortage of qualified personnel and the inability of workers and peasants to comprehend fully the principles of self-management made this experiment in socialism more a myth than a reality.

Ben Bella's style of rule did not instill confidence among a war-weary population. He quickly attempted to increase his personal standing and power. In April 1963 he took over the position of general secretary of the FLN. Subsequently, he engineered the passage of a constitution creating a presidential regime with the FLN as the sole political party. In September 1963 he was elected president for a five-year term. He also assumed the title of military commander in chief while becoming head of state and head of government.

This consolidation of personal power and apparent move toward dictatorial government aroused opposition and the reemergence of factionalism. Ferhat Abbas, the president of the assembly and the leading spokesman for a more liberal policy, resigned from the presidency and was subsequently expelled from the FLN. In the Kabyle, where discontent was accentuated by Berber regionalism, sporadic disturbances broke out, and a revolt had to be quashed by police action and political compromise.

In April 1964, the long-awaited third congress of the FLN was held in Algiers to sort out the ideological differences among various competing groups within the ruling establishment. Toward this end the Algiers Charter, as it came to be called, was formally adopted. The charter defined the relationship among the state, party, and army and supported traditional Islamic principles as theoretical guidelines for Algerian socialism and the policy of *autogestion.*

The congress, however, exacerbated the feud between Ben Bella and Boumediene. Ben Bella attempted to strengthen the leftist organizations in the hope that they would help him against the army, while Boumediene tried to unify the army against Ben Bella by resolving the conflict between the former *wilaya* leaders and the newer officers of the ANP.

Ultimately Ben Bella lost. Despite his numerous efforts to institutionalize the revolution and its socialist ideology, his popularity among the masses, and his status as one of the historic chiefs of the revolution, he was never able to overcome the many rivalries, challenges, and controversies that faced his regime. In addition, his ouster of the traditional leaders, his repeated political attacks on the General Union of Algerian Workers (UGTA), his failure to make the FLN an efficient mass party, his suspicion of plotters behind every door, and his increasingly dictatorial tendencies alienated many political leaders and interest groups. Furthermore, Ben Bella's constant improvisation in policy offended even his closest supporters. Once the army had turned against him, he was left virtually powerless and vulnerable, and in June 1965 he was ousted from power.

The military takeover hardly caused a ripple in Algerian society. The constitution was suspended and power was smoothly and efficiently transferred to Boumediene and a twenty-six-member Council of the Revolution, which was designated as the supreme political body. Boumediene was named prime minister and minister of defense, and Abdelaziz Bouteflika, a close ally of Boumediene whose foreign affairs portfolio was being threatened by Ben Bella on the eve of the coup, continued as foreign minister. According to the council, the aims of the new regime were to reestablish the principles of the revolution, to remedy the abuses of personal power associated with Ben Bella, to end internal divisions, and to create an authentic socialist society based on a sound economy.

For his base of support, Boumediene relied on the *moudjahidine* veterans of the war of independence, the ALN officers, and a new class of young technocrats, a reflection of his more somber and low-key style of authority. The shy, introverted Boumediene was a reformist and organizer who stressed the need for planning and reflection and was wary of radical change. During the first two years of his rule, he initiated no bold new initiatives. There was little attempt to resuscitate national political life, and the Algerian National Assembly remained in abeyance. The FLN was incapable of action.

Despite Boumediene's cautious administration, opposition against him began to crystallize among left-wing ministers, the UGTA, the students, and some sections of the army—notably the former *wilaya* leaders. The opposition favored the syndicalist approach to socialism embodied in *autogestion* rather than the more centralized and technocratic system being developed by Boumediene. It also feared that collegial rule was being supplanted by a dictatorship of Boumediene and the small group around him.

On December 14, 1967, Colonel Tahar Zbiri, army chief of staff and a prominent former *wilaya* leader, launched an armed uprising in the countryside. It was quickly and efficiently suppressed by forces loyal to Boumediene, but other groups, especially dissident students, continued to demonstrate their opposition to the new regime by striking and staging street demonstrations. There were reports of guerrilla activity in the Aurès and Kabylia regions, and on April 25, 1968, there was an unsuccessful attempt to assassinate Boumediene.

Between 1968 and 1972, however, the regime managed to consolidate its power, thereby enabling it to initiate bold policies of development in the industrial, agricultural, and political fields. The second stage of the reform of governmental institutions, for example, was put into operation in 1969 when the government held elections for the regional-level administrative units (Popular *Wilaya* Assembly or APW). Both the APC (Popular Communal Assembly) elections that had been held in February 1967 and May 1969 APW elections clearly indicated how Boumediene envisioned the organization of the

Algerian state and its political institutions. Specifically, his idea was to implement a system of decentralized local government counterbalanced by a single centralized party, the FLN, and a well-established administration.

It was also during the 1968–1972 period that the regime gave priority to the development of heavy industry, particularly of the petroleum and gas industry. At the end of 1971 a major attempt was also made at agrarian reform in order to improve the lagging agricultural sector, which had received only secondary attention when the emphasis had been on boosting industrial productivity.

In the political sphere, the lack of political representation and popular participation in the first five years of Boumediene's rule, despite the creation of local and *wilaya* assemblies, led him to reassess the status of the nation's political institutions, particularly its single-party governing structure, the FLN. The regime's successful creation of a stable political environment had been achieved at the expense of public participation in the political process. The FLN had been allowed to become moribund and overly bureaucratized. Thus, on June 19, 1975, (the tenth anniversary of his ascent to power) Boumediene announced the preparation of a national charter and constitution that would provide for political institutions that were either to be created or reactivated.

In May 1976, Boumediene submitted the charter to public debate. The extensive and surprisingly candid discussions at party gatherings, trade union meetings, and assemblies of the burgeoning peasants' association reflected widening public participation in political life and reaffirmed the power of Boumediene and his regime.

On June 27, 1976, the new National Charter was overwhelmingly approved by a referendum. The charter represents an ideological inventory of Algeria's socialist history and indicates the direction the country intends to pursue. It also delineates the popular and institutional basis of the future Algeria, giving renewed prominence to the FLN as the nation's only authentic representative of the people's will. Emphasis is also placed on the participatory role of citizens in a socialist society.

In November 1976 Algerians again went to the polls and overwhelmingly approved a new constitution that reactivated the national assembly, now to be called the Popular National Assembly (APN), and restored the country to constitutional rule for the first time since the July 1965 suspension of the 1963 constitution that had been promulgated under Ben Bella. The new constitution was a lengthy document, containing a preamble and 199 articles; it ushered in what has become known as the Second Algerian Republic (the first republic lasted from 1963 to 1965). In theory, the National Charter and the new constitution signaled the return of constitutional government, but because Boumediene personally led and encouraged the public debate that favored both new documents, the votes approving them were in fact votes of confidence in the man himself and his personal system of rule.

A month after approval of the constitution, Boumediene, the only candidate on the ballot, was overwhelmingly elected president of the republic. According to the constitution, Boumediene, as president, officially became head of state, head of government, commander in chief of the armed forces, head of national defense, and nominally the head of the FLN—all of which significantly extended an institutional power that was already well-fortified by his support from the military.

Finally, as provided for in the new constitution, elections for the new Popular National Assembly were held on February 25, 1977. Although all the candidates were chosen by the FLN, there was a certain amount of debate over the choices between the grass-roots militants and the party leadership. The representatives elected to a five-year term in the new assembly included six government ministers, diplomats, army officers, peasants, industrial and office workers, civil servants, party workers; several of these were women. Emphasizing that the new assembly was composed of a majority of peasants and workers, government officials described the APN as the final step in the construction of a socialist state that had begun a decade earlier with local elections.

On April 27, 1977, the assembly formed a new government. The president remained firmly in control, however, since all twenty-four ministers and three secretaries of state were considered to be the president's men, loyal, obedient, and, for the most part, competent. Because Boumediene did not designate a prime minister—a constitutional role of his office—he further enhanced the presidential prerogative within Algeria's political system.

In addition to creating the important institutional and participatory bases of Algerian political life, Boumediene's main accomplishments as leader of Algeria during the years of his tenure included: stabilizing the nation's leadership, consolidating government control over the economy, introducing comprehensive economic planning, capitalizing on petroleum and gas revenues, and generally aiming at rapid industrialization.

Boumediene's sudden illness in November 1978 and his death a month later from a rare blood disease left Algeria without a designated successor. As stipulated in the constitution, National Assembly President Rabah Bitat, the last surviving and politically active of the nine historic chiefs, assumed interim responsibilities as chief of state while a special congress of the FLN was convened to select a candidate. The congress's choice of Colonel Chadli Benjedid—a senior military officer—as presidential candidate and secretary general of the party reflected the preeminence of the military officer corps as a predominant political force in Algerian political life.

In the five-year period from Chadli's uncontested election to the presidency in February 1979 to the renewal of his five-year mandate in January 1984 (with over 95 percent of the popular vote in both instances), Algeria has evolved away from the ideological militancy and economic austerity of the Boumediene era into a more liberalized phase of decentralization, deconcentration, and (limited) democratization that have become the salient features of the current regime. Through a series of broad measures in virtually all sectors of politics and economics, Chadli Benjedid has taken the Algerian ship of state toward a different, more pragmatically oriented direction in clear distinction to the volatile romanticism of Ben Bella and the heavily ideological orientation of Boumediene. Thus a full two decades after independence Algeria's revolution has been institutionalized with Chadli's no-nonsense, businesslike demeanor representing a new style of governance.

President Chadli Benjedid—his nom de guerre—was born on April 14, 1929, in a family of modest farmers in the *wilaya* of Annaba. He completed his early education in Annaba where it was said he was involved in clandestine proindependence activities. Early in 1955 Chadli joined the forces of the ALN; there his organizational as well as military and political skills were recognized, allowing him to advance rather quickly within the military hierarchy. He was named head of a military region in 1955 and vice-head of a larger military zone in 1958. Two years later Chadli headed the thirteenth ALN battalion in the northern zone close to the Tunisian border. When the Army General Staff of the ALN was created in February 1961, Colonel Boumediene, who headed the staff, appointed Chadli as assistant chief of operations in Ghardimaou (Tunisia), a position that he held until July 1962.

On the eve of independence Chadli was sent from his base in Tunisia to Algeria but was arrested along with others of the external army by guerrilla fighters of the *wilaya* II district. Their arrest presaged the upcoming conflict among the various military wings of the nationalist movement. After his release Chadli assumed the post of military commander in Constantine at the end of 1962.

In June 1964 Benjedid assumed the important position of commander of one of the five military districts in which the country was
divided at that time. From his position as leader of the Oran *wilaya,*
Chadli was able to establish a popular base of support among both
the military and civilian populations. He was still head of the Oran
district when he was nominated as the single presidential candidate
by the special FLN congress in December 1978. Two months later
he was elected the country's third postindependence president.

Chadli was essential in assisting Houari Boumediene's ALN in
overcoming resistance by the internal guerrilla forces and subsequent
dissident groups that arose in July 1964 and December 1967. Chadli
fully backed Boumediene's coup d'état against Ben Bella in June 1965
and became one of the twenty-six members of the Council of the
Revolution, which assumed total political power following the dis-
solution of the National Assembly and the suspension of the country's
1963 constitution.

As reward for his loyal service Chadli was promoted to the
rank of colonel in June 1969, which, at the time, was the highest
military grade in the Algerian armed forces. Noted for his devotion
to Boumediene and his military professionalism, Chadli did not at
first appear as a likely candidate for the presidency. He became the
army's choice, however, when it became clear that bitter conflicts
between ideological factions of the party and governmental leadership
could not be satisfactorily resolved without undermining the political
legitimacy of the state. Chadli's noncontroversial career and unsullied
record, despite unconfirmed reports that while commander in Oran
he had greatly enriched himself and his relatives, made him ideally
suited to take over the reins of power. In the period since his first
election he has developed an independent identity, disengaging himself
from the personalities and policies of his predecessor. As such Algerian
politics and policies in the 1980s have assumed a very different cast,
with gradualism, reformism, and economic productivity operating in
a more enlightened social environment, constituting the central hallmarks of the Chadli regime.

The remaining chapters of this book will be treating in detail
the specifics of Algeria's current political, social, and economic development. It is sufficient at this point simply to provide an outline
of Chadli's accomplishments in the first half decade of his rule.

After pursuing a cautious policy of "change within continuity"
in the years immediately following Boumediene's death, Chadli Benjedid later undertook a number of wide-ranging initiatives. These
enabled him to consolidate his power and take full control of the
state, party, and military apparatus on the eve of his reelection to

the presidency in early 1984. As a result the process of "de-Bou-medienization" has virtually been completed, and Chadli's men and policies are now firmly in place. This has been achieved through a combination of liberalization measures, policy shifts, coercive pressures, changes in key personnel, and modifications of the rules of the game.

Popular measures that Chadli implemented almost immediately after assuming power in 1979 included the elimination of the much hated exit visa that had been required of all citizens and foreign residents for travel abroad; the release of politically innocuous prisoners such as Ben Bella, who had been placed under house arrest following the 1965 coup; the return of noted exiles such as Tahar Zbiri, who had conspired to overthrow Boumediene in 1967; the lifting of controls against certain dissidents at home like Ferhat Abbas and Benyoussef Ben Khedda, who had come out in 1976 against Boumediene's foreign policies, especially Algeria's relation with Morocco; and the implementation of a massive anticorruption drive directed against well-known public figures who governed under Boumediene like Abdelaziz Bouteflika, who had been the country's long-term foreign minister from 1963 to 1979, as well as against numerous other high-ranking officials and their subordinates. Besides opening up what had become an increasingly oppressive and corrupt society, these measures also enabled the new regime to eliminate loyalists of the previous government whose devotion to Chadli was uncertain.

Also important were the many policy shifts that Chadli undertook in the economic, administrative, and foreign policy realms. Almost all large state enterprises, for example, accused at once of being overly centralized, inefficient, and parasitic, were broken up into smaller, more manageable parts. Similarly "super" ministries were reduced in number. They would thus be not only more accountable but also more controllable. Potentially ambitious bureaucrats would not be able to use ministerial or subministerial authority to accumulate power into their own hands. Other changes included opening up the Algerian economy to certain types of limited foreign investment, expanding and revitalizing the country's private sector in both agriculture and consumer industries, diversifying arms purchases away from the Soviet Union and toward such western manufacturers as Britain and the United States, and lowering of Algeria's once highly visible profile in global and Third World affairs.

None of these liberalizing efforts, however, have been allowed to challenge the regime's central authority. Thus when it has become necessary, the regime has used sweeping coercive measures to suppress uprisings, demonstrations, and other forms of antistate behavior. In this regard the government has come down hard on university students, Islamic fundamentalists, and ethnic Berbers who have challenged the education, religious, and language policies of the regime. In almost every instance, however, a firm response has been quickly followed by a conciliatory gesture aimed at appeasing discontented groups. In combination the carrot and stick approach has managed to control and contain effectively the limited antigovernment actions that the country has experienced in recent years.

There have been a number of personnel shifts since 1979 that have also succeeded in firming up Chadli's power. These shifts have taken place in all the key institutions of the state such as the cabinet, the National Assembly, the Political Bureau and the Central Committee of the FLN, the military, and the directorships of the nationalized companies. Through elections, reductions in numbers, forced retirements, and movements to symbolic, but politically insignificant, positions at home and abroad Chadli's regime has virtually eliminated all serious contenders to his increasingly "sultanic" authority. Finally in both the armed forces and the political party Chadli has changed certain rules, especially the powers of appointment, to ensure that his people are placed in decisive positions.

The frontal assault on a sluggish, corruption-ridden, and bloated bureaucracy that had made the Algerian economy so inefficient these many years (despite the existence of ample hydrocarbon reserves) has been now undertaken without fear of challenge or opposition. To the initial call for A Better Life, which constituted the motto of the extraordinary party congress in 1980, has now been added Discipline and Hard Work to Guarantee the Future, which was advanced at the December 1983 fifth FLN congress. Efficiency, accountability, and productivity are the hallmarks of the new Algeria. In order to counteract unemployment, low food production, rapid population growth and overurbanization, the current regime has reoriented its domestic development away from heavy industry, except for energy, toward agriculture, light industry, consumer goods, and the social services such as housing, education, and health care. The mistakes of the past—which include unrealistic concentration on heavy industry, excessively rigid socialism, and the loss of private business initiative—have all been recognized and attempts are now being made to correct them.

As we have seen, Algeria has experienced a turbulent and violent history over several centuries with each post-Islamic phase adding some distinctive dimension to what was eventually to become the independent Democratic and Popular Republic of Algeria. The traumatic experience of colonialism and the bloody decolonization process have all left their legacy of confusion and disorientation and engendered suspicion and a conspiratorial mind-set among the many competing nationalist forces that emerged at independence. An initial period of charismatic but chaotic rule under Ben Bella was quickly replaced by a rigidly bureaucratic system of socialist rule under Boumediene. In the last half decade of his presidency, however, political life became more institutionalized as a new constitution and a national charter were promulgated and parliamentary and presidential elections were held.

It was not until the rule of Chadli Benjedid that a more "mature" form of development began to take hold. Secure at home and abroad, the current leadership is devoting more of its energies to the tasks of modernization, social rectification, and improving the quality of life of its citizens. The next decade will be crucial in determining whether or not these processes will evolve productively or whether mismanagement will once again prevent Algeria from assuming its proper role. As one of the more advanced of the newly industrializing countries Algeria is attempting to follow its own distinctive path toward development without compromising either its cultural heritage or its national identity.

NOTES

1. Alistair Horne, *A Savage War of Peace: Algeria, 1954–1962* (Middlesex, England: Penguin Books, 1977), p. 40.

2. Ibid., p. 27.

3. Wilfred Knapp, *North West Africa: A Political and Economic Survey,* 3d ed. (Oxford: Oxford University Press, 1977), p. 76.

4. Charles F. Gallagher, *The United States and North Africa: Morocco, Algeria, and Tunisia* (Cambridge: Harvard University Press, 1963), p. 95.

5. Mostefa Lacheraf, *L'Algérie: Nation et Société* (Paris: Maspero, 1976), p. 195.

6. Clement Henry Moore, *Politics in North Africa: Algeria, Morocco, and Tunisia* (Boston: Little, Brown, 1970), p. 86.

7. Horne, *A Savage War of Peace,* p. 141.

8. Alf Andrew Heggoy, *Historical Dictionary of Algeria* (Metuchen, N.J.: The Scarecrow Press, 1981), p. 145.

9. William B. Quandt, *Revolution and Political Leadership: Algeria, 1954–1968* (Cambridge: The M.I.T. Press, 1969), p. 93.

10. Harold D. Nelson, ed., *Algeria: A Country Study,* 3d ed. (Washington, D.C.: Government Printing Office, 1979), p. 53.

11. William B. Quandt, *Revolution and Political Leadership,* p. 100.

12. Eric R. Wolf, *Peasant Wars of the Twentieth Century* (New York: Harper and Row, 1969), p. 241.

13. Horne, *A Savage War of Peace,* p. 230.

14. Gallagher, *The United States and North Africa,* p. 115.

15. Horne, *A Savage War of Peace,* p. 562.

16. Gerard Chaliand, *Revolution in the Third World* (Middlesex, England: Penguin Books, 1978), p. 72.

4

Culture and Society
in Transition

Culture and society in the Algeria of the 1980s are undergoing fundamental change as exhibited in the multitude of hidden and open conflicts, contradictions, and tensions that beset everyday existence. Algerian traditional life both in the countryside and the city and at the personal, familial, and local levels has been affected profoundly by 132 years of colonial rule, including nearly 8 years of war and revolutionary struggle, and the broad mobilization policies of the postindependent leadership. These conditions have endangered Algeria's cultural continuity and created a mobile, often rootless society that only Islamic belief and, secondarily, populist ideology have prevented from disintegrating into open conflict or social chaos.

Precolonial society, although reflecting a relative coherence in the spiritual, economic, and social aspects of its culture, had been unprepared to meet the challenge of Europe. Nothing within the indigenous culture could stimulate Algerian society as a whole. "Its population growth was too late and too abrupt; there was not enough vitality in urban crafts or foreign commerce; and there was no intellectual renewal."[1] Colonialism fractured, disoriented, and redefined Algeria according to its own dynamics. Although a "strong historical continuity of the leading segments of Algerian rural society from Turkish times to the early twentieth century [withstood] the multiple calamities of conquest, epidemics, colonization and rebellions,"[2] the Algerian traditional order was, in the final analysis, recast in fundamental and profound ways. The war of independence, including the mass resettlement program undertaken by the French, had cataclysmic impact on the society as a whole. It destroyed traditional institutions but did not automatically create or even accelerate the creation of new ones.

Desert nomads outside the oasis town of El Goléa.

  At independence the country was free, but the society was adrift. The colonial legacy revealed a continued fragmentation of the traditional order resulting in a disjunctive rather than functional pattern of development. Radical socialist forms appeared and state-centered and state-directed policies aimed at creating a modern industrial system took shape, further alienating an already disrupted society. A victim of all these historical forces was the traditional order—its central value system, its enduring norms and beliefs that gave meaning to human existence. What kind of society was destroyed by these multiple impacts and what has taken its place?

  Traditional rural life has long been characterized by poverty and a certain degree of physical insecurity, at least until the early twentieth century. Within such a hostile environment there developed a tough and hardened population whose values encouraged armed strength, virility, and masculinity. Self-contained and culturally distinct from urban society, the settled cultivators and nomadic herdsmen who inhabited the countryside lived in small, ethnically homogeneous groups, the largest of which was the village or tribe. Kinship ties were the basis of social organization, and cohesion the result of patriarchal authoritarian rule.

Group identity in such communities was highly pronounced. Economic relations tended to be autonomous, and there was a limited use of money. Local products were exchanged for the few goods that were needed from outside the village or tribe—everything else was produced within the group. Local fields, orchards, and flocks were the source of foodstuffs, with clothing and footwear coming also from sheep and goats.

The family constituted the center around which all tradition-oriented life revolved. The family, with the individual subordinated to it, was and, in many ways, still remains today the basic social and economic unit. Typically the Algerian traditional family is extended, patrilineal, patrilocal, patriarchal, endogamous, and, increasingly less and less so, polygynous. In such an extended family the husband and wife, their unmarried children, and their married sons with their families all live within the same house or proximate dwellings. The oldest male member possesses complete authority over the family. He is empowered by tradition and custom to make all major decisions that affect the family's standing with the outside world. He is also entitled to punish any family member who acts against the reputation or welfare of the family. Finally, succession of authority and the inheritance of real property passes through the male in both the Arabic- and the Berber-speaking communities.

One cannot emphasize enough the power and importance of family ties and loyalties, which override most other obligations even among those groups that are undergoing social change. In such an environment, personal life is stifled by the social life of the family. The importance of the family in Algerian society is well summarized by a leading French sociologist.

> The family is the alpha and omega of the whole system: the primary group and structural model for any possible grouping, it is the indissociable atom of society which assigns and assures to each of its members his place, his function, his very reason for existence and, to a certain degree, his existence itself; the center of a way of life and a tradition which provide it with a firm foundation and which it is therefore resolutely determined to maintain; last but by no means least, it is a coherent and stable unit situated in a network of common interests whose permanence and security must be assured above all else, even, if necessary, to the detriment of individual aspirations and interests.[3]

Religion has always played a significant role in traditional society. The atmosphere of Islam permeates virtually all of life in Algeria—

religious, intellectual, private, social, and professional. Algerians are not a particularly religious people in the sense of abiding by dogma—for example, few Algerians, whether in the countryside or in the cities, say their prayers five times a day as religious teachings instruct. Yet they scrupulously observe prescriptions that are secondary from the point of view of religious doctrine, such as taboos concerning food and alcohol and practices like circumcision and wearing of the veil.

These various rituals are important in the religious life of the community. Among the more backward strata of society, rites associated with pagan beliefs, sacred stones, and other forms of divine intervention provide proximity to God. Such practices are far removed from the orthodox strictures of the Koran that remain remote, inaccessible, and impenetrable for most country folk.

Traditional rural people and large segments of the urban society in Algeria lived this way until the 1900s. Then thorough and profound changes took place: French colonialism and massive European settlement disrupted economic, social, and political life. Agriculture was exploited to the detriment of the Algerian peasant. French-controlled commercial activities, especially in the modernized urban sectors, squeezed out the small Algerian middle stratum of merchants and artisans. In the countryside dispossessed Algerian landowners in the more fertile areas were often reduced to the status of sharecroppers or landless laborers. Hunger and malnutrition plagued rural communities, whose population growth of 3 percent per annum fast outpaced dwindling food and land resources. Living conditions were forced to the point of crisis as employment dropped steadily. The rural masses became paupers on the land, which was stripped each year of its youth who sought work in the major cities and abroad. One source describes this process in the following terms:

> A rapid increase in population, coupled with alienation of cultivated and pastoral lands to European settlers, created tremendous pressures on the cultivable land. Displaced villagers and tribesmen flocked to the cities, where they formed an unskilled labor mass, ill-adapted to industrial work, scorned by Europeans, and isolated from the extended family and larger kin units that formerly gave them security and a sense of solidarity. As the area available to nomadic sheepherders decreased, many herders were forced to adopt a partially sedentary way of life or to migrate to coastal areas to seek work.[4]

The war of national liberation, with its devastation and intensity, catalyzed further social changes that would become very difficult, if not impossible, to reverse. In brief, war completed what colonial politics and commerce had begun: rural exodus and entry into employment centers. The massive bloodshed, forcible removal of populations, destruction and razing of thousands of villages, burning of forests, slaughtering of cattle, mass migrations within and across the country's borders, and the disappearance of the kin-based residential communities created deep-seated social, gender, generational, occupational, and educational dislocations and cleavages that, more than twenty years later, have yet to be fully overcome. The result of these actions was the swelling of the country's already overcrowded coastal cities—terminals for Algerians fleeing the pauperization of the rural areas and for emigrant laborers pausing in their outward journey to metropolitan France.

The regime that assumed power at independence aggravated rather than ameliorated many of the pressures that had destroyed important traditions of the past without providing adequate substitutes that could give meaning and purpose to contemporary social existence. By propagating policies that called for the radical technological modernization of society while simultaneously promoting cultural and personal beliefs predicated on the country's Arab-Islamic heritage and traditional family structure, postindependence Algeria was left suspended in its development, straddling two different worlds without being fully in either.

In many parts of the country today the Algerian world remains split dramatically between the women's world of hearth and home and the man's world of mosque, marketplace, and coffeehouse. In rural areas life continues to revolve around the family; in the cities the family, along with other traditional institutions, now competes with more modern, individualistic voluntary groupings that are supervised from above by the state. Even in remote areas of the country formal political and social institutions of the state—police headquarters, party office, health center, school—have begun to replace the clan. These dualistic structures and competing allegiances have caused great disquiet among contemporary Algerians. "Clear guidelines for behavior and belief no longer exist for the millions of Algerians caught between a tradition that no longer commands their total loyalty and a modernism that cannot satisfy the psychological and spiritual needs of young people in particular."[5]

Few areas of society have managed to escape these wrenching pressures, save for two Berber tribal groupings, the Mozabites and the Tuaregs, located at the northern and southern ends respectively of the country's Saharan zone. These tribes' physical isolation, small numbers, religious insularity, and strong social cohesion have made

Open market in Ghardaia. Note the absence of women.

them immune to conquest, colonization, conflict, and ideological conversion.

More than anything else, urbanization has changed the national spectrum of traditional life and labor. Increasingly the new social order, discontinuities and all, is located in the sprawling urban areas that today constitute over 50 percent (1982: 52 percent) of the country's population concentration. Within such urban conglomerations as Algiers, Oran, and Constantine potentially disruptive class structures and other social groupings and aggregations have formed. At the top a small but influential stratum of highly educated technocrats constitute the core of a new salaried and bureaucratized class, which includes managers of national industries, directors of state enterprises, teachers, professors, administrators, scientific experts, engineers, lawyers, and army officers. Modernist, populist, and egalitarian in ideological orientation, this technocratic elite is the greatest beneficiary of the industrialized complex that state capitalism, using its ample hydrocarbon reserves, has created in the last generation.

Below them rests a relatively large, but politically impotent, petite bourgeoisie involved in running small shops, tea and coffee houses, and small family businesses and whose sons are clerks in commerce, teachers, and lower-echelon public servants. This group

Rug dealers in Ghardaia market square.

controls the 75 percent of the retail trade that remains in the private
sector in an otherwise socialized economy. Another segment of the
urban class structure includes blue collar workers involved in non-
agricultural activities in industry, construction and public works,
services and administration. Many in this group are workers regularly
employed in state-owned factories. Others are a shifting stream of
low-paid day laborers.

The lowest group are the hard-core jobless made up of displaced
former peasants who have flooded the cities in search of work and
social opportunity but who possess neither the skill nor temperament
to achieve either. This emerging underclass of former mountain dwellers
from Kabylia, shepherds from the High Plateaus, and gardeners from
the oases of the Sahara have all converged into the coastal cities,
accelerating a trend that began in earnest during the period following
World War I. Originally propelled by the shattering of the economic
and social equilibrium in their rural districts, the migration of these
urban "nomads" is a result of the socialist regime's industrialization-
first policies. The neglect of agriculture and rural development has
made work on the land less attractive and rural exodus the only
escape from a life of abject poverty. Although these members of this

new proletariat often lived in districts within the cities according to their origin and preserved close contacts with their home villages, they were in fact detached from the rural society without being truly integrated into the urban society.

That state and society have not collapsed under the weight of these divided class structures and social cleavages can be attributed just as much to the reactivation of traditional values as to the extensive coercive capacities of the state. In the last decade as social and psychocultural pressures have mounted in an increasingly alienating urban environment, individuals and groups have returned to their traditional values as expressed in family solidarity, public morality, religious fundamentalism, and the Arab-Islamic heritage to provide guidance and direction in an otherwise turbulent world. More than anything else Islamic belief and practice, providing the means to ameliorate many of the social tensions generated by vast class cleavages, remain at the core of Algeria's culture.

ISLAM

Virtually all Algerians are Sunni Muslims. Yet, as we have seen, Islam's importance is not the orthodox observance of the faith; rather, Islam is the source of cultural identity. The religion in this broad societal sense is a key to understanding not only culture and society but politics and economics as well.

During the long period of colonial domination—especially at the time of the protracted struggle for independence—Algerians gained strength, identity, and national cohesion from their Islamic belief. Islam served both as the language of refusal against French oppression and as a symbol of self-assertion against colonial power and policy directed, as part of its "civilizing mission," at debasing and dismantling Islamic practices and institutions. There can be no doubt that, however profound the Islamic identity at the individual or community level remained, it was the disruptive nature of French colonial policy that ultimately provoked the aggressive reassertion of an indigenous Algerian identity with strong ties to native Islamic culture. The result was that Islam became an integral part of incipient Algerian nationalism.

At independence the secular authorities sought to incorporate this identity into a more revolutionary ideology directed toward socialism and rapid modernization. For nearly twenty years this strategy of incorporation appeared to be working, but by the late 1970s serious tensions and discontinuities developed within the body social as a radicalized "populist" Islam emerged to challenge the "official" Islam of the state. Islam's politicization had thus become a central fact of Algerian society.

In discussing the role of Islam three diverse forms find expression in contemporary Algeria: maraboutic Islam, state or official Islam, and populist, or fundamentalist, Islam. Each will be discussed in turn.

Maraboutism

Islam in Algeria, as indeed in all of the Maghreb, has been interlaced with the indigenous Berber culture to produce a characteristic style of religious belief and practice. Throughout history Algerians have accepted the presence of mysterious powers and invisible beings. In fact, the mystical element identified in early Islam was a continuation of pre-Islamic Berber practices in the countryside. For centuries an important element in local religious belief has been the coalescence of special power in particular living human beings, that of *baraka*, a transferable quality of personal blessedness and spiritual force. Such persons who possessed *baraka* came to be known as marabouts, derived from the Arabic meaning, "those who have made a religious retreat."

Marabouts, "a quintessentially Maghrebin social type,"[6] were thought to be individuals on whom God had bestowed intercessory and intermediary powers. If this condition of blessedness could be substantiated through performance of apparent miracles, exemplary human insight, or genealogical connection with a recognized possessor, the individual marabout would be viewed as a saint. These ascetic, saintly men and women, preoccupied in channeling God's power and blessing into the world, would withdraw from mundane affairs. Their faith was expressed in festivals, magical practices, and ecstatic ceremonies. Venerated as mystics and teachers locally, marabouts gathered a circle of disciples who propagated their beliefs within religious orders or brotherhoods. Each brotherhood followed a particular "way," or *tariqa*, with its own rituals and rites—conducted in addition to the ordinary observances of Islam. When rural life remained disorganized and far removed from the centers of power located in the cities, these brotherhoods and maraboutic movements were instrumental in making Islam accessible to the masses.

Through their simple, emotional, and popular rituals marabouts had particular appeal among the plain country folk whose lack of education made it difficult for them to assimilate the Koranic teachings and dogma practiced by the orthodox Islamic clergy and ulema classes in the cities. Indeed, much of maraboutism's populist appeal was in direct reaction to the aridity of orthodox Islam and the moribund schools of Islamic theology patronized by the religious legal scholars.

Essentially intuitive and transcendental in their theology, the marabouts, stressing community solidarity, mutual assistance, and self-defense, offered psychological reinforcement to the masses who followed them in a way that the mosques, schools, and courts could not.

Their popularity and significance in the organization of religious life in the countryside had wide political and social implications: marabouts became important community figures acting in various roles such as tribal leader, arbitrator in family and clan disputes, businessman. Eventually maraboutic brotherhoods emerged, constituting a kind of "corporate institutionalization of folk religion."[7] During its peak period between the fifteenth and mid-seventeenth centuries, maraboutism functioned as a vast rural revivalist cause. Beyond the control of whatever putative central authority existed in urban centers, the religious brotherhoods served real organizational and social functions whose legitimacy was enhanced by religious sanction.

Both external and internal forces, however, were eventually to undermine and destroy the marabouts' independent political power. French colonialism, for example, by pacifying and incorporating the countryside within its colonial administration, undercut the numerous broker, social, and political functions performed by the marabouts. Although they reduced the organized political power of the marabouts, the French allied themselves with certain brotherhoods in an effort to cut the strength of the orthodox ulema whose promotion of Islamically inspired nationalist appeals among native Algerians challenged French hegemony in the country. Inevitably such association with colonial authorities discredited the marabouts—many of them were attacked as "colonialist collaborators" and as "religious frauds."

The brotherhoods' greatest opposition, however, came from within, among the Muslim reformers who rejected completely institutionalized mysticism and other forms of saintly worship and popular superstitions. Religious reformers like Ben Badis and his Association of Algerian Ulema saw orthodox Islam as an essentially creative force that could integrate national life through the religious courts and the religious schools. Orthodox Islamic belief has always emphasized God's unique and inimitable majesty and sanctity and the equality of access to God for all believers, leaving no room for saintly spokesmen of the faith. From the perspective of Islamic orthodoxy, mystical beliefs and maraboutism were heterodox elements that encouraged local dissidence.

Attacked from without and within, maraboutism seemed essentially a spent force by the time of Ben Badis's death in 1940. The nationalist movement and its successor regime incorporated reformist Islam in the state's official ideology and, as such, fully rejected maraboutism as a valid expression of the Algerian identity. Nonetheless the mystical tradition remains alive, for the history of Islam in Algeria has always been one of division: the Islam of the mosque and ulema and the Islam of the rural folk and the marabouts. Between these two extremes a wide middle ground has emerged in which scriptural and Sufi (that is, mystical) aspects of Islam have been integrated; this middle ground may well constitute the norm of Islamic belief in both rural and urban Algerian society. As one observer has commented, Maghrebi Islam can only be understood as a "coexisting blend of the scrupulous intellectualism of the ulema and the sometimes frenzied emotionalism of the masses."[8]

In concrete sociopolitical terms as well, there is evidence to show that maraboutism is not the spent force once assumed. One scholar, for example, has noted that despite the hostility toward maraboutism of the state's official Islam, "the success of members of maraboutic families in local and departmental elections has been a major feature of politics in the Jurjura region of Greater Kabylia since 1967."[9] Since the late 1960s the government, in an effort to incorporate Berber Algeria within the modern state sector, has spent large sums and devoted human resources to the region. Therefore, the ability of maraboutic families to preserve and, in some cases, enhance their social status is quite remarkable. Much of this has been accomplished through an adept climbing of the "several bandwagons of modernization."[10] By entering into the critical sectors of state-sponsored modernization—education, medicine, politics, and even religious training—individuals claiming maraboutic lineage have managed to incorporate new, officially sanctioned powers to themselves while preserving their traditional status.

Ultimately, of course, this situation cannot last; more and more people are becoming educated and modern, thus challenging the new found prestige of maraboutic families. Maraboutism in the 1980s remains a local, rather than national, force with limited political possibilities. What remains unchanged, however, is the attraction of the mystical and the mysterious. As they have throughout the centuries, the presence of mysterious powers and the satisfaction in the magical approach of marabouts to solving human problems continue to attract Algerian rural society. Whether benevolent or malevolent, these powers must be "greeted, honored, propitiated, or avoided."[11]

La Mosquée des Ketchaoua, constructed in 1794 but converted by
the French into a Catholic church
in 1832. After independence it was
reconverted into a mosque. Located in old Algiers at the base of
the Casbah, fronting the Place des
Martyrs.

Official Islam

The second major expression of Islam in Algeria is that of official
Islam or state reformism. Its origins lie with the Muslim reformers
associated with Ben Badis and his Association of Algerian Ulema,
discussed in Chapter 3 as one of the three strains of Algerian
nationalism that emerged during the interwar period. Algeria's Islamic
reformers came from the Constantine area at the beginning of the
twentieth century—Ben Badis from Constantine, al-Ibrahimi from
Sétif, al-Okbi from Biskra—and directed their attack simultaneously
against French assimilationist tendencies and the heterodox practices
of the marabouts and religious brotherhoods. It was within the many
religious schools founded by the association of ulema that a sense
of Algerian identity was instilled among the nation's youth.

Although by the 1930s and 1940s the Muslim reformers had
relinquished control of the nationalist movement to secularly oriented
political figures, Islam remained a powerful symbol of national unity
and pride both during the colonial struggle and after independence.
In particular, the government of Houari Boumediene undertook a
concerted effort to restore and promote Islam to its rightful place in
Algerian culture and society. Islam, or rather *laïcité islamique* ("Islamic
secularism"), as one French scholar has described it,[12] became the

civil religion; Christian churches and cathedrals, for example, were (re)-converted to mosques and Christian religious symbols dismantled and replaced by Arab-Islamic ones. In principle and practice Muslim reformism was embodied as the official religion of the postindependent state with the government presenting itself as the "only legitimate heir to [Ben Badis]—the greatest figure of Algerian [Islamic] reformers."[13]

From the outset as with everything else in Algeria, religion came under the direct and complete control of the centralized authorities. State reformism as such constituted the only form of religious organization granted official sanction; maraboutic Islam was reduced to virtual insignificance in the countryside. From the perspective of the revolutionary leadership Islam was to serve as an identity-forming instrument, not as a legal code by which to order state and society. Ideologically, it was one of the dominant themes in the Algerian nationalist consciousness but had no influence on political structures. The *sharia* (body of Islamic legal principles) had been seriously undermined during 132 years of colonial rule, and the leaders of independent Algeria saw no reason to activate the sacred law as a means of organizing society. A secular state with an Islamic cultural component would thus be the manner in which a nationalist synthesis would be achieved; hence, there is no apparent conflict in the country's constitution, which states in Article 1, for example, that Algeria is "socialist" (that is, secular and revolutionary) and in Article 2 that "Islam is the state religion."

Within this framework, official Islam was promoted as a complementary aspect of the developmental process by religious authorities mobilized to advance such an ideology. According to state-appointed reformist-minded ulema, modernization and Islam were compatible inasmuch as the latter "stressed a puritanical observance of the Quran and a transformation of society at the same time."[14] In such a manner the technocratic elites in power hoped to expand their legitimacy "by claiming that [they] alone could lead both in upholding religion and in modernizing the country."[15] Their objective was clear enough: "the intercessor between God and development [was] no longer a [marabout], a prophet, or a *mufti*, but rather, the state apparatus."[16] The organization of religion in the state reflected this new reality. Religious affairs were institutionalized at the highest levels of government, with a minister for religious affairs constituting the state's official spokesperson on religious practice. Organized along the lines of a civil service bureaucracy, this ministry has been given virtually total power over religious matters, including the authority to hire and fire religious leaders, administer all religious schools and other centers of Islamic study, control the *habous* (religious endowments) and mosques, determine the kind and quantity of religious books published and circulated, and monitor the content of Friday sermons throughout the country. The principal objective in these multiple efforts has not been only to raise the level of national religious consciousness as a moral prerequisite for revolutionary advancement, though this remains important. The objective has also been to ensure that Islamic symbols and appeals are not confiscated by autonomous forces hostile to the current regime and its secular policies.

The four individuals who have held the religious ministry position since independence represent the prototype of the subservient bureaucratic functionary who directs religious affairs in the state. Tawfiq al-Madani was the first person to be appointed minister for religious affairs after independence. As a former leader in the ulema association of Ben Badis and, later, a member of Algeria's preindependence provisional government (GPRA), he possessed the kind of sectarian-secular balance that the new regime was looking for. His successor, Mouloud Kassim, who assumed the post in the 1970s, devoted himself to showing how the government's socialist policies were not contrary to Islamic principles.

Boualem Baki was appointed minister in Chadli Benjedid's first government in March 1979. Like his predecessors Baki had been directly involved in the principal political movements (PPA and MTLD) struggling for independence. He had also been arrested and imprisoned by French authorities for his political activities. His directorship of several private Koranic schools in Sétif in the 1950s qualified him for the religious affairs portfolio until the growing power of Islamic fundamentalism forced the regime to select a personality more visibly identified with Islamic activism.

Abderrahmane Chibane was brought into the cabinet that was formed in July 1980 and has been the minister for religious affairs ever since. He survived a major government reshuffle in June 1982 and the creation of a new cabinet in January 1984. A former teacher of Arabic language and literature at the Ben Badis Institute in Constantine, Chibane had been associated with the reformist movement and served as a high-ranking official in the wartime FLN. With impeccable Islamic and ideological credentials, Chibane represents the kind of pliant bureaucrat favored by the secular authorities in that "he is the perfect symbol of the official dualistic formulation of legitimacy: the cultural *and* the historical, the reformist *and* the revolutionary, the religious *and* the political."[17]

A decade and a half after independence it seemed that the national leadership, through its uncontested authority, had thoroughly integrated reformist Islam into the official ideology of the state. Controlling religious officialdom, institutions, teaching, and values, the central government had simultaneously adorned itself with the mantle of legitimacy that Islam could provide and halted any potentially disaffected groups from exploiting religious symbols as instruments of protest and opposition.

By the late 1970s, however, state cooptation of religion began to unravel when discontented groups found official Islam sterile to their daily lives and limiting in their attempts to arrive at an authentic sense of cultural identity. In response, a more populist, puritanical, fundamentalist, or "folk" Islam emerged and severely challenged the secular authorities. The populist argument went as follows: "State reformism [had led] to the glorification of the state rather than to the glorification of Islam. The nation-state [had] nationalized religion, to the detriment of the community of all Muslim believers. In so doing, the state [had] worked counter to the plan of the Prophet: to have all Muslims under one banner within one entity, the *umma* [the community of Muslim believers]."[18]

Populist Islam

As elsewhere in the Middle East and North Africa there has been a re-Islamization of politics in Algeria during the last decade. Although several forms of Islamic expression exist, only one has assumed national significance with widespread implications for state and society.

Referred to by several alternate labels—"popular puritanism," "Islamic fundamentalism," "militant Islam," "Muslim radicalism"— the reactivation of Islamic principles differs markedly from the mysticism and saintly worhsip of maraboutism, which provides little meaning to contemporary urban life, and the official Islam of the state whose recasting of transcendant religious values in modern form has increasingly worn thin. No doubt the revolutionary experience in Iran, where Muslim militants took over power in 1979, has had a lasting impact on Algerians as on other Muslim peoples of the Arab world. Yet the rise of populist Islam in Algeria has more to do with local considerations than with any external experience, however appealing or galvanizing.

The government could not long pursue policies of secular development based on industrialization, urbanization, mass education, and bureaucratization, while espousing Islamic principles, without eventually creating between principle and practice a gap that alienated many Algerians. Partial modernization left its mark on society, and neither the secular ideology—socialism—nor the state-sponsored religion—official Islam—provided the kind of psychological palliative necessary for a people to overcome the stressful and dislocating consequences of rapid social change. As a result widespread frustration and resentment of the sacrifices made in the name of modernity have inspired a reaction and a demand for a return to the proven basis of cultural tradition—Islam.

Fundamentalist or populist Islam, with its call for a more scripturalist interpretation of Muslim life, has set the standard for so-called authentic Islam. Unlike the Muslim reformers of the first half of the twentieth century in the Middle East who called for reform of the faith so as to better deal with the West—the names of Jamal al-Din al-Afghani, Muhammad Abduh, and Rashid Rida come to mind in this regard—fundamentalist Islam completely rejects Western concepts and any kind of accommodation with Western intellectualism. The intense rejection of the West—its ideals, values, material possessions—is uncompromising. Action-oriented and directed at achieving specific programs, militant Islam is equally unaccepting of socialist slogans that supposedly cohere with Islamic beliefs in some general, theoretical way. The government's socialist rhetoric pointing to the congruence of Islam and socialism has sounded increasingly hollow. As one observer has commented: "The vague identification of socialist policies as being somehow Islamic was not definite enough. The need was for specific actions that could be recommended which would clearly and unambiguously show that they were Islamic."[19]

For Algeria's fundamentalists all economic and social problems are at bottom moral problems. Thus the bases of a good and powerful Muslim society are not institutions or political structures per se, however rational or effective they may appear to be, but belief in Islam by a people with virtuous impulses who are committed to religious law in a direct and comprehensive manner—in other words, by those determined to live out Islamic principles. Indeed the key to the fundamentalist style in Algeria

is an insistence upon a rigorous and uncompromising adherence to the rules found in the Quran and the traditions of the Prophet. This adherence is expressed in a relatively literalist application of Quranic regulations and precedents. Such a literalist application [provides] a set of clearly visible actions that could be taken as a way of showing adherence to authentic Islam. The special punishments prescribed in the Quran for particular crimes . . . represent clearly visible policies or actions that can be taken as a way of showing that a person, government or opposition group is explicitly and authentically Islamic.[20]

Distinctive of Muslim fundamentalists, as opposed to other dissident groups, in Algeria is not only their interpretation of the Koran and other sources of Islamic doctrine for themselves but also their determination to act on their beliefs. This determination makes them violently oppose the established order in an attempt to realize the City of God on Earth. Very different from the fundamentalist thinking of an earlier generation identified with such groups as the Muslim Brotherhood in Egypt or the Wahhabis in Saudi Arabia, the populist movement in Algeria is more radical socially and politically. "There is a willingness to advocate a total restructuring of society based on a comprehensive and holistic vision of what the Quran requires for society as a whole, rather than a list of Quranic rules and regulations."[21]

As a sociopolitical movement, populist Islam, bent on "purifying" what it sees as a less than devout society, has swept through urban Algeria since the late 1970s. Although not nearly so well-organized as the mullahs and ayatollahs in Iran, Algeria's fundamentalists do have a modicum of organization and recognized leadership. They have been particularly active in the following areas: pressing for conservative female dress codes, exhorting the faithful and thereby increasing mosque attendance, demanding a ban on the use of all alcoholic beverages in public places, insisting on expanded Koranic religious schooling, pushing for an intensification of Arabization language policies, and urging increased broadcast hours of Islamic topics on radio and television.

It is on university campuses in particular where fundamentalist activity has been most visible—and violent. In the last half decade, for example, there have been repeated clashes between left-wing students and Muslim radicals involving bloodshed and loss of life. In 1979 and 1980, for example, militant Muslims attacked groups whom they labeled as "Marxists" and "Berberists." They have also physically assaulted individual female students for allegedly dressing in less-than-proper Muslim attire. Encouraged by the tactics of intimidation and physical coercion on campus, the fundamentalists have also begun to coordinate demonstrations off campus. This was the case in June 1980 when Muslim radicals in the eastern towns of Biskra, Batna, and El Oued ransacked hotels, cafés, and restaurants suspected of serving alcoholic beverages in violation of Islamic tenets.

Most disturbing of all from the perspective of government officials has been the growth of unauthorized mosques that have escaped the control of the Ministry for Religious Affairs. In these "streetside" mosques it has not been uncommon to hear imams (religious leaders) attacking the government and its socialist policies. Neither Chadli's

Peaceful street scene in oasis town of Laghouat, locale of clash in 1981.

assertion that "no one can give us lessons in Islam," recalling that religious faith fueled the Algerians' struggle against the French, nor statements that "our ideology is Islam," have proven satisfactory to the religious zealots. The fundamentalists have even gone as far as to oust officially appointed imams and to replace them with ones of their own: Indeed in October 1981 in the northern Saharan oasis city of Laghouat a police attempt to close down a "usurped" mosque in which a popular imam was sermonizing led to a bloody clash in which one policeman was severely beaten.

The most serious disturbances in recent years involving Muslim fundamentalists took place in November 1982 both on and off the several campuses of the University of Algiers. In tracts, pamphlets, and booklets fundamentalist students had been making demands for a drastic reduction in Western influence on Algerian society. Specifically, they were demanding the creation of an "Islamic government" and the abrogation of the National Charter of 1976, the state's official ideological blueprint. Instead, they insisted that the Koran should replace this secular document as the basis of explaining the philosophic, socioeconomic, and political life of the nation. In addition, they were demanding certain purification measures such as eliminating coeducational schooling, forbidding girls to continue formal education after the age of twelve, rejecting completely Western values, and prohibiting alcohol. Although these demands had been made before, they were now being promoted as much through organized violence as through moral persuasion. Nor was the violence limited to isolated or uncoordinated attacks against particular individuals or female students. One was now witnessing a developing social movement utilizing collective violence as a means to achieve ideological ends.

It was within such an intensely polarizing atmosphere that campus violence erupted. In early November residence hall committee elections on the University of Algiers' suburban campus of Ben Aknoun were contested by Communist students who were dissatisfied with the results by which a Muslim majority had won the elections. The Communist students challenged the outcome; this quickly degenerated into direct clashes between the groups, and one leftist student was killed and several others were injured. The police arrested more than 400 fundamentalists. Word of their arrest, which spread quickly throughout the capital, led to the convergence as a sign of protest of some 100,000 Muslim-supporting demonstrators at the Friday prayer of the university's downtown campus mosque. Populist Islam had become a potentially dangerous force that directly challenged the regime's very existence. The government's response was one of intense coercion followed by gestures of conciliation.

The scope and intensity of the 1982 demonstrations, rooted as they were in populist Islamic appeals, sent shockwaves throughout the state for they challenged two fundamental assumptions of state legitimacy: the uncontested monopoly of coercive force in the society through an expansive military and police network and the monopoly of religious symbols and vocabulary through the control of the religious institutions. Populist imams preaching violence against "heathen" authorities in makeshift mosques to massive gatherings were unlike any other challenge the postindependence state had confronted.

The early liberalism of the Chadli government—granting greater permission for public expression on a variety of issues, for example— was superceded, by the early 1980s, with a no-nonsense policy of swift retaliation, imprisonment, and (alleged) torture of radical Muslim fundamentalist leaders. In December 1982, for example, the government branded those that had inspired the disturbances and mass rallies the month before as a "band of criminals" and "agitators" who, with the assistance of "hostile foreign powers," had conspired to disrupt public order. Police sweeps supposedly uncovered large quantities of explosives and weapons assembled by clandestine organizations allegedly intent on overthrowing the legitimate government. Whether true or not, these accusations provided the justification for imprisoning hundreds of known Muslim militants.

Police crackdowns and further arrests continued throughout 1983 in an attempt to stamp out all potential centers of Muslim dissidence in the cities. Yet it was readily apparent that force alone would not be a sufficient deterrent to fundamentalist-inspired agitation. This was confirmed in March 1984, for example, when an estimated 25,000 (pro-Muslim sources cited nearly 400,000) people attended the burial of Shaykh Abdellatif Sultani, a prominent leader of the fundamentalist movement who died of apparently natural causes (he was eighty) while under house arrest following his incarceration for involvement in the 1982 disturbances. The highly emotional funeral and rally outside Algiers was the first public Islamic demonstration in Algeria since 1982.

Ignoring the protests of international organizations about violations of human rights, the Algerian government has kept up its arrest and imprisonment without trial of suspected Muslim "agitators." However, it is becoming increasingly evident that no single power center of such fundamentalist activity exists; activists and sympathizers alike are located throughout urban society—on university campuses, in factories, in schools, within religious institutions, and in the government bureaucracy itself. Hence, along with its hard-line coercive policies, the authorities have instituted conciliatory measures in order to preempt and preclude potential sources of discontent based on Islamically inspired appeals.

The government's attempt to recapture the Islamic initiative away from populist imams and Muslim fundamentalists has involved, among other things, greater use of a religious idiom in the official speeches, public statements, and government pronouncements of President Benjedid and his subordinates. Religious Affairs Minister Chibane, for example, recently praised Chadli for striving to "reestablish the hierarchy of values by placing faith in Allah above any other allegiance." Chibane himself stated at a seminar on Islamic thought that the Koran "is the source of our civilization and the impulse for our renaissance."[22] This kind of language, which has been repeated on a regular basis, represents an official effort to overtake and embrace fundamentalism before it takes any further dissident paths of its own.

In more concrete terms there has been a concerted effort to establish a national network of Islamic institutes and teaching centers intended to train Muslim clergymen. The prior financial neglect was apparent in 1982 when more than 3,000 of the 5,000 registered imams were inadequately trained, ill-prepared, or even illiterate. Since then the authorities have rapidly increased both the numbers and funding levels of Koranic educational centers and accelerated the recruitment of younger people into an otherwise aging profession. In 1982, for example, there were only 2 functioning institutes for the training of religious personnel: 1 in Meftah (not far from Algiers) where 100 students were in attendance, and another in Tamanrasset, deep in the Algerian Sahara, which was opened in January 1981 with only 50 students (of whom 20 were non-Algerians from other African countries). Today, by contrast, the following projects are either in planning stage, undergoing construction or in full operation: 160 pilot mosque-Koranic schools situated in the local administrative districts (*daira*); 2 national-level Islamic academies located in Oran and Algiers; Islamic cultural centers situated in each of the forty-eight regional administrative districts (*wilayas*) in which the country is divided; and 3 Islamic science institutes, in Tlemcen in the country's far west, Mascara in the middle west, and Medea, slightly southwest of Algiers.[23]

The centerpiece of this whole enterprise, indeed the virtual touchstone of this extensive exercise at religious legitimation through the control of education, is the recently completed Emir Abdelkader University for Islamic Sciences (ex-Higher Institute for Islamic Studies) located in Constantine, the birthplace of Ben Badis. Possibly the largest mosque-university of its kind on the African continent, the Constantine center, which was begun in June 1971 and took nearly fifteen years to complete (the first students were admitted in October 1984), has been constructed at enormous cost. It is a massive architectural achievement with impressive artistic elaboration, providing extensive classroom, library, and amphitheater space for its nearly 1,000 registered students. Intended as the nationwide institute for religious training and education ranked above all other similar centers, the Abdelkader University's stated mission is to "relate education more intimately to the realities of society and its needs both in material as well as spiritual and intellectual terms."[24]

In reality, of course, the overriding objective is to ensure that no future unofficial imams are allowed to preach unauthorized sermons in unsanctioned mosques. All Muslim clergymen are now required to possess a degree from the appropriate religious institute. The Ministry for Religious Affairs has the sole authority for assigning certified religious leaders to positions throughout the country. The ministry is also involved, more than ever before, in sponsoring annual national seminars on Islamic subjects, publishing religious journals and periodicals, broadcasting religious instruction and Muslim prayer on radio and television, organizing the yearly hajj, or pilgrimage to Mecca, by the Algerian faithful, and monitoring a wide range of religiously related activities, all in strict conformity to the national dictates established by the secular authorities.

Given the emotive nature of the fundamentalist movement and the danger that a new, independently minded clerical class may evolve out of these training institutes and challenge the authorities themselves, not unlike what happened in Iran, it is unlikely that religious symbols and semantics can ever again be completely monopolized by the state—especially so long as serious socioeconomic problems and cultural tensions confront Algerian society.

What emerges from all these conflictual developments surrounding the re-Islamization of politics is the volatile and unpredictable nature of the religious idiom in political discourse. As we have seen, for historical and religious-cultural reasons Islamic concepts and rhetoric seem almost universally adaptable as a language of *both* social protest and political legitimation. The role of political Islam in Algeria today is thus best understood as a "roving" phenomenon, broad enough to encompass virtually all strata of society. Political Islam can be used by groups opposing the regime in power and also by the ruling elite as a means to put down system challengers.[25] However, unlike opposition groups invoking Islamic appeals to challenge the bureaucratic state, the state can ensure compliance with official ideology and policy by exercizing the power of its military, administrative, and party organizations. Of course it can also invoke Islamic concepts. Thus, although Islam remains important as an instrument of political challenge in Algeria today, it should not be exaggerated in terms of its capacity, in and of itself, to mobilize large numbers of people in a full effort to overthrow the incumbent regime. The situation in Iran is sui generis and applies hardly at all to the Algerian case.

STATE SECULARIZATION

State cooptation of the religious idiom has not been limited to questions of containment and control of its use by potentially antigovernmental elements in the society. The rejuvenation of Algeria's Arab-Islamic heritage is also related to a general effort at promoting a more authentic cultural identity. Equally important, however, has been the concomitant but contradictory effort at creating a "new" Algerian man—one who will be educated to participate in a modern, technologically advancing, and secular society. Educational policy has thus been developed with these dual objectives in mind. To date, however, the results have been less than satisfactory both for identity-formation and for state modernization.

Education

The government's educational efforts since independence have been impressive, if not spectacular, at least in statistical and quantitative terms. In 1962, for example, there were only about 750,000 Algerian children enrolled in primary school; two decades later, in the 1983-1984 academic year, more than 5,000,000 students, or about 90 percent of the total primary school age group in the country, were registered. Given the much greater complexity of the secondary school curriculum and the need for more extensive equipment and more instructors, progress at the secondary school level has been even more impressive; the figure of 32,000 at independence was multiplied nearly thirtyfold by 1983-1984, with more than 900,000 enrolled, constituting over 35 percent of all children of secondary school age. Finally, although there were only 3,000 Algerian university students enrolled in 1962, by 1984 that figure had reached 107,000, distributed unevenly throughout the country's four major universities and numerous university centers, with over 70 percent on full government scholarship.

For the past decade more than 30 percent of the Algerian national budget and 11 percent of its gross national product (GNP) has been spent on education. In the Middle East–North Africa region, only Tunisia compares favorably in this regard. Despite marked regional, social, and economic imbalances (for example, in 1977-1978 only 63.8 percent of Tiaret's primary school age group was enrolled in school while Tizi-Ouzou had a 95 percent enrollment figure), a comprehensive higher education network has been established. There are full-scale universities (Algiers, Oran, Constantine, and Annaba), regional university centers (in 1977-1978 Tizi-Ouzou, Sétif, and Batna in the east, Mostaganem, Bel-Abbes, and Tlemcen in the west, and plans for establishing at least one university or university center in each of the country's forty-eight *wilayas* by the end of the century), and technical, agricultural, vocational, and teacher-training institutes as well as army, navy, and air force military academies. The goal is to serve all the nation's educational needs, including those of its adult, female, religious, and peasant populations.

At the university level, scientific, technical, biological, and medical studies have been encouraged the most, with nearly 50 percent of all university students in the 1979-1980 academic year, for example, specializing in these fields. Indeed by the early 1980s a national glut of doctors had developed, leading officials to discourage student specialization in this field. Nevertheless, the country's overall health needs remained woefully inadequate, due in great measure to the unwillingness of many newly licensed physicians to accept positions in distant and difficult areas of the country. Beginning in 1987, for example, only 2,000 medical school candidates will be accepted per year for the next twenty years while other fields of science, technology, and mathematics will be given priority. The purpose is to create the technical-scientific cadres needed to staff the swelling administrative machinery of the state. In the meantime, however, interest and concentration in the humanities, social sciences, and juridical studies continue to be high among university students.

Algeria's general educational policies are directed toward four different sectors of society and reflect varying pedagogical philosophies, levels of human and material investment, and expected outputs. Among the mass of illiterate peasants, bedouins, and seminomadic groups, for example, the government has been working conscientiously—with mixed results—to establish a minimal functional literacy, regarded as necessary for effective participation in the country's modernization and development process. At a slightly higher level, there is another mass-oriented effort involving vocational training, special institutions, and other nonacademic programs that could prepare teenage and adult "drop-outs" for jobs that would provide acceptable benefits to the individuals involved. This program would also supply blue collar labor for the state's numerous industrial and manufacturing enterprises. A third category of mass education involves those pursuing formal academic programs paralleling or slightly exceeding secondary school standards, designed ultimately to train the bulk of bureaucratic, technical, administrative, and clerical personnel that the public and, increasingly, the private sector will need in the coming decades. In a sense this politically obedient, clerical-administrative stratum constitutes the base of the regime's expanding technocracy.

At the apex of this educational pyramid stands the 1 to 3 percent of Algerians who are destined, because of their family and personal connections, acquired wealth and influence, type and level of education, multilingual fluency, and technical-scientific accreditation, to assume the top- and secondary-level decisionmaking positions in each of the principal institutional components of the technocratic system: government, party, military, bureaucracy. These four sectoral targets reflect the mass-elite dichotomy characterizing educational policy in Algeria today. Thus, the overwhelming thrust of educational efforts is to create a minimally educated, participant but obedient public, trained to assume the technical requirements of a scientifically developing society although maintaining, indeed reinforcing, the Arab-Islamic cultural identity. For a very small segment of the society, however, an elite-oriented educational structure exists to train the managers of this technological system. Yet this latter process is directed more at producing administrators than politicians, doers than thinkers, imitators than inventors, technicians than scientists, and organizational men rather than independently minded and creative decision makers.

How successful has this educational system been in creating the modern Algerian? Pedagogically, Algeria's university system is in a stage of painful transition from its colonial heritage to an independent, academically credible, and culturally authentic national system of higher education. This transitional stage is undergoing serious discontinuities and conflicts regarding its impact on student socialization. For example, although foreign instructors (mainly French) have been virtually eliminated from the primary and, to a lesser extent, secondary school systems, they still predominate (over 50 percent) at the university level at ranks (associate and full professors) and in fields (science, technology, law, and economic sciences) that have policy and prestige significance. That is, French language competence—notwithstanding the government's official Arabization policy—continues to ensure access to disciplines and academic specializations that are most rewarded in the economic market place. Indeed, increased Arabization of primary and secondary school curriculums without concurrent language uniformity at the higher levels has created enormous frustrations for those Arabized students unprepared to cope effectively with lectures in French. These students are destined for dead-end jobs, since nearly all openings in the public and to a lesser extent the private sectors require some level of bilingualism or in certain fields trilingualism.

Here immediately one sees the practical problems inherent in a dual system aimed simultaneously at providing technical training and at establishing the foundation for a culturally meaningful sense of national identity. The creation of parallel Arabophone and Francophone sections in many faculties and disciplines at the four major universities has led to severe competition and conflict between the sections in regard to academic status, job opportunities, cultural authenticity, and nationalist credibility. Sometimes these conflicts have turned violent, as occurred in 1974, 1975, and 1976 at the University of Constantine, where representatives of both groups clashed, technically over the question of which legal system the country should adopt—traditional Islamic or modern secular. More intense demonstrations took place in winter 1979-1980 at the University of Algiers where Arabic-language students, who constitute 25 percent of the student body and tend to come from the lower socioeconomic classes, went on a two-month strike to protest discrimination and lack of employment opportunities in government and business. In every instance such eruptions reflected increased student dissatisfaction with the quality, purpose, and usability of an all-Arab education in Algeria when government decision makers regard bilingual training and other features of modern, secular education as integral to the overall development process. Even in a minor ministry such as the postal and telephone service, for example, Arabization has barely taken hold.

The attempt by religious fundamentalists to forge an alliance with the student protesters added an element of urgency to the situation and forced decisive government action. In January 1980 the Chadli government broke the impasse by a combination of restrictions and concessions. The courts were ordered to Arabize, and 600 young Arabic-speaking law graduates were appointed to judgeships. Further measures affecting educational policy and personnel were implemented to secure support of Arabized elements. Well-known officials like Redha Malek, once minister of information and culture under Boumediene and later Algerian ambassador to the United States, and Mustapha Lacheraf, a respected westernized intellectual who headed the Ministry of Primary and Secondary Schooling in the late 1970s, both noted for their moderate views on language and cultural matters, were dismissed from positions of authority and influence by the Chadli government. In their place strong advocates of intensified Arabization policies were promoted to cabinet-level posts. Mohamed Cherif Kharroubi and Rafik Abdelhak Brerhi, for example, were appointed, respectively, ministers of education and higher education in 1980, retaining these crucial portfolios in the cabinet reshuffles of 1982 and 1984. Under their authority numerous organizational, instructional, and personnel changes have been pushed through, often in unthinking and unplanned fashion, causing much havoc and resentment throughout the nation's educational system.

As a result, the policy of Arabization in the nation's school curriculum has had some undesirable effects. Although the government has achieved impressive quantitative results since independence in the number of schools, institutes, and universities built and in the large numbers of students attending them, there have not been comparable qualitative results. The gradual loss of French academic influence in the training of professionals, for example, has led to some deterioration in the administrative and technological capacity of the governing elite. The shift to the Arabic language and viewpoint in education, intended to pacify traditional elements in the society and forge a sense of nationalistic unity, has begun to undermine the development of middle managerial and technological cadres.

A more serious failing in the regime's educational policies in general and Arabization program in particular is the alienation of

and potential opposition from the country's minority Berber population. Fearing cultural suffocation and economic decline, Berbers of
Kabylia have come to distrust the Arabization policies of the regime.
For many among the poorer Berber communities French language
competence has historically provided the only avenue of economic
escape to France and other parts of Europe where menial yet adequately
compensated jobs could be found. Remittances from the large migrant
labor force in France (by the end of 1982, over 805,300 Algerian
residents, including family members, were living in France, according
to a French government census) have often allowed otherwise destitute
villages in the Kabyle region, for example, to survive and even prosper.

The imposition of an all-Arabic language policy in education
and professional training threatens this essential lifeline. Similarly,
the government's official Arabization policy is perceived as threatening
the distinctive character of Berber culture and identity. These fears
have boiled up into open conflict involving bloody clashes with police
and army such as occurred in April 1980 and every year thereafter,
in the city of Tizi-Ouzou, the regional center of the Kabyles in the
northeast.

The intensity and scope of Berber discontent forced a strong
government response involving the use of riot police followed by
conciliatory gestures. Eleven years after having formally abolished
the teaching of Berber languages in Algerian universities, for example,
a Department of Popular (that is, Berber) Literature and Dialects
within the Institute of Arabic Language and Culture at the universities
in Algiers, Oran, Constantine, and Annaba was formally established
in September 1981. Additionally a professorial chair in Berber studies
was created at the university center in Tizi-Ouzou. Finally, the
government leadership has been consciously invoking the distinctive
contributions of Berber society and leaders to the historical development of the country. The most notable example was Chadli's
references in December 1983 at the FLN's fifth party congress both
to the great pre-Islamic Berber warrior, Jugurtha, and to the nationalist
hero, Emir Abd el-Kader. Chadli alluded to the bond uniting these
"Algerians" in their struggle during periods of conquest and colonization.

These conflicting demands, which have erupted with disturbing
regularity, have not yet been resolved to the complete satisfaction of
Muslim militants, supporters of intensified Arabization, bilingual
students, or ethnic Berbers. Piecemeal reforms, ad hoc arrangements,
and manipulative symbolism have only aggravated existing grievances
and possibly engendered new, more violence-prone frustrations. The
educational system, with its renewed emphasis on a revitalized Islam,

Arabization, and selective gestures to Berber constituents, is having serious political consequences for the future as antagonistic classes of elites and nonelites confront each other in competing economic, social, and cultural arenas. One observer's description of this phenomenon in neighboring Tunisia is equally appropriate to the Algerian case. A bilingual or trilingual, modernist, westernized, technocratic elite may increasingly be "faced by a coalition of the frustrated Arabic-speaking subelite—public servants in some ministries and lower cadres of the party, the alienated intellectual proletariat that is being turned out by the universities, the rejects of the school system who have expectations but no qualifications, and the millions of unemployed and underemployed."[26]

Communications and Culture

Beyond the extensive educational network state secularization policies are being advanced through an expanding communications system intended to inculcate a nationalist culture that is at once "authentic" (that is, Arab-Islamic) and "scientific" (that is, modernist).

Daily communications and routine face-to-face encounters at all levels of society are conducted in Algerian colloquial Arabic or the appropriate Berber dialect, thus facilitating elite-mass contacts. The government's official policy of Arabization, Algerianization, and Islamization gives additional expressive and symbolic meaning to Arabic language use by all. Instrumentally, however, and in terms of the scientific needs of the society, French language competence is considered essential. Current language policy that advocates and partially implements Arabization principles but allows the enormous state machinery to function in French—only the ministries of justice and religious affairs conduct their business strictly in modern literary Arabic—has created tensions and discontinuities.

Among the bilingual incumbent elites these arrangements pose far less of a psychological or practical problem. Indeed, unlike their counterparts in Tunisia and Morocco, Algerian elites are not particularly enamored with or mesmerized by the cultural trappings and civilizing qualities of French language and society. Bitter experiences from the past and hostile encounters in the present make Algerians extremely suspicious of all things French. Yet a curious love-hate relationship continues between Algerian elites and French culture, language, and society. As a result, use of French is viewed essentially in pragmatic and utilitarian terms. In other words, within a cultural environment in which the Arabic and Islamic components of national identity continue to be emphasized, Algeria pursues a practical policy of bilingualism. Those in and out of power view Algeria as Muslim,

Central post office in downtown Algiers (being refurbished in 1978).

Arabic, socialist, revolutionary—however much many of these ideas continue to be communicated in French.

The danger of such a bilingual approach, however, is that too many young people may be emerging from secondary schools with an incomplete command of both literary Arabic and functional French, thus condemning them to the lowest levels of political, economic, and social organization and effectively removing them from mainstream participation in the system. Even the psychocultural benefits that are supposed to accrue through increased Arabization may be undermined by the inadequacy of language training in literary Arabic, theoretically the only effective means by which enlightened cultural values, national symbols, and political ideology can be communicated.

As presently constituted, the communications system is essentially an instrument for mass socialization and indoctrination, not a means by which knowledge and information are freely disseminated among elites and between elites and the masses. The government owns and operates, either directly or through the FLN, all formal communications media—the press, radio, television, films, and book publishing and distribution. Government leaders regard the media as instruments to support the socialist (under Boumediene) or nationalist (under Benjedid) revolution and to promote its goals among the masses. Although the media remain free to criticize shortcomings that interfere with the implementation of this national objective, they are not permitted to challenge either the objective itself or the social and political concepts that provide the framework for its attainment.

Probably the most important and widespread formal informational channel is the radio, of which there are an estimated 10 million receivers with a potential audience equal to the country's population of 22 million. Algerian Radio-Television (RTA) is operated as an autonomous institution under the supervision of the Ministry of Information and Culture, which has a monopoly on broadcasting. The radio network covers the entire country with three channels— Arabic, Kabyle, and international (French, English, and Spanish)— twenty-four hours a day.

Yet, with all this, the radio's role as a means of indoctrination remains limited. For listeners in the rural areas, for example, much of the broadcast material contains information and concepts that are outside their experience. In addition, comprehension of news and commentary on economic and political matters is circumscribed by the fact that the literary Arabic used in broadcasting is not easily understood by many, if not most, Algerians. For most elites, local radio broadcasts serve diversionary rather than informational needs. The latter are more adequately served via foreign shortwave broadcasts originating from France and other parts of Europe.

The television network covers most of Algeria and bordering portions of neighboring countries with a single Arabic/French channel that has recently been converted completely to color, with equipment capable of receiving Eurovision programs. Programming is a mixture of educational programs, news, and entertainment. On balance, news is presented without much overt distortion or propaganda, although how and what news is reported leaves little doubt as to the government's official position, especially on foreign policy issues. Domestic politics are presented in functional rather than political terms, as in the daily reporting of official public functions performed by various ministers or their subordinates. As a result one learns very little about political life or political events within Algeria by watching Algerian television, a fact well understood by the leaders themselves, who turn elsewhere for nonbiased sources of information about political processes within their own country's borders.

Newspapers and periodicals are slightly more important sources of information for Algerians, although for the press too the tight control allows little room for serious political debate. Reporting of domestic events is overwhelmingly concerned with the trivial details and technical aspects of some feature of social, economic, industrial, or labor policy; thus, for example, extended coverage is often devoted to ways by which potato production can be improved, water shortages ameliorated, a socialist ethic instilled among passive rural villagers, the problems confronting the building of the trans-Saharan highway can be overcome, and so forth.

With the revival of institutional life, the formal procedures of government are receiving more attention, especially the work of the various commissions of the National Assembly. This coverage may be intended to demonstrate to Algerians and foreigners alike that democracy is alive and well in Algiers. Perhaps with enough perseverence and reading between the lines something significant about politics can be squeezed out of this type of formalistic, institutional journalism. More revealing perhaps are the regular editorial attacks made against public corruption, bureaucratic inefficiency, and social irresponsibility so manifest in Algerian daily life. These social sermons do not constitute serious analytical pieces that demand reform or policy changes, however, but are more in the nature of pedagogical reprimands directed at an indifferent mass public in need of civic education. Needless to say, broad policy objectives or political ideology are never open to criticism in the press or elsewhere for that matter. More than 50 percent of press coverage is devoted to foreign affairs in a manner consistent with Algeria's Third World orientation and nonaligned posture.

The highly restrictive nature of all formal communications channels and media structures inhibits the free flow of information between leaders and followers but not within the top elites themselves, who hold a privileged status in the overall communications network. Algerians at the political and social top have access to virtually all significant Western and non-Western sources of information through constant travels abroad, personal newspaper and journal subscriptions, direct telephone dialing to France and other parts of Europe, contacts with foreigners in Algeria, and other individualized means which, in combination, have resulted in the formation of one of the most sophisticated and knowledgeable elites in the Third World.

The disparity between leaders and masses in access to independent sources of information would be even greater were it not for the large numbers of Algerian workers and students traveling back and forth on a regular basis between Algeria and Europe. The privileged communications status of society's elite is also moderated by the pervasive influence of word-of-mouth information, which remains an extremely important source for the transmission of news and ideas at both the elite and mass levels. The evident discrepancy between unofficial information as gained from independent and third-party sources and official government propaganda has discredited the latter in the eyes of most urban, educated Algerians, especially in areas of political reporting.

Despite the porousness of the mass-oriented communications system and the availability of independent sources of information, the government continues to pursue a cultural policy predicated on a single, unitary ideology. In such a setting, secular intellectuals who are unwilling to be identified with official government policies have no real influence or prestige. Even those respectable scholars (e.g., Mustapha Lacheraf) who have been involved in the process of rediscovering the cultural roots of Algerian identity, debating the merits and difficulties of bilingual education, or assessing the validity of European pedagogical techniques operate under the direct juris-diction and close supervision of the government. Because the official ideology is pervasively Arab-Islamic, religiously oriented scholars enjoy prestige and importance, not as independent actors, however, but rather as officially approved religious "bureaucrats."

Intellectuals willing to compromise their artistic and literary talents find employment available in the appropriate ministries where they are asked, inter alia, to romanticize the heroic past and the ubiquitous independence fighter–folk hero in stories, poems and filmscripts. Inevitably, this leads to ideological clichés and human stereotypes. Moreover, official encouragement of the literary treatment of the socialist revolution has given rise to idealized but sterile descriptions of social and economic progress and soporific language use. Like the religious bureaucrat, the intellectual also has been co-opted into the role of technician to make ideas serve bureaucratic-propagandistic ends rather than act as creative forces for social change.

Where timely thematic choices and innovative language dealing with questions of social conscience, human solidarity transcending national boundaries, the status of women in postindependence society, the challenge of social transformation, individual dilemmas in a changing society, and the alienated condition of man in a technological environment have appeared, they have all been in French and com-municated to a very small and selective audience.

Given this restrictive—some would say oppressive—intellectual atmosphere it remains remarkable how many French language Algerian writers, novelists, essayists, and poets have managed to publish works of genuine depth and creativity that have been recognized both inside and outside Algeria. An impressive literary tradition was begun in the period prior to independence, with the writings of such distin-guished Algerian authors as Jean Amrouche (1906–1962), the Kabyle poet-essayist convert to Christianity who eloquently described the heart and soul of Algeria; Mouloud Feraoun (1913–1962), a Kabyle who wrote extensively and sensitively about his own people and society; Mouloud Mammeri (b. 1917), another French-educated Kabyle who has given literary expression to such political themes as the war of independence and Algerian nationalism; Mohammed Dib (b. 1920), born in Tlemcen but currently residing in France, whose prolific writings, including poems and novels, deal with a variety of subjects relating to Algeria, past and present; Kateb Yacine (b. 1929), a former journalist whose most famous novel, *Nedjma*, received international acclaim; and Malek Haddad (1927–1978) who, like Yacine, was born in Constantine and educated in French schools. A wide-ranging novelist, journalist, and poet, Haddad wrote extensively on questions dealing with national identity, cultural authenticity, and personal alienation. He remained active in the political and cultural affairs of the state until his death.

In the more recent period the names of Mourad Bourboune (b. 1938), Rachid Boudjedra (b. 1941), Rachid Mimouni (b. 1945), Nabile Farès (b. 1941), Ali Boumahdi (b. 1934), and Assia Djebar (b. 1936), whom some have called the "Françoise Sagan of Muslim Algeria," represent a vigorous new literary trend despite the fact that most of their writings are published abroad, mainly in France, with only limited circulation within Algeria itself. An Arabic language literary tradition exists in Algeria but remains modest, although the more thorough application of Arabization policies in recent years may eventually produce quantitative if not qualitative results and contribute to the enrichment of Algerian intellectual life.

One art form that has earned popular and critical acclaim by Algerians and non-Algerians alike has been the documentary and feature film. Delicate or controversial themes, often left purposely untreated by government-controlled communications and information agencies, have been tackled directly in sensitive and dramatic fashion by Algerian filmmakers whose efforts have received worldwide recognition. Mohamed Lakhdar Hamina, an internationally acclaimed film director, for example, has received numerous film prizes—the most recent was a 1982 Cannes film festival award for his film, *Vent de sable (Desert Wind)*, a piercing and at times brutal depiction of the harsh social realities confronting Algerian women living in traditional society.

On balance, state efforts to reconcile competing sectarian and secular demands through the instruments of the mosque, national education, the communications system, and language policies have created an ambiguous cultural identity. In their different socializing milieus young people receive contradictory messages—traditional-

Islamic at home and in the mosque; scientific-secular in the school; participatory in the centrally controlled political arena; modernist, traditionalist, diversionary, and instructional in the press, radio, and television; Western ideas through travel, work, and study abroad— that all combine to produce a condition of discontinuous political socialization with potential for serious social unrest. Further exacerbating this condition of cultural ambiguity is the continuing decline in the quality of life in urban and rural Algeria.

SOCIAL PROBLEMS

Intense industrialization during the Boumediene era when the emphasis was on the development of the hydrocarbon and capital-intensive industries to the detriment of agriculture and consumer goods has caused a serious fractionalization of Algerian society. Extensive urban decay, derelict social services, substandard education, severe housing shortages, inadequate food supplies, and a general low level of the quality of life have been the consequences. These conditions have spawned waves of social discontent among important groups in the society, groups that will have to be appeased if the regime is to proceed with its development plans in a nonviolent environment.

In many ways life in urban Algeria is a microcosm of all that has gone wrong with agrarian society bent on transforming itself within twenty years through rapid and intensive heavy industrialization. Since independence successive Algerian governments have struggled to provide Algiers with such basic services as water, electricity, food, housing, education, health care, and transportation, but they have been overwhelmed by a population that has doubled in the last decade. Today, for most of the capital's two-and-one-half-million inhabitants, living conditions remain woefully inadequate. The appalling urban problems in Algiers and also Oran, Constantine, and Annaba come from uncontrolled population growth.

Mass movements away from rural areas occurred because of the centralization of government, the neglect of agriculture, and the rush to industrialize as well as the high birth rate. The country's annual population growth rate of 3.2 percent is one of the highest in the world. This phenomenon was virtually ignored until recently by the few policymakers concerned with family planning and population control. A special cabinet-level commission was created in June 1983 to investigate the problem and recommend solutions, but much of the damage has already been done. Today, for example, 60 percent of Algeria's estimated population of 22 million is under the age of eighteen. A projection from current demographic trends shows that instead of the more than 5 million school-age children the country had in 1980, there will be more than 9 million by the year 2000. To meet these student needs, a school a day must be built; yet in 1982, for example, only 4,000 of the 5,500 projected classrooms had been built (including 128 middle-level schools, 27 high schools, and 1 technical school).

Education remains mandatory for all children under the age of sixteen. The large numbers thus involved have simply overwhelmed schools, services, and staffs—with deplorable academic results. In 1983, for example, only 18,000 out of the 100,000 candidates passed the baccalaureate exam required for high school graduation and eligibility to university. In the society as a whole 60 percent of the population remains illiterate, with the figure even higher among women.

Overcrowding in the schools in combination with the large school drop-out rate and unchecked rural migration has made the streets of Algiers resemble, in many ways, one permanent and massive school playground. Students attend classes in two-hour shifts and are disgorged into the streets where they spend the remaining hours of the school day playing soccer or, increasingly, involved in various criminal acts. Although major crimes such as murder and rape remain rare, petty crime is becoming an increasingly serious problem, with attacks on property, especially automobiles, apartments, and houses, causing particular concern.

Twenty percent of the country's population live in the capital, creating an urban macrocephaly—a "head" abnormally large and totally out of proportion to the size and population of the country. Swollen by the peasant exodus from the rural areas, Oran and Constantine are quickly following the grim model of Algiers. Until a few years ago a disproportionate share of government resources was being poured into encouraging industrialization within and around urban centers. Meanwhile deteriorating conditions in the agricultural sectors were forcing more and more farmers to seek work in the cities or as foreign workers in France. Recent efforts at decentralizing industry and, to a lesser degree, government have failed to halt the decline of the quality of life for the urban poor. Increasingly, these negative trends are also beginning to affect the lifestyles of the urban middle class and managerial elite. Everyone is touched by the urban crisis. Because of the extraordinary discomfort of using public transport, most Algerians buy a car at the first opportunity. The resulting traffic jams then force the government to spend scarce resources on new highways. The problem of air pollution is closely associated with the traffic not only because cars spend hours moving slowly but also because the city's poorly serviced buses spew out thick, black diesel fumes.

Although Algeria lacks the kind of oppressive slums, or *bidonvilles*, that surround Morocco's major cities, for example, it is estimated that more than two hundred thousand people currently live in precarious housing—often constructed in one night—without legal title of occupation or approval by appropriate authorities. In the government's current urban cleanup (*assainissement urbain*) campaign many of these slums are being systematically destroyed. At dawn, for example, it is not uncommon to see the fog that regularly covers Algiers thickened by the smoke of fires destroying these illegal slum dwellings. Despite such efforts at reversing many of these destructive trends, the growth of Algiers stands as a warning that Third World development models based on rapid and uncontrolled industrialization produce huge, unmanageable cities.

The status of women is also causing concern as female activists see their situation gradually regressing in an already chauvinistic environment. In Algeria, unlike Morocco and Tunisia, many Muslim women continue to wear the veil. Only in the major cities is some progress evident. There, many more young girls and women are going to school and university today than ever before, and many more are working in offices and shops. But Algeria is still a man's world. Indeed, Algiers, as all Algerian cities, has become a notoriously unpleasant place for women on the street. Hence the usefulness of wearing the *haik*—a long, white cloth thrown over the hair with a handkerchief hiding the lower half of the face—as self-protection, a signal that the woman wearing it does not wish to be molested, harassed, or importuned by men who seem to be carried away with the notion that liberalized manner and Western dress mean that anything goes. For many otherwise urbanized men, "Algerian women are considered incapable of behaving 'decently' once 'liberated.' "[27]

It took over twenty years before a "family code" was promulgated, and it is one replete with traditional and conservative biases that work against the liberation of Algerian women. Initial government attempts to introduce a relatively liberal and modern family code were undermined by Islamic forces in the government and out. The earliest postindependence effort was in 1963–1964 in the form of a draft proposal that never saw the light of day. Subsequent legislation was advanced in 1966, 1973, and 1980. The terms of the bill for a new family code, which was drawn up by the government on September 29, 1981, were extremely conservative, so much so that the bill finally had to be dropped because of vigorous protests from Algeria's feminists.

Street scene in the Casbah ("the fortress"), the old quarter of Algiers in which overcrowding, squalid living conditions, and lack of water led to serious rioting in April 1985. Note woman in *haik*.

Public demonstrations against it were organized by the UNFA—the National Union of Algerian Women under FLN sponsorship—and held in front of the parliament building in Algiers.

In the wake of intensified fundamentalist and Arabization pressures on the society as a whole in the early 1980s, another proposal was put forth in 1984. It was formally adopted by the National Assembly in May and made into law on June 9, 1984. Although promoted as a "progressive" code by the justice minister, Boualem Baki, the fact is that the new document is explicitly based on Koranic precepts and Islamic law (*sharia*). For example, although women are granted the right to work, laws regulating marriage, divorce, rights of inheritance, guardianship over children, and the like all favor the man. Polygyny is permitted, although only sterility or incurable illness of the first wife can allow the husband to take another spouse. Algerian men can marry any women they wish, but Algerian women are forbidden to marry non-Muslim men. Even though adoption is legal, the child cannot take the name of the adoptive parents. Additionally, inheritance rights have been modernized somewhat, but female children still cannot inherit so much as their brothers. Without turning its back on Islamic principles, the new code, according to the justice minister's interpretation, takes note of changing times and modern demands.

Only time will tell whether this legislation will fundamentally alter the status of women in Algerian society. Until then, however, women remain subject to traditional Islamic dictates and the chauvinistic attitudes that the latter engender within Algerian men. Repudiation of wives and desertion of families have long plagued Algerian society, for example, and it seems unlikely that this situation will soon change.

The subordinate status of women is but one element of a broader divergence developing between the mass public and ruling elites in Algeria. On the one hand, the masses are becoming more alienated from secular culture and turning to religious belief systems for personal guidance and social purpose, and on the other, higher status elites continue to move in an opposite direction. Algerian high government officials, party cadres, military officers, and professional technocrats are all more and more preoccupied with the technicalities of making and concluding business deals with Western firms or of putting Western equipment into place. In Algeria probably even more than elsewhere in the Arab world, the nonpolitical or pragmatic technocrat is increasingly replacing yesterday's passionately nationalist intellectual as the representative of the priorities of the Algerian state. The influence of the hardheaded men running the nationalized industrial section of the economy, who have been openly nonideological, is expanding. The oil and gas revolution and Algeria's determination to modernize and industrialize rapidly have stimulated the rise of a cosmopolitan class of experts and state entrepreneurs bound together by the same ultramodern technological and commercial culture: the same ambitions, the same skills, the same language, the same instrumental ethics, and the same impatience with "irrational" ideology and politics. From this situation a new polarization of society is emerging, pitting the radicalized masses (more of fundamentalist than revolutionary coloration) against the technocratic, commercialized elite.

It is in part to rectify this dangerous social imbalance that the Chadli government has instituted major policy changes. The objectives of many of the reforms incorporated into the Five-Year Development Plan of 1980–1984 and projected into the current plan (1985–1989), along with the numerous administrative laws put into effect in recent years have been to overcome what the leadership perceives as the excesses of the technocrats who had assumed prominence during the Boumediene period. The technocrats were the planners, economists, engineers, and technicians whom the military and party elites appointed to run the economy once the decision was made to proceed with the industrialization-first policy. These technocrats, who now number in the thousands and proliferate in the second and third levels of government, especially in such ministries as finance and industry, as well as in the many state corporations and their recent autonomous offshoots, remain largely faceless to most Algerians.

Accusations, mostly about the massive projects associated with oil, gas, and heavy industry, have been leveled at the technocrats. Government critics in the current regime accuse the technocrats of having created an industrial disequilibrium that has made Algeria excessively dependent on imports, especially agricultural foodstuffs. To reduce the impact of imports, the technocrats sought to build an industry diversified enough to produce most of the country's consumer goods. However, imports kept rising because the industries still had to import machinery, components, expertise, and some raw materials.

Additional criticisms relate to the many state-owned companies that were created by and for the technocrats but that became overstaffed and inefficient. Within such enterprises the technocrats were also accused of favoring the emerging professional middle-class and middle-income Algerians, many of whom receive special benefits, notably year-end bonuses of one, two, or three months pay. The wages of the middle class rose faster than those of the lowest paid, widening an already significant gap in income distribution.

Yet no one could detract from the single accomplishment of the technocrats: They have constructed one of the developing world's most sophisticated networks of roads, telecommunications, gas and oil pipelines, liquefaction plants, and electric power facilities. This network services a widely diversified industrial base that could enable Algeria to outperform most other countries in the Afro-Asian world. Notwithstanding this impressive achievement, critics within the Chadli regime still accuse the technocrats of being men with a "vision of an imaginary country." The technocrats are described as "dominated by the fascinating exercise of abstract planning, by optical illusion of centralized decisions and macroeconomic theories, by the rapture of important and sophisticated decisions, incompatible with the Algerian reality and the reality of its modest standards and incomes of its peoples." More serious has been the charge that the technocrats ignored the needs of the population in the drive to industrialize the country. "They were trying to imitate the development of the advanced world—to become the Germany of Africa—and failed at improving the life of its people."

Another social problem stems from the development, below the diffused but still powerful technocratic stratum, of a new generation of Algerians that has grown up since independence. Educated in a secular, Western tradition, yet without the "rituals" of their forefathers, these "angry young men" view colonialism as history; however, its successor, neocolonialism (i.e., economic domination by foreign powers) is not. The political awakening of this young, primarily urban generation has largely coincided with falling living standards caused by a population explosion and blighted productivity.

There is a struggle under way in Algeria, indeed as elsewhere in the Arab world, for a new start, a struggle waged by Arabs who have never experienced the traumas of colonialism but who yearn for catharsis and whose populist leaders speak of redemption and a major revival; ergo, Islamic revivalism. Yet these same leaders' aspirations derive less from any profound feeling for Algerian traditions than from an amorphous, inarticulate sense of the need for rectification. If there is a common theme among this new generation, it is a desire for a new beginning and self-advancement in a world unable to produce either.

The current relationship between the technocratic elite and the mass of semiliterate Arab masses is uneasy, tinged with hurt pride, envy, and ambiguity. Islamic appeals, purist exhortations, and revivalist aspirations all revolve around this need for redemption, rectification, and an authentic sense of identity.

The specter of mass upheaval is partly the creation of the ruling elites, who have redeemed the promise of independence by providing once denied educational opportunities. But these have spawned unmet aspirations. The great mass of Algeria's youth has received only the most basic education, enough to nurture expectations but not enough to provide the skills necessary to fulfill them. Many of the secondary school graduates are unemployed or underemployed, and university students represent a radical faction that the current government fears as an automatic threat, a genie that cannot return to its bottle. Algeria's hard-line crackdown in recent years on university students (closing campuses), Islamic fundamentalists (arresting and imprisoning leaders), and Berber groups attests to the government's determination that no Iran or even Egypt will take place in Algeria. In this regard, Chadli's informal personal style and his support for selective liberalization measures in society and the economy should not be interpreted as a preliminary step toward pluralistic politics or genuine democratic freedoms.

NOTES

1. Lucette Valensi, *On the Eve of Colonialism: North Africa Before the French Conquest* (New York: Africana Publishing Co., 1977), p. 80.

2. Peter von Sivers, "Indigenous Administrators in Algeria, 1846–1914: Manipulation and Manipulators," *The Maghreb Review* 7, nos. 5–6 (September–December 1982), p. 117.

3. Pierre Bourdieu, *The Algerians* (Boston: Beacon Press, 1962), p. 97.

4. Richard F. Nyrop and others, *Area Handbook for Algeria* (Washington, D.C.: Government Printing Office, 1972), p. 144.

5. Harold D. Nelson, ed., *Algeria: A Country Study*, 3d. ed. (Washington, D.C.: Government Printing Office, 1979), p. 98.

6. Allen Christelow, "Saintly Descent and Worldly Affairs in Mid-Nineteenth Century Mascara, Algeria," *International Journal of Middle East Studies* 12 (1980), p. 139.

7. Nelson, *Algeria*, p. 21.

8. Ibid.

9. Hugh Roberts, "The Conversion of the Mrabtin in Kabylia," in *Islam et Politique au Maghreb*, ed. Ernest Gellner and Jean-Claude Vatin (Paris: Editions du Centre National de la Recherche Scientifique [hereafter CNRS], 1981), p. 101.

10. Ibid., p. 109.

11. Nelson, *Algeria*, p. 116.

12. Henri Sanson, *Laïcité Islamique en Algérie* (Paris: Editions du CNRS, 1983).

13. Jean-Claude Vatin, "Revival in the Maghreb: Islam as an Alternative Political Language," in *Islamic Resurgence in the Arab World*, ed. Ali E. Hillal Dessouki (New York: Praeger, 1982), p. 235.

14. Ibid., p. 233.

15. Ibid.

16. Ibid.

17. Jean-Claude Vatin, "Popular Puritanism versus State Reformism: Islam in Algeria," in *Islam in the Political Process*, ed. James P. Piscatori (Cambridge: Cambridge University Press, 1983), p. 111.

18. Ibid., p. 106.

19. John O. Voll, "Islamic Dimensions in Arab Politics Since World War II," *American Arab Affairs*, no. 4 (Spring 1983), p. 114.

20. Ibid.

21. Ibid., pp. 116–117.

22. Paul Balta and Claudine Rulleau, *L'Algérie des Algériens: Vingt ans Après* (Paris: Les Editions Ouvrières, 1981), p. 171.

23. Daniel Junqua, "Le Maghreb entre le modernisme et l'intégrisme— Algérie: défendre l'islam authentique," *Le Monde*, January 28, 1982.

24. *El Moudjahid* (Algiers), February 5, 1984, p. 1.

25. Ira M. Lapidus, *Contemporary Islamic Movements in Historical Perspective*, Policy Papers in International Affairs, no. 18 (Berkeley: University of California—Institute of International Studies, 1983).

26. Charles A. Micaud, "Bilingualism in North Africa: Cultural and Sociopolitical Implications," *Western Political Quarterly* 27, no. 1 (March 1974), p. 103.

27. Juliette Minces, *The House of Obedience: Women in Arab Society* (London: Zed Press, 1982), p. 89.

5

The Political Economy
of Development

INTRODUCTION

Two factors have dominated Algeria's political economy since independence: an impressive supply of hydrocarbon reserves (with more natural gas than oil) upon which a policy of accelerated heavy industrialization has been predicated and an agricultural sector that has been so abused and mismanaged that food dependence from overseas sources has reached crisis proportions. The strength of one sector—industry—has been vitiated by the weakness of the other—agriculture—causing serious structural dislocations in Algeria's economy. The agenda for Algeria's future development is thus clear: how to utilize better a valuable but diminishing natural resource while regaining control of food production. This chapter will focus on these two critical interrelated elements of Algeria's political economy in order to predict the country's pattern of development in the coming decades.

More so than in most countries, the Algerian economy is dependent on politics. This dependency is only partially due to geography and history, which have combined to give the economy its political character; more influential has been the deliberate decision of Algeria's technocratic elites to bring the economy under the direction of the state.

In the decade following independence in 1962, Algeria nationalized all major foreign business interests as well as many private Algerian companies. Nationalization ranged from the assumption of a controlling interest in some cases to complete takeover in others. Today the Algerian economy is almost totally government controlled. State enterprises and government agencies run much of the foreign trade, almost all of the major industries, large parts of the distribution and retail systems, all public utilities, and the entire banking and credit system. Despite recent government measures to deconcentrate and decentralize the massive state bureaucracy and to create new incentives for private sector initiative, there has not been a single major enterprise denationalized and returned to private ownership in the whole of the postindependence period.

The Algerian commitment to a state-centered technocratic thrust evolved out of the radical nationalism of Houari Boumediene and his group, who took power in mid-1965. They were convinced that true national independence could only be realized through control of natural resources, especially hydrocarbons, and through rapid industrial development—objectives that, in the context of global economic relations and the dominance of advanced industrial societies, could be achieved only through nationalization and state control of the economy.

The 1965–1971 period witnessed an intensive state-directed public sector expansion. Initially the state created new industrial ventures with public investment. Simultaneously foreign firms were taken over. Later a portion of the self-management or *autogestion* sector was absorbed into state enterprises. The banks, insurance companies, and some mines were socialized in 1966. Two years later the state nationalized sixty-six of three hundred French enterprises that were operating in diverse fields such as construction materials, fertilizers, electrical supplies, textiles, and foods. State control of marketing of gas and oil products, the first step toward state control of the oil and gas industry, was effected in 1968, and takeover was completed in this crucial sector in 1971.

In 1965 an Algerian national oil and gas corporation (SONA-TRACH) was created, followed by a network of state industrial combines. By 1967 thirteen other state corporations had been set up, including the National Iron and Steel Company (SNS), the National Company for Textile Industries (SONITEX), and the Algerian Insurance Company (SAA). These and related state corporations formed later constituted the underpinning for the Algerian development strategy: Secure full control over the natural resource base, and convert the oil and gas revenues into a broad-based industrial sector.

Since the late 1960s, industrial development has been given priority over agricultural development, and within the industrial sector most investment has gone into basic industries. Although the current five-year plan (1985–1989) gives more attention than did previous plans to social programs, water projects, and agricultural resources, investment in the petrochemical sector remains very high. In the past this industrialization-first strategy was defended by two arguments.

First, continued emphasis on the export of raw materials and agri-cultural products would prevent Algeria from achieving the type of economic independence deemed necessary to make political inde-pendence truly meaningful. Second, not only could Algeria's petroleum and gas resources finance industrialization, but they could also be used to develop a petrochemical industry that would be the foundation of the entire strategy of industrialization.

THEORY

The industrialization-first strategy has its theoretical roots in the notion of *industries industrialisantes* ("industrializing industries") as articulated by G. Destanne de Bernis, a French adviser to Algerian industry. He argued that given Algeria's limited agricultural resources, the rural population could not maintain a reasonable standard of living and therefore had to find employment in the industrial sector. In any case history had shown that an agricultural revolution followed, never preceded, an industrial revolution. Once industry was in place it would supply the fertilizers and machinery for agriculture, as well as form a market for the resulting agricultural output. With Algeria's impressive hydrocarbon base, this industrialization-first approach seemed compelling. In addition, Algeria planners had always rec-ognized that although better endowed than many other Third World states, Algeria's endowment consisted of diminishing resources. The planners' dilemma, therefore, was how best to convert these resources, before they were exhausted, into a self-sustaining and self-propelling economic infrastructure capable of supporting the country's expanding population at increasing levels of per capita income.

The manner in which this industrialization-first program would achieve effective self-sufficiency would be as follows:

> Some industries, particularly the power-producing ones, have stimulating capacities [which] give rise to a series of associated industries, both up-stream and down-stream. The entire national economy is thereby stimulated. The industrializing industries include energy-related indus-tries, petroleum and gas, which provide fuel, feedstocks and finance for the industrialization process with petrochemicals representing the basis for a whole range of new industries: iron and steel, metallurgical and mechanical industries and chemicals, e.g., phosphates. They are huge capital intensive projects based on Algeria's own natural resources and utilizing the most modern production processes. They act as the "motor" of the development process producing raw materials and machinery for other sectors of industry engaged in the production of finished goods such as vehicles, farm machinery, pumps and irrigation

equipment, electrical goods and plastics thus strengthening the inter-industry matrix. In turn the products of the new industries will contribute to the modernization of the more backward sectors of the economy, notably agriculture, forging new linkages that will eventually create an integrated economy reducing Algeria's dependence on the world capitalist market.[1]

The implementation of this economic strategy was begun with the three-year program of 1967–1969. It was expanded upon in the two back-to-back four-year plans (1970–1973, 1974–1977), according to which industry was supposed to place at the disposal of the socialized economy the basic requirements of energy and heavy industry, to meet important needs of the population, and to achieve the greatest possible capitalization of the country's natural resources. The 1967–1969 program was actually a "pre-plan" with modest objectives. Nevertheless, it was during this period that the structure of state-directed industry was built up and the major national companies, purchasing and marketing agencies, cooperatives, and other institutions were created. Special development programs were also begun during this three-year period.

The thrust toward industrialization began in earnest with the four-year plan of 1970–1973, which marked the first real effort at comprehensive economic policy in the postindependence era. The conceptual framework within which this four-year plan was devised rested on a number of fixed objectives: the top priority of heavy industry; the increasing substitution of domestically produced consumer goods for imported ones (import substitution); and the training of the various specialized personnel required by a rapidly developing economy. The plan allocated 45 percent of total capital investment to the establishment of a capital-intensive industrial sector that was to be the basis of economic growth. Only 15 percent went to agriculture, while 40 percent of investment was allocated to social and economic infrastructure. The investment strategy was called "planting Algeria's oil" (*semer le pétrole pour récolter l'industrie*), thereby using petroleum revenues to create a strong industrial base. At the same time, an agrarian revolution policy, as it was called, aimed at improving efficiency through land reform and a system of cooperatives. The latter program was not only undercapitalized but, owing to resistance from the rural population, it failed to increase agriculture's percentage of the GNP, which in fact declined from 13 percent in 1969 to 9 percent in 1973.

The second four-year plan (1974–1977) attempted to remedy the apparent imbalance and malfunctions of the previous plan without jeopardizing the heavy emphasis on rapid industrialization. The new plan, nevertheless, placed more emphasis on developing consumer industries that would create jobs, fight regional economic disparities, encourage small and medium-sized industries, and promote land reform. The 1974–1977 plan also placed a major emphasis on housing, an area that had been conspicuously neglected in the first four-year plan.

HYDROCARBON POLICY

Algeria's development strategy of rapid industrialization has been made possible by petroleum and gas revenues. The country owns the world's fourth largest proven natural gas resources—after the Soviet Union, Iran, and the United States—and significant reserves of crude oil. It is the seventh largest Middle East–North Africa oil producer (preceded by Saudi Arabia, Kuwait, Iran, Iraq, the United Arab Emirates, and Libya) but accounts for only 4 percent of the total output (725,000 barrels per day in third quarter of 1983) of OPEC (Organization of Petroleum Exporting Countries), which it joined in 1969, and no more than 2 percent of total world output. The development of these reserves has been central to economic planning since independence in 1962. Despite (or because of) policy shifts since 1980 toward decentralized decisionmaking in the hydrocarbon and other large industrial sectors, the strategy of using these natural resources to finance other industrialization continues to govern energy policy and helps explain Algeria's constant determination to obtain as high a price as possible on world markets for its natural resources.

Under the regime of Houari Boumediene (1965–1978) the emphasis was placed on as rapid and as extensive exploitation of energy resources as technology and world market conditions would allow. The underlying concept of the hydrocarbons development plan of the period as articulated by Belaid Abdesselam, the once powerful minister of energy and heavy industry, who for twelve years directed Algeria's program of massive and accelerated industrialization (1968–1980), and by Ahmed Ghozali, the longtime former head of SONATRACH (*Société Nationale pour la Recherche, la Production, le Transport, la Transformation et la Commercialisation des Hydrocarbures*), was that essentially all of the presently known reserves of oil, condensate, and liquefied petroleum gas (LPG) and most of the known gas reserves would be used up over the next thirty years or by the early 2000s. According to the reasoning of the time, because the sale of a large portion of the country's hydrocarbon reserves was necessary for the creation of a large and integrated industrial base for the national economy, it was important to maximize the production rates of gas, crude oil, LPG, and condensate, consistent with obtaining the highest total recovery of hydrocarbons as economically as possible.

A significant shift in policy took place with the ascent of Chadli Benjedid to the presidency of the republic in February 1979. In December of that year a special parliamentary commission was established to investigate the Algerian oil ministry's sales of liquefied natural gas (LNG) to the El Paso Company of Houston, Texas. A year later, on December 25, 1980, the commission submitted its report, holding El Paso "morally responsible" for causing SONATRACH to lose earnings estimated at US$290 million in the ten-year period following signing of a contract in 1969. These charges led to the dismissal of Abdesselam and Ghozali and the discrediting of their policies.

Several days later, at crucial meetings of the Central Committee of the FLN on December 29–31, 1980, a new energy policy that gave greater emphasis to resource preservation and energy conservation, and improved the means by which Algeria could control and utilize its natural resources and hydrocarbon industry was formulated. In addition, the Central Committee emphasized the need for creating new industries that would be self-generating and less vulnerable to external energy and market considerations.

The energy policy that emerged had carefully identified aims including:

- Much more emphasis on the use of natural gas for domestic purposes in industry and residential homes
- A broader national effort at energy conservation by preventing unnecessary energy waste
- A broader and more intensive effort at discovering and exploiting national energy resources and a concomitant development of indigenous technical and scientific expertise
- A concerted effort at discovering and developing alternate energy sources such as wind, geothermal energy, and solar power, along with increasing mining of coal and nuclear raw materials
- The creation of more efficient and extensive capacity for hydrocarbon storage, distribution, and transportation
- More careful monitoring of domestic hydrocarbon output in relation to the world market supply-and-demand balance
- Continued firmness and determination in pursuing price increases for hydrocarbons

- Diversification of export markets for hydrocarbons
- Greater coordination and cooperation with other hydrocarbons producers and exporters in achieving a "just" price for natural gas exports
- A restructuring and more efficient management of the hydrocarbon industry, beginning with the state oil and gas company
- Accelerated development of domestic technological expertise in the oil and gas industries so as to reduce the dependence on foreign technical assistance
- Improving the coordination between the scientific, technical, diplomatic, security, and defense institutions in matters relating to hydrocarbons
- The establishment of a Higher Energy Institute empowered to coordinate national energy policy and monitor its impact on the economy as a whole

Despite its modest reserves of petroleum deposits and its rather late entry into the OPEC club, Algeria has consistently argued for a maximum return on its oil exports. This attitude is in part due to rational economic calculations but also has strong emotional and ideological roots. Even during the war of national liberation the Algerian revolutionary movement made reference to French oil exploration in the Sahara, and awareness of the possibilities of an oil industry increased the insistence of the FLN on the unity of Algerian territory. After independence oil came to occupy a crucial place in Algerian political emotions. There was a strong sense that the natural resources of Algeria belonged to the Algerian state. To this was added the aspiration to economic independence without which political independence was not truly meaningful and the resistance to "back door" imperialism or neocolonialism.

By 1972, a mere decade after independence, all petroleum exploration and production facilities, natural gas concessions, and gas and oil pipelines and other transport facilities had come under the control of the Algerian state. The historic turning point had occurred on February 24, 1971, when Boumediene, in announcing that Algeria had decided to "carry the revolution to the petroleum sector," nationalized 51 percent of all French oil companies operating in the country and 100 percent of all natural gas concessions. This "victory" in the oil battle against French and other multinational petroleum companies enhanced Boumediene's prestige at home and abroad and became a constantly recurring theme, associated with the cultural and agrarian revolution, in his speeches. The nationalization decrees opened the door to a new era in the international oil industry, allowing other OPEC members, for example, to take control progressively of their own hydrocarbon resources.

The quadrupling of oil prices following the 1973 Arab-Israeli war enabled foreign exchange derived from petroleum expenditures to reach US$5 billion, dramatically increasing Algeria's investment opportunities for national economic growth. Since that time Algeria has consistently argued within OPEC for higher prices. Except for the 1977–1978 slack period preceding the overthrow of the Shah of Iran and the 1981–1984 period, Algeria has successfully raised the price of its oil. During 1979 the price of its highest-grade crude was increased from $14.10 per barrel at the beginning of the year to $30 in December. Two further increases in 1980 and one in 1981 brought the price by May 1981 to $40, to which was added a $3 surcharge for oil exploration. The surcharge was intended as a way by which foreign oil companies would be encouraged to participate with SON-ATRACH in oil exploration.

By early 1982, however, world oversupply of oil forced Algeria to drop the surcharge and, in line with other OPEC producers, charge $37.50 per barrel. This trend of decline continued through 1983: OPEC ministers agreed in March to set their oil reference price at $29 per barrel, and the price for high-grade Algerian oil was set at $30.50. Algeria joined Venezuela in supporting Iran's request in mid-November 1983 to raise OPEC prices by as much as $5 a barrel, arguing that the group's $5 price reduction eight months earlier had failed to revive oil demand. Short of a major global oil reduction caused by war or political turmoil in the Middle East or elsewhere, it seems unlikely that Algeria can succeed in reversing the downward trend of oil prices in the immediate future. (Indeed, by late 1984 Nigeria broke ranks with its OPEC partners and unilaterally reduced the price of its oil to $28 per barrel, placing additional pressures on price "hawks" like Algeria.) As a consequence crude oil sales as a percent of total hydrocarbon export earnings have been declining precipitously in recent years. Revenues from sales of crude oil accounted for 61 percent of Algeria's total hydrocarbon export earnings in 1980, 52 percent in 1981, 30 percent in 1982, and less than 25 percent for 1983. The dramatic change in the composition of Algeria's hydrocarbon exports caused by the continuing oil glut worldwide and the recognized paucity of Algerian reserves vis-à-vis other OPEC and non-OPEC producers have led Algeria increasingly to shift attention to its expansive natural gas reserves as the instrument for implementing its developmental policies.

With the decline in Algeria's oil production and the remaining doubt about substantial future expansion of recoverable petroleum reserves, natural gas is quickly becoming Algeria's most valuable export. The 3.5 trillion cubic meters (1982) of proven recoverable gas reserves (4 percent of the world total) are for the most part unassociated with the oil fields. This unassociated gas is free of sulfur and, consequently, both easy to handle and inexpensive. It is not only suitable for commercial and domestic uses but also readily adaptable to petrochemical transformation by the extraction of a condensate and for liquefaction for shipment abroad.

The exploitation of natural gas in Algeria on a massive scale is a relatively recent phenomenon of the postindependence era. Taking advantage of new gas technology, particularly in the transport across the sea by liquefaction (which confines the transport to a limited number of liquefying and deliquefying points of entry and exit), Algeria has taken the lead in a new world industry. SONATRACH has been responsible for the planning, management, and financing of pipelines and liquefaction plants. The result has been the creation of a state-of-the-art industry that has been economically worthwhile, thus justifying the large-scale capital expenditure. Yet it is these huge capital outlays and the increasing dependency on gas for export earnings that have led Algeria to seek substantial price increases for its LNG to bring it to par, based on energy value, with the price of crude oil.

Algeria has bargained stubbornly with potential customers for its expanding natural gas exports. Shifting exports from the fluctuating oil markets to the more stable demands for gas has been a central part of Algeria's international economic strategy in the last half decade and a principal means of financing development. The current minister of energy and petrochemical industries, Belkacem Nabi, a member of the FLN's Central Committee and a former counselor for economic and petroleum affairs in the President's Office, has been in the forefront of Algeria's efforts to achieve parity with oil prices. Nabi's position is supported by SONATRACH officials who argue for the adoption of a pricing formula that would automatically align the price of gas to oil, thus increasing OPEC's control over the structure of world energy costs.

The attempt to organize a worldwide gas cartel similar to OPEC and the use of tactics involving threats of boycotts, embargoes, and cessations of oil deliveries, as well as promises of greatly increased (or threats of decreased) trade and bilateral commercial agreements, have all been part of a concerted effort to increase the price Algeria charges for its natural gas. Failure to extract the necessary economic and political benefits from this policy can have serious implications for the country's 1985–1989 development plan, upon which so much of Chadli Benjedid's socially oriented programs are predicated. To date this strategy has led to three major "successes" with the Belgians, French, and Italians and four "failures" with German, British, Spanish, and U.S. companies, save for a few minor contracts. As global energy needs have receded and new discoveries of natural gas been made elsewhere, even signed and already implemented gas contracts originally negotiated at above-market prices are now being challenged by such close economic partners of Algeria as France and Italy.

The manner in which the Algerians have negotiated or renegotiated gas contracts with Western customers reveals much about the political economy of development being pursued by the current Algerian leadership. Pricing disputes with U.S. contractors began less than a year after the first LNG deliveries to the United States had been made. SONATRACH requested in early 1979 that the price paid to the Algerians be renegotiated, complaining that in the decade since the contract was originally signed SONATRACH's costs had substantially increased. After several months of intense negotiations the U.S. companies gave in, approving a not insignificant increase over the original price of Algerian natural gas entering the United States.

For his part, the newly appointed energy minister, B. Nabi, indicated that the price of energy was still too low. Accounting for shipping and regasification, the cost of Algerian gas at the pipeline entry was $3.43 per million BTUs (1 million BTUs [British Thermal Units] equals about 30 cubic meters of natural gas). The minister wanted gas priced according to a new principle: namely, a price equivalent to the energy content of Algerian crude oil at the point of export. Because shipping gas in liquid form is more expensive than shipping oil, and because the liquid must be regasified, the delivered gas would be higher in price per BTU than oil.

Nabi initiated talks with Gaz de France in early 1980 to renegotiate the price of LNG from US$3 per million BTUs to $6 per million BTUs. He subsequently made the same demand to El Paso Natural Gas, giving it until April 1, 1980, to accept a doubling of the price of the 1.05 million cubic meters of gas the company had planned to buy in 1980, from $2.30 per million BTUs to between $5 and $6 per million BTUs. Algeria also told customers in West Germany, Belgium, and Italy that they too would have to accept a doubling of prices for future gas deliveries.

Unwilling to renegotiate contracts, the major U.S. and European customers were cut off from all supplies of Algerian gas in the first week of April 1980. A month later, the Algerians stepped up their campaign to make gas prices rise in line with oil prices by threatening to close their gas-exporting business altogether unless they received substantially higher prices. They also threatened to cancel plans for a third liquefaction plant (at Arzew), which was to be built by the Foster Wheeler Corporation of the United States. (Ultimately it was cancelled for economic reasons.) As part of Algeria's strategy Nabi argued that oil sales alone were sufficient to meet all of the country's foreign currency needs.

By September 1980 it was evident that Algeria's campaign to raise the world price of natural gas and to create a cartel of natural gas exporters like OPEC was failing. Algeria unilaterally cancelled a twenty-year contract to supply LNG to the Netherlands and West Germany, hoping to apply pressure on its customers to accept a doubling of the world price of natural gas. Algeria took the offensive again in November 1980 when SONATRACH informed France that the ten-year contract to sell 230,000 barrels of oil a day to the French-controlled *Compagnie Française de Pétroles* would be abrogated unless France accepted higher prices for the 4 billion cubic meters of Algerian natural gas that it had planned to import in 1980. In linking oil supplies with higher gas prices in this way, the Algerians hoped to exploit the increased importance of their oil contract with France after the latter had lost roughly one-fourth of its normal supplies in September 1980 when Iraq stopped exporting oil because of its war with Iran. By the end of 1980, it had become clear that none of these measures had produced the desired results, and Algeria was losing millions of dollars in foreign revenue.

Algeria had its first partial success when it completed renegotiation of its long-term natural gas supply contract with Distrigaz of Belgium in April 1981, raising the price of gas supplied to the company to around $5 per 30 cubic meters (an increase of 400 percent) and adding an escalator clause based on oil prices. Nabi proclaimed that the Belgian Distrigaz agreement would be used by Algeria to set minimum conditions for renegotiations with French and U.S. customers. According to him the contract had effectively fulfilled Algeria's target of parity for gas prices with oil prices, with the escalator clause ensuring that the price of gas would rise in line with future increases in prices for crude oil. No mention was made of the possibility that oil prices would decline, although the escalator clause was meant to operate in either direction. For the Algerians crude oil price increases were the reality; oil price decline was mere theory or the private fantasy of Western oil importers. In any case to Algerians the principle of indexation was a safer way of ensuring continued price rises than ad hoc negotiation even if oil prices were themselves subject to temporary fluctuation.

The major breakthrough occurred in February 1982 when the new socialist government of François Mitterrand agreed to a "political" price for Algerian natural gas. For two years, negotiations between Algeria and the previous French government of Valéry Giscard d'Estaing had failed to achieve agreement on price and quantity of gas sales. Following political talks between Chadli Benjedid and François Mitterrand in late 1981, a new agreement was struck. According to contract terms *Gaz de France*, the French state gas utility, agreed to pay about US$5.20 per million BTUs, with the price indexed to a basket of six crudes, for 9.63 billion cubic meters per year. That price was well above the $4.28 that France paid for Algerian gas in 1981 and much higher than the $3.70 to which the price would otherwise have fallen in 1982 under a formula that had linked the price of natural gas to the cost of certain grades of crude oil. *Gaz de France* itself would pay only about $4.65 of the $5.20, with the balance coming from the French foreign aid budget. In essence nearly 14 percent of the contract was to be subsidized by the French government as a sign of political goodwill.

The agreement constituted a major victory for Algeria in its long campaign to increase gas prices so that they would be equivalent in energy terms to world oil prices. France's decision also greatly reinforced Algeria's hand in negotiations with Italy for the supply of 13.02 billion cubic meters of Algerian natural gas annually through a pipeline under the Mediterranean (Transmed—see the discussion in Chapter 7). Agreement was reached with the Italians at a base price of $4.41 per million BTUs at the Algerian-Tunisian frontier indexed to a basket of eight internationally traded crude oils. Gas flows through the pipeline began in mid-1983. The gas sold after various price negotiations with other customers is expected to equal most of Algeria's exporting capacity well into the 1980s and probably beyond.

Several developments in recent years make uncertain whether Algeria's strategy of price parity between oil and gas will pay off in the long run. Currently there is a worldwide glut of natural gas and relatively weak demand. In addition, exploration and discovery of new sources, along with continuing efforts in the Soviet Union, Saudi Arabia, and elsewhere to bring to market large quantities of natural gas, make it increasingly difficult for the Algerians to maintain their hard-line bargaining position. The contracts that have been signed with the nearly dozen foreign customers tend to be relatively small in volume. The U.S. market, which constitutes the greatest potential customer, has been effectively removed as a major importer since El Paso pulled out in 1981. The Panhandle (Houston) and Distrigas

(Boston) agreements are exceptions, but they constitute miniscule percentages of total U.S. gas imports. Even recently concluded contracts with French, Spanish, and Belgian customers are being renegotiated. They are all seeking substantial reductions in contracted supplies because of weak demand. Finally, Algeria's indexation formula is now detrimental to the country as a result of the movement of the market. Since OPEC's March 1983 pricing agreement the unit price of Algerian gas has been declining.

These setbacks come at a particularly critical time for Algeria. The country's development goals have been predicated on Algeria's hydrocarbons policy as originally put forth by the Boumediene regime and later modified by Chadli Benjedid. In both cases first oil, then natural gas, were to be the financial catalyst for an industrially based development. Given Algeria's limited crude oil reserves and the depressed demand for OPEC oil in the world market, the role of natural gas has assumed increased importance in Algerian economic calculations. Belkacem Nabi has been given the unenviable task of articulating and implementing a broad-based political strategy of maximizing natural gas revenues through a system of indexation and long-term contracts with Western customers. In such agreements the customers are tied to specific pricing formulas but are only "promised" increased commercial and trade agreements with Algeria.

The complexity of the natural gas industry and the massive investments and large capital outlays involved, including over US$3 billion in equipment, terminals, and specialized giant tankers, have made it difficult for the Algerians to shift quickly or radically their energy policy. It is therefore expected that in future contract dealings the Algerians will be exhibiting greater flexibility. This appears to be the case in current negotiations for contract modifications with the U.S., Belgian, French, and Spanish customers although a protracted pricing dispute with Spain's national gas company, ENAGAS, has forced the Algerians to go to the International Chamber of Commerce for arbitration. Spanish attempts to extricate itself from earlier contracts—now considered "exhorbitant"—have led to Algerian trade reprisals and a worsening of Spanish-Algerian economic relations. Despite an amicable resolution of this dispute in mid-1985 to the official satisfaction of both Madrid and Algiers, it is a pattern that may soon be repeated with other European customers. In the meantime what the Algerian leadership cannot afford to do is to reduce significantly the outlays for the socioeconomic programs that have been identified in the current development plan. These programs constitute the centerpiece of Chadli's new economic strategy of liberalization, private sector initiative, and other forms of decentralization, deconcentration, and democratization, and they are being promoted as the solution to the country's numerous social, economic, and bureaucratic problems.

DEVELOPMENT PLANNING IN THE 1980s

By the time Chadli Benjedid assumed power in 1979 many of the shortcomings associated with Boumediene's centralized development strategy had become evident. The strategy based on heavy industrialization had created dualistic economic structures, threatened Algiers and other coastal cities with hyperurbanization, caused intolerably high unemployment in both rural and urban areas, exacerbated income inequalities despite theoretical salary ceilings, and so neglected domestic food production that it increasingly failed to meet the country's needs. The new government gave priority to alleviating these problems and deferred further heavy industrial investment until a later date. Also Algeria's substantial foreign debt, contracted mainly to pay for industry, was causing concern, particularly because it implied an unwelcome vulnerability to pressure from overseas. Following nearly two years of debate, the FLN at its extraordinary session in June 1980 put forth a Five-Year Development Plan (1980–1984) which was intended to overcome many of these problems.

Toward a Better Life became the principal theme of the FLN special session. It was meant to signal the shifting away from the previous emphasis on heavy industry to a concern for the social needs of the people, notably in the fields of education, health, and housing, and on developing food and consumer industries. These policies and other proposals put into effect in the four years following 1980 did not mean the dismantling of Algeria's socialist structure or the forfeiting of its revolutionary commitments. Repeatedly Algerian officials have assured their people and foreign observers that this self-induced internal revolution was not to be interpreted as a return to "liberal" society, "in the sense that society as a whole would be made to suffer for the sake of the individual." In the words of the secretary general of the planning and regional development ministry, "the main lines of the Plan were meant to follow the options and political orientations already chosen for the country's development strategy. Algeria remains committed to creating a modern, stable and independent economy which is capable of generating its own internal development." And despite the decisions to halt construction of more LNG plants, to slow investment in other heavy industries, and to channel more funds into agriculture, light industry, and public services, the secretary general indicated that it was "vital for Algeria's economy to continue the development of basic industries in the future. For this reason a high rate of investment would be maintained in both basic and consumer industries. This represented about 40 percent of Algeria's gross national product which, although less than the 55 percent of the last few years, was still very high."[2]

These and other statements confirm the notion that Chadli's Toward a Better Life policies have not meant liberalization or democratization; instead, Chadli's directive has made decentralization and deconcentration the keys to effective utilization of Algeria's human, natural, and industrial resources. The tilt toward pragmatism that resulted from disenchantment with centralized development planning has been viewed as an issue of management and administration, not politics. This view has led to a search for technical solutions, managerial reforms, and mechanistic adjustments that would create the appropriate incentives for self-discipline in the workplace, accountability, and higher productivity. The critical factor of a nonauthoritarian political environment where democratic forces are allowed free play is visibly absent in all these exhortations and policy directives. Nonetheless, the new strategy of decentralization, involving several important changes from previous policies and practices, moves forward.

According to current Algerian development planners, the fundamental problem is how to raise productivity—which has been running at 40 percent or even lower in some plants. The major decision taken in this regard has been the restructuring of state companies, many of which had become too big and overcentralized. Restructuring has meant creating offshoots to take over subsidiary activities or, in other cases, separate, autonomous regional bodies. Thus, the division of the mammoth, state-run oil and gas company, SONATRACH, which has 100,000 employees, began in mid-1982. By late 1983 ten of the planned thirteen companies had already been created and put into place. Although the central SONATRACH organization remains, responsibility for many of the huge company's auxiliary activities have been delegated to the new companies, some of them headquartered outside Algiers.

This process of restructuring, involving numerous other big state corporations, has proceeded rapidly. In late 1982, for example, the four main state construction companies were reorganized and replaced by new, autonomous, smaller, regional companies specializing in building, research, or industrial activities. Twenty-one new state companies have been formed from the old *Entreprise Socialiste pour le Développement National de la Construction* (ESDNC). The former *Société Nationale des Travaux d'Infrastructure et du Bâtiment* (SONATIBA) has been split into five new companies based in Algiers, Annaba,

Constantine, Oran, and Skikda. Other state corporations currently undergoing restructuring include the National Iron and Steel Company (SNS), which is being split into thirteen autonomous companies; the National Company for Mechanical Construction (SONACOME), which is broken up into eleven companies specializing in trucks, cars, and agricultural machinery and which employs 50,000 people; and SON-ELEC, the National Company for Electricity and Electronic Equipment, which is to be divided into eight companies involved in electronics, cables, and various household appliances.

A related measure has been to allow state industries to form their own capital base. Previously, state companies borrowed all their money from the government, and therefore had little incentive to make profits. Now that they are allowed to plow back their profits, the government hopes they will behave a little more competitively. Overtly these measures at decentralizing old state monopolies have been aimed at increasing productivity, but they have also served the important political function of reducing the power and prestige of many of the Boumediene loyalists who ran them. Thus decentralization achieves the subordination of the technocratic class to the army-government elites currently in dominance.

A second factor constraining higher productivity, besides the massive size of state corporations, has been the serious lack of skilled personnel. Although Algeria has created a high quality core of top management officials, many of whom have been educated abroad in France, the United States, or the Soviet Union, there has been a major gap in the number of qualified middle-level managers. An increasing emphasis is now being placed on management training, with larger sums being made available for vocational education. The purpose is to create a competent middle management that would enable the government to reduce the heavy dependency on foreign technical expertise. Although foreign companies operating in Algeria have always been required, as part of their contracts, to provide training for Algerian personnel, these efforts have not always produced impressive results. Current government plans therefore are to encourage Algerian management to stand on its own feet.

Another measure introduced as an incentive to production is that of production bonuses. Wages in the state industries now consist of three components: a basic wage (Algerians have a guaranteed minimum wage, which in 1982 was approximately US$0.85 an hour for nonagricultural workers), a supplement to take account of working conditions, and a production bonus. Industrial workers can earn up to 20 percent more just by fulfilling their production norms. They can get another 30 percent by exceeding them. If the shop floor as

President Chadli Benjedid inaugurating a paint factory located in the Sig-Masacara industrial zone, in October 1984. (Algerian Press Service)

a whole produces more than its norm, the workers can get another 20 percent. It is estimated that since the introduction of this scheme in early 1982 industrial production has gone up 11 percent.

A crucial element in the decentralization strategy is that of regional development. Until recently industrial development had been concentrated in the overcrowded northern cities of Algiers, Oran, and Constantine. Industrial units are now being moved to rural areas in the central and southern regions of the country as a means to provide both jobs (to stem the rural exodus) and services and amenities in regional centers (another incentive for people to stay on or near the land). An interesting political consequence of this regional development plan is the potential for increased power and importance of the *wali* (head or governor of a *wilaya*, an administrative district of which there are forty-eight) as his sphere of responsibility and decisionmaking expands. This consequence may provide the foundation for a more autonomous democratization process at the local level because the *wali* will have real resources and services under his jurisdiction. Some ministerial power may devolve incrementally to administrative heads whose districts become the centers of regional industrial enterprises. These developments will have to be followed closely in the years ahead.

The government has also increased the scope for private sector growth. In a speech in May 1982 Chadli encouraged Algeria's small, but energetic, private sector to expand in the retail, housing, and tourism industries. It is estimated that Algeria's private sector accounts for a third of the economy. In addition to the half of farming that is privately owned, trade is wholly in private hands. So are about half the country's building and textile firms. The government wants the private sector's help in creating jobs and tapping savings for investment. At present private fortunes are often stashed away or smuggled abroad. Some 95 percent of all investment is by the state. New laws are seeking to pinpoint the areas private industry can invest in without fear of interference. The criteria governing private sector development are that private companies should not be allowed to occupy a strategic position in any industry—either by being the sole source of supply of a key component or by being jointly able to exert a monopoly over price. Some planners have gone so far as to say that private industry "is an ally of the revolution." One should be careful not to exaggerate the importance of this development, however. Algeria remains essentially a socialist state whatever critics may think of its socialist pretensions in other areas of state behavior.

The government is also acting to establish more joint-venture companies with foreign concerns. In particular, Western businesses are being given tax holidays to encourage them to invest in consumer goods industries, housing, and electronics. Yet most foreign businesses remain wary of the Algerian market. Foreign companies can repatriate profits worth up to a quarter of their investment, but they still must pay stiff taxes.

The agricultural sector has been severely neglected in the past, with disastrous consequences as the next part of this chapter will demonstrate. In theory, Algeria should be able to feed itself. In practice, it imports half of its grain, is the world's biggest importer of eggs, and ships in huge amounts of meat and dairy products. Chadli's development plan envisions the building of twenty dams for irrigation. Farmers, who have suffered under state-run collectives, are being given more credits and encouraged to till small plots that they can eventually own. A new agricultural bank has been established at Blida, and steps are being taken to break up the two thousand *autogestion*, or self-managed, state farms into several thousand smaller units. These and other measures being recommended will require time before any substantial results will be seen.

It is not yet certain whether all these highly publicized efforts at streamlining the Algerian economy in response to accumulated social grievances are part of a broader, more permanent shifting of

Late afternoon gathering in El Goléa's central market.

the system from a "center-down" to a "bottom-up" strategy of development. As early as 1971, for example, the Boumediene region had begun a campaign against poor governmental performance, which it said was caused by excessive centralization. The government then mobilized party ideologues, representatives of the mass organizations within the FLN (such as UGTA, UNFA, UNPA—the National Union of Algerian Peasants), and the state-controlled mass media to push for decentralized planning and administration. Yet by the time of Boumediene's death in late 1978 little of a concrete nature had been accomplished. The decentralization effort remained at the level of rhetoric.

Benjedid's team was quick to support the principle of decentralization but began to act only after political power had been effectively consolidated. Clearly many of the components necessary for a viable decentralization process oriented to the local level are already in place. Land reform, better structures for communal decisionmaking, private-sector incentives, industrial restructuring, regional development, priority to projects for basic needs rather than production for export, and other policies favoring peripheral and rural areas already can be seen, if only in embryonic form. A significant step was taken in administrative reorganization when, in December 1984, the government approved a measure increasing the number of *wilayas* from thirty-one to forty-eight. The increase in regional units should impel local economic development and make the administration more accessible and accountable, thereby benefiting the public.

The theme of Work and Discipline to Guarantee the Future marked the FLN's fifth party congress held in December 1983. Among its many objectives was the continuation of the government's efforts at streamlining the economy so as to make it more efficient and responsive to populist needs. The broad outline of the next five-year plan was also discussed. It was given concrete meaning at the twelfth session of the FLN's Central Committee, which convened in May 1984, and officially approved by the cabinet in early July 1984. On balance, the 1985–1989 plan reflects the government's determination to shift economic priorities from state-centered to society-centered needs. Other principal features of the new plan include increasing the degree of horizontal integration of Algerian industry by promoting intersectoral exchanges, on developing import-substitution manufacturing, and on improving storage facilities and the distribution system, the deficiencies of which have long plagued Algerian bureaucracy.

In order to tackle the serious problem of overurbanization in the major coastal cities projects are to be implemented that will stimulate new industrial development in the High Plateaus and the south. It is hoped that this development as well as the setting up of family planning clinics throughout the country will decongest already overpopulated cities. Continuing the programs begun in the previous plan, the new development scheme will emphasize social and communications infrastructure, especially housing and rail transport. A priority issue that has already caused controversy and may give authorities political problems in the future is the plan's decision to reorient secondary and higher education in order to meet more closely the economy's evolving manpower demands and employment possibilities. (As noted earlier, attempts to limit enrollment in training for certain popular professions such as medicine and law as well as the effort to keep students at regional rather than urban universities so as to achieve more regionally balanced growth have already created anxiety among many of the nation's youth.)

It will be some time, however, before the whole package of reform measures originally introduced by the Benjedid government and spelled out in the two five-year plans will be adopted in any comprehensive or integrated fashion. The hydrocarbon industry, for example, continues its financial domination of the economy. The focus on industrial investment has not been significantly lessened but merely supplemented by new policy orientations. Yet it is too soon for an objective evaluation. As protracted gas and oil contractual negotiations have revealed, the Algerians possess quite a long time frame for policy implementation. Nonetheless the trend to subnational policy initiation and follow-through comes into conflict with Algeria's historic urge for organic unity and the need for central direction and close supervision. It is thus too early to decide whether an effective transformation of elite political culture has taken place or whether the current push toward decentralization is mere managerial tinkering.

In the meantime, society's multiple dilemmas continue to mount, and the problems of an unproductive and deteriorating agricultural sector cause particular alarm. Not only has domestic food production overwhelmingly failed to satisfy the basic food needs of Algeria's 22 million people, but the drain on human and financial resources has been enormous, having a negative impact on the effort to achieve an integrated and self-sufficient development. What created this condition, how has the government responded, and what are the implications for Algeria's political economy in the future are the questions we seek to answer next.

AGRICULTURE: THE ECONOMY'S ACHILLES' HEEL

On February 2, 1984, the United States and Algeria concluded a historic five-year accord on agricultural cooperation and trade. It was a wide-ranging protocol involving increased sales to Algeria of U.S. agricultural products (especially wheat), enhancing Algeria's capacity to absorb and utilize better the agricultural goods being received, and introducing U.S. scientific and technical know-how to the many areas of Algerian agriculture that are currently experiencing difficulties.

In a dramatic and decisive way the agricultural agreement represented a fundamental shift in Algerian developmental priorities from one based exclusively on an industrialization-first policy to one more and more concerned with reviving the country's long-neglected agricultural sector. The change was necessary to ease the dependence on agricultural imports to meet basic food needs. This dependence was having and continues to have profound economic, social, and political consequences on the country's overall development.

Although industry has not been supplanted as the leading sector of national investment in the 1980–1984 or the 1985–1989 five-year development plans or in the country's annual operating budgets, agriculture, food production, the condition of rural life, and the education and training of Algerian peasants have all shifted to the top of Chadli's developmental agenda. The appointment of Abdallah

Khalef (until recently, better known by his nom de guerre, Kasdi Merbah)—one of Chadli's closest aides, whose ties with the president developed during their military careers together and who was previously assigned the crucial functions of vice-minister of defense in charge of military industries and, from January 1982, minister of heavy industry—as agriculture minister in January 1984 signaled the president's reordering efforts.

How serious has the food dependence problem become and what is the state of Algerian agriculture in the early 1980s? Why have Algerian authorities felt compelled to initiate bold and unprecedented action to remedy a problem that has been around for nearly two decades and one to which successive government leaders have given regular attention in their speeches, party statements, and other official documents? A few representative facts about the country's agricultural situation will dramatize the dimensions and depth of the problem.

Food Dependency

Algeria's dependence on food imports has increased dramatically over the years from a state of complete self-sufficiency at independence in 1962 to 75 percent dependency today. Since the end of the 1960s cereal imports have increased fourfold, flour thirtyfold, meat fortyfold, vegetables fivefold. In 1969, 70 percent of Algerian food needs were being satisfied by domestic production. Less than five years later (1973) that percentage was reduced to 55; it declined further in 1977 to 35 percent. It is estimated that today Algeria produces only 25 percent of its total food needs.

Algeria has always imported agricultural products, but its export of wines, citrus fruits, and dates left its agricultural trade balance either in equilibrium or in surplus. But by 1971 major imbalances between agricultural imports and exports began to develop. The country had a serious food deficit—not to mention the immense financial burden this was placing on the economy. In 1977, for example, Algeria's total food import bill was US$1 billion; this was nearly doubled to $1.9 billion by 1982 and is estimated to have been $2.3 billion for 1984. Steadily increasing hydrocarbon-derived revenues, beginning with the quadrupling of oil prices following the October 1973 Arab-Israeli war, were able to pay the bulk of this bill. This income, however, has leveled off considerably in the 1980s as market pressures, overproduction, new discoveries, global conservation, and OPEC greed have had the collective impact of depressing oil prices and thereby reducing Algeria's ability to pay for foodstuffs, the costs of which have continued to rise. It is estimated, for example, that the value of net food imports has amounted to nearly 35 percent of revenues from oil exports in 1983. The figure will rise to 50 percent in the next half decade should world hydrocarbon prices remain unchanged or decline while food imports and prices continue to rise.

Overpopulation, urbanization, rural exodus to the cities, and an uncontrolled net population birth rate of 3.2 percent per annum have placed added pressures on food production and therefore food imports. Agricultural shortages have not been limited to a handful of products; the country is currently dependent on a wide range of imported foodstuffs to satisfy the increasingly sophisticated consumption needs that higher national incomes have engendered. For example, butter, milk, cheese, coffee, tea, sugar, eggs, and meat are all being imported in greater and greater quantities at greater and greater cost.

Cereals, more than any other single commodity, reveal the dimension of the problem: Their import has risen steadily over the years. Indeed, Algeria in 1984, with 22 million people, produces less cereals than it did at the beginning of the century when its population was only 5 million. From 1961 to 1965, annual imports of cereal were about .46 million tons, and from 1971 to 1975 such imports reached approximately 1.4 million tons a year. Since then, imports have been as high as 2 million tons per year, and it is estimated that these could reach between 4 and 4.5 million tons annually by the end of the century if production techniques do not improve in the interim. Overall food imports have shown even higher rates of growth. During the early 1970s, they grew by an average of 31 percent a year, and during the mid-1970s, the growth rate soared to 450 percent.

The picture is clear and the implications unmistakable: If nothing is done to reverse drastically this condition of massive food dependence, the country will become vulnerable to enormous political, economic, and social pressures both internally and externally. Such pressures will inhibit Algeria's ability to develop and industrialize in the manner and at the speed its people and leaders desire.

How has Algeria reached this dangerous condition in such a relatively brief period? A wide range of geographical, climatic, historical, structural, and political factors combine to provide an explanation. Although agricultural development has long been restricted by problems such as erosion, adverse weather conditions, especially drought and flood, primitive methods of production, and underemployment, the decisive factors have had to do more with regime policies and programs than with the limitations imposed by nature and history.

El Kantara gorge in the Aurès mountains, a historic gateway to the Sahara Desert.

Constraints

Algeria confronts one unchangeable fact about its topography—more than four-fifths of its nearly 2.4-million-square-kilometer land surface is composed of desert. Of the remaining areas only between 2 and 3 percent can be considered suitable for cultivation. Thus, although the third largest country on the African continent—after Zaire and the Sudan—in terms of total land surface, Algeria has one of the smallest percentages of arable land in the world. Of the absolute amount of cultivable land, only about 4 million hectares of the 6.5 million hectares actually suitable for crops are being cultivated, with the balance being held in fallow. As there are no large reserves of fertile land that can be brought into cultivation, this shortage of usable agricultural areas will remain a more or less permanent condition facing Algerian agricultural planners.

Agricultural development is also restricted by erosion and adverse weather conditions compounding the destructive effects of overcultivation, overgrazing, and deforestation over the centuries. The combined impact on usable agricultural land is that the hectare amount theoretically available to every Algerian has declined dramatically as the population has soared. In 1962, for example, there were approximately 0.75 hectares of arable land for every man, woman, and child in Algeria. This ratio fell to 0.59 hectares per person in 1966, 0.48 in 1973, 0.41 in 1977, 0.37 in 1980, and by 1990, with a projected population of 26 million, there will be one person to every 0.29 hectares.

The amount and frequency of rainfall has historically been a crucial factor in determining agricultural output in the three northern zones of the country—Constantinois, Algerois, and Oranie regions—where the bulk of Algerian cultivation is done. The early 1980s witnessed an extended period of drought that had a negative impact on production. The situation was ameliorated somewhat in 1983 and 1984, although production increases were as much due to reforms in the organization of agriculture, especially the renewed emphasis on the private sector and the operation of market forces, as to improved weather conditions.

Limited arable land and unpredictable and meager rainfalls by themselves could not explain the sorry state of Algerian agriculture since 1962. The colonial experience and the ensuing decolonization process, war of independence, and massive flight of colon farmers must be added to the factors helping to explain the severe crisis in Algerian agriculture.

With their arrival in 1830 the French severely dislocated existing agricultural arrangements by bifurcating the agriculture of northern Algeria into modern and traditional sectors. Government-supported settlers pushed the original communal or individual landowners out of the productive coastal plains and intermontane valleys onto the slopes of the surrounding hills and mountains and the grazing lands of the high plateau between the Tell Atlas and the Saharan Atlas ranges. Around Algiers as well, potentially rich swamplands and bottomlands were reclaimed by the Europeans. Colon farmers had thus wrested the best land and most of the irrigation facilities for themselves. Additionally, the modern-sector farms were run on a commercial basis, benefiting from the use of technical skills and counsel, mechanized equipment, fertilizers, insecticides, and imported seeds. This sector was integrated into the French market system, supplying France with large quantities of wines, citrus fruit, olives, and early vegetables. As supply and demand conditions changed, the modern sector had credit facilities available to enable it to increase and update its plant and equipment. In almost every respect the modern-sector farm represented the economic elite of the colony.

In stark contrast was the situation in the traditional sector where a typical farm averaged around 10 hectares (compared to 120 or so hectares on the average modern-sector farm), of which several hectares were likely to be unproductive and several more might at any one

Camels grazing in the High Plateaus.

time by lying fallow in the traditional two-year cereal-fallow rotation. Typically such farms supported a family unit of ten or more persons. "Subsistence cereal culture, eked out by the growing of olives, figs, and dates (mainly in southern Algeria) and by nomadic stockraising, formed the basis of the traditional agriculture, but the land available for cropping was submarginal even for cereal growing under the prevailing traditional cultivation practices."[3]

The Algerian small farmer in the traditional sector lived at the edge of subsistence. Burdened by accumulated debt, he was neither able to save from his own output to afford improvements in capital or personnel nor given access to institutional credit with which to acquire improvements on an installment basis. This situation was worsened by a rapidly growing population which, because of Islamic inheritance laws, tended to fragment the farm unit and force more and more of the labor force off the land in search of a better life in already overcrowded coastal and metropolitan cities. Although the modern sector was productive and profitable—in 1954, for example, agriculture contributed 34 percent to the GNP, compared to less than 7 percent today—the traditional farms remained consistently unproductive. The crisis of underproduction was severely aggravated by the war of independence, most of which was fought in the countryside, the massive and forced dislocation of the rural population into regroupment centers, and the widespread destruction of livestock and of farm and forest lands.

The trend of agricultural production continued at independence when European capital, management, and skill fled the country virtually in their entirety. The rupture of the previously intimate economic relations between France and Algeria following the European exodus caused a serious breakdown of Algerian exports, especially wines, to the important French markets.

As crucial as topography, climate, and colonialism have been in limiting agricultural production, none of these factors by themselves or collectively have been so decisive as the policy of rapid and heavy industrialization pursued by successive postrevolutionary regimes. Indeed, the distorting role of the industrialization-first policy has, in one way or another, created the conditions inhibiting the functional development of Algerian agriculture.

This was not how development planners had intended it to be. Following the comprehensive program envisioned in G. Destanne de Bernis' idea of "industrializing industries," agriculture was to have an important and integrated role in economic development. "It was required to produce foodstuffs to feed the growing population so that foreign exchange could be reserved for imports of industrial equipment; it could supply important raw materials for the industrial sector; and it provided a large potential market for the products of Algeria's new industries—fertilizers, pesticides and farm equipment."[4]

According to the theory, extensive investment in large-scale industrial projects, despite its lack of short-term economic rationale, would help provide a range of development possibilities to all sectors of society. Petrochemical plants, for example, could provide insecticides, fungicides, and plastics for use in irrigation pipes, greenhouses, and packaging, as well as fertilizers. Steel plants could produce Algerian-made agricultural equipment. Given the country's availability of impressive amounts of hydrocarbon resources and the modernization thrust of socialist decision makers, it was understandable why the industrialization-first policy was readily adopted.

Yet despite the claim that the country was seeking a balanced development between industry and agriculture and that both sectors were intimately linked, the proportion of investments in agriculture as reflected in the various development plans was markedly smaller than that allocated for industry. In both the three-year pre-plan of 1967–1969 and the first four-year plan (1970–1973) investment allocated to the agricultural sector was only 15 percent, while industry received 51 percent. The former percentage declined to 11 percent in the 1974–1977 four-year plan and increased to only 11.7 percent in the first five-year plan (1980–1984) despite the fact that agricultural issues and problems of food production had become central concerns of the new government (February 1979) of Chadli Benjedid. Actual investment fell even more dramatically in the 1966–1983 period because the agricultural sector was unable to utilize fully the moneys made available to it.

Government pricing policies have also reflected the favoritism given to industrialization. Until 1974–1975, for example, the official pricing policy for agricultural commodities discouraged the intensification of agricultural production—the only way by which output could be increased, given the absence of additional irrigated land. "Prices were held stable at a time when the cost of farm machinery, fertilizers and labor rose substantially. These distortions in the terms of exchange between agriculture and industry discouraged investment and resulted in low incomes for peasant farmers."[5] Concerned about accelerating industrialization and feeding its swelling urban population at the lowest cost possible, the state attempted to maintain the price of agriculture as low as possible, even if that involved the massive importation of food from abroad at higher world market prices. Producer prices of cereals, for example, increased only 15 percent in the decade from 1967 to 1977. Under such conditions the small farmer was unable to make an adequate living and was thus forced to look for work elsewhere, normally in the larger towns or cities of the country.

A World Bank study identified government pricing policy as one major causal factor in the problem of low agricultural growth in Algeria.

> Increased Algerian demand for food caused by rapidly rising per capita incomes and population growth did not cause agricultural producer prices to increase which would have stimulated production. Instead, producer prices were kept artificially low by Government, and demand satisfied by imports. Government's objective was social rather than economic: to subsidize food consumption, without excessively burdening the Government budget by combining low retail food prices with low agricultural producer prices.[6]

For the last decade there have been new attempts at increasing producer prices, which have risen more rapidly than costs of agricultural inputs. Not all products have benefited from such increases, however, for the price of fertilizers and pesticides, for example, have responded slowly and intermittently, thus discouraging farmer productivity whether in the private or government-managed sectors.

Given the importance of the urban-directed industralization efforts, agriculture was made to pay for the inflation caused by industrialization and urbanization. Similarly, despite an official parity in the minimum wage paid agricultural and industrial workers, pay differentials in the two sectors have been wide and dramatic. A 1974 report, for example, revealed that 30,000 SONATRACH workers received an aggregate salary of close to 600 million Algerian dinars (DA) in 1972 while 250,000 workers and employees of the self-management agricultural sector were paid just under 450 million DA.[7]

The inequality between the industrial and agricultural sectors has gone even beyond pricing and pay differentials; it has also included investment, affecting salary bonuses, social security, health, education, and professional training. In combination limited educational and training opportunities, inadequate services and recreational facilities, and pricing and pay disincentives have accelerated the pace of the rural exodus—which has proceeded unchecked since the turn of the century. More importantly, those leaving the land are normally the most skilled and youngest of the rural population, those whom the countryside can least afford to lose, leaving behind an aging and unproductive peasantry.

Results of the 1977 census reveal in dramatic terms the drop in the active agricultural work force, which in 1966 constituted 918,000 persons but which fell to 692,000 a decade later; a decline from 54 to 29 percent of the total active work force, this despite a net annual birthrate of 3.2 percent. Similarly, the median age in 1977 of all workers in the country was 34, but it was 39 for farmers. In the 20–45 age group, of the 58 percent represented in the labor force population as a whole, 54 percent were involved in agricultural pursuits. Finally, although only 6.5 percent of the total work force was over 60 years old, 12 percent of that age group was working on the land.[8] In some sectors of agriculture this latter figure is currently as high as 50 percent. Thus, both qualitatively and quantitatively agriculture has been unable to retain those it most needs.

Another serious problem has been the competition between industry and agriculture for scarce water resources. This competition has resulted in the loss of valuable irrigated land and a sharp decline in water resources available for agricultural use. In a country in which the total arable surface is already small compared to its national population and where the land most conducive to intensive production is limited, it is in these very circumscribed regions that industrial zones and, with them, urban centers have been created. Since independence, nearly 250,000 hectares (including 5,000 ha of irrigated land) have been removed in this manner from agricultural use.

Water, like land, has been used disproportionately by industri-alization-urbanization measures. The once fertile area of the Mitidja, for example, which the French had so fully developed, is slowly being undermined as the water needs of Algiers, Rouiba, Blida, and other urban areas and industrial zones have increased unchecked. Despite government awareness of the problem, the competition for scarce water resources among factory, city, and farm remains keen.

To all the difficulties identified above, one must add those of massive bureaucratic delays, overcentralized decisionmaking, inade-quate cadres of native-trained personnel, serious production shortfalls in agricultural machinery, and poor performance in the repair and return of farm equipment.

What has been the response of government to these multiple causes of agricultural decline? A number of differing farming systems (self-management, cooperative, private) and policy strategies (mech-anization, mobilization, market incentives) have been put forth, none of which, however, has constituted the basis of a coherent national agricultural program. Indeed, until very recently, government agri-cultural policy had been characterized by a great deal of revolutionary rhetoric but relatively little investment of resources and manpower.

Agricultural Structures

At the heart of the problem of agriculture has been the prevailing structural asymmetry between government-controlled and privately held lands. Despite public commentary to the contrary, the structural duality of land ownership inherited from French colonialism has not been fully discarded. The socialist or *autogestion* ("self-management") sector, for example, representing the best lands that were vacated (*biens vacants*) by the departing French colon farmers at independence, remains a privileged area. Modern farming methods and equipment are used there; its ownership is Algerian, but its management style and mode of operation remain little changed from colonial days.

This was not what revolutionary theoreticians had in mind when a unique system of worker management of *biens vacants* was proclaimed by governmental decrees in March 1963. The decree followed a brief period of rural chaos and economic uncertainty in the aftermath of the precipitous exodus of European owners, managers, and technical staffs. *Autogestion* was originally conceived as an economic system based on workers' management of their own affairs "through elected officials and cooperation with the state through a director and national agencies. The State had the function of guiding, counseling, and coordinating their activities within the framework of an evolving national plan." As a theory of economic management and social organization, *autogestion* was seen as a stage in the "transformation from a colonial to a socialist economy. The guiding forces during the transition were designated as the peasants, workers, and revolutionary intellectuals united in the tasks of planned social action, civic formation, and economic development."[9]

In the short space of fifteen months—July 1962 to October 1963—the *autogestion* concept absorbed nearly 3 million hectares of the richest and best-farmed land in the country. Not only did the lands that came under *autogestion* contain the most valuable fertile properties but they also constituted the technologically most advanced sector of the former colonial agricultural economy, whose productive units were rationally organized and geared toward a world market. In principle, *autogestion* introduced a system of autonomous collective management of the means of production by all the permanent working personnel and a doctrine of social organization with implications for the restructuring of community and national life.

Although the Algerians who replaced European farmers in the self-management system elected their own committees of management, actual ownership of these properties passed to the state. Gradually from mid-1966 on, the government established effective control of the *autogestion* farms, which thereafter came to be known as the socialized sector. What had begun as a spontaneous occupation of farms by agricultural laborers and had led quickly to the expropriation of the total settler-owned modern agricultural sector and the initiation of collective ownership and management was ultimately bureaucratized and subordinated to the all-powerful control of state technocrats who put agricultural profitability ahead of political mobilization of the peasantry. The March 1963 decrees installed the elements of a new managerial system and the October 1963 decrees secured the full possession of colon estates, but the patterns of land use and work and the hierarchy of occupational categories, responsibilities, and status were left virtually intact. Thus, although *autogestion* was eminently successful in meeting the general work and production norms set by the preindependence economy, it did not constitute a fundamental reordering of the existing structural imperatives or productive and human relations of the agricultural system. Unguided by revolutionary leadership, farm laborers and agricultural workers on self-management farms reverted to long-accustomed patterns of social behavior that had been formed under generations of colonial rule. Whatever revolutionary potential the *autogestion* experience may have had as a bold attempt at democratic decisionmaking quickly gave way to the demands of a domineering state-centered technocracy. The urban proclivities and industrially oriented developmental objectives of this technocracy made it suspicious of any independently minded populist rural sector whose resource base was considered essential for Algeria's economic growth.

Today the socialist sector, covering 27 percent of the country's total arable land and 44 percent of its irrigated areas, consists of approximately 2,300 mechanized state farms that cover more than 2 million hectares of the best agricultural land. The state farms employ about 180,000 permanent and 100,000 seasonal workers, or about 20 percent of the agricultural labor force. The land is not owned by the farmers but is worked by them, and in return they receive help from state organizations. Through the Ministry of Agriculture, the state appoints a manager for each farm whose role is to ensure that land development conforms with national planning objectives. The state farms account for about 60 percent of total agricultural output. They utilize the most mechanized and modern farming methods and concentrate on the most intensive crops.

Overcentralized government planning and direction have been a problem and have prevented these farms from achieving their potential. Yet from the outset the socialist sector was "assigned objectives at once ambitious and contradictory. It has been called upon to maintain and even increase the level of production for export and at the same time to satisfy local needs which involves the gradual replacement of export crops."[10] Also, although socialist farms are large—the individual farm units cover on average 1,158 hectares— and can thus benefit from economies of scale and mechanization, they have been difficult to manage at skill and technical levels necessary to make them fully productive. Aware of this problem, the agricultural ministry has taken steps in recent years to split the farms into five to six thousand smaller units in order to make them more manageable. In addition, about one hundred experimental farms are being established to study better methods of management and to demonstrate modern agricultural techniques. In conjunction with this, the government has taken steps to train 3,000 people in specialized agricultural fields such as agribusiness and agronomy.

To be sure, such measures reveal a new government awareness of the problem and the need for broad level reforms. Yet the first decade of independence witnessed little fundamental change in agricultural management. The mechanized socialist sector constituted the focus of government attention more as an instrument of narrow economic policy than as a way of transforming rural society, ideological rhetoric notwithstanding. Numerous programs of agrarian reform have been put forth in the past by Algerian intellectuals—the preindependence Tripoli Program of May 27, 1962, calling for the reform and modernization of agriculture, was probably the most explicit in this regard—but none of these have effectively tackled the structure of ownership or the relations of production in Algerian agriculture. By 1971, however, a number of factors caused the government of Houari Boumediene to confront the issue of agrarian reform and launch, with much fanfare and publicity, a three-phased program of national action: the Charter of the Agrarian Revolution.

The first phase (January 1972–June 1973) abolished sharecropping, cancelled sharecroppers' debts, and distributed some 700,000 hectares of state land to 54,000 peasant farmers. These were organized into small production cooperatives supported by service cooperatives that provided modern means of production, storage, marketing, credit, planning, and extension work. In the second phase (mid-June 1973–mid-June 1975) large privately owned Algerian farms were nationalized by the state, and 650,000 hectares were redistributed by the communal governments to 60,000 landless peasant families. The third phase, beginning in 1975, was aimed at livestock reform in the pastoral steppe. All pastureland was nationalized and livestock redistributed to 170,000 herdsmen who are now being resettled in new cooperative villages.

One thousand "socialist villages" are also being built to provide accessible urban-industrial amenities and facilities to the rural population to stem the exodus to the larger cities. A fourth phase to restore and manage the use of forests is in the transition stage between planning and implementation. An 18-million-tree Green Belt forestation program is now underway to hold back the Sahara, combat land erosion, and increase production of fruit and wood products.

By 1980, the agrarian revolution had resulted in the establishment of nearly 6,000 production cooperatives, 730 communal farming co-ops, 177 service co-ops, and 671 socialist villages. But employment, production, and earnings of the cooperatives have fallen far short of expectations: Only a minority of production cooperatives appear to be profitable, and they have had little impact on production or productivity. State farm workers receive higher wages, especially the administrative and technical employees. Rural underemployment remains high, and many migrate to urban areas. Government incentives to remain on the farm have not stemmed the migration to the cities; indeed, bureaucratic and logistical problems have impaired potential agricultural productivity.

Why was it necessary to launch the agrarian revolution in the first place? Several reasons have been put forth. First, there was the need to bridge the gap between the increasing industrial production and the lagging aggregate demand. This lag was considered a function of the inadequate employment and income-generating capacity of the capital-intensive industry and of a stagnating agricultural sector. It was becoming increasingly clear by the late 1960s that "not only was agriculture failing to produce sufficient raw materials for Algeria's developing industries or enough foodstuffs for its rapidly expanding population, but that it was also failing to generate an adequate demand for industrial products. The industrializing industries strategy was being threatened by a weak market for those products geared towards agriculture."[11] Thus any planned industrial expansion programs would be effectively frustrated if an internal market for the growing industrial output were not expanded. Rehabilitating the private agricultural sector would be one way of expanding that internal market. There was also the need to change rural ways of life so that they would approach urban standards. This change would control the exodus of peasants from the countryside into already overcrowded and under-serviced cities.

Finally, there was the important political goal of mobilizing the Algerian rural masses toward greater consciousness and participation in national life using such institutions as the National Liberation Front (FLN) and, as soon as it was founded in 1974, the National Union of Algerian Peasants (UNPA). As perceived by the national decision makers themselves, there was great concern for the incorporation of the "somewhat refractory population of the countryside into the national political community by responding to its material needs—thereby reinforcing the legitimacy of the regime—and bringing it more firmly within the purview of the State apparatus in several ways at once: in production, distribution, education, health, religious and cultural life, and so on."[12]

In its attempt at transforming the private sector of agriculture, the Boumediene regime hoped to achieve broad, indeed radical, changes in economic and political life, thereby giving substantive meaning to Algerian revolutionary socialism. Yet by the end of Boumediene's rule in 1978 most of these theoretically interrelated objectives had not been achieved. The impact of the agrarian reform program on the rural sector of the economy, for example, has been limited at best: It has neither raised production levels nor effectively slowed down the rural-urban exodus.

For some observers, however, the short-term economic failures were less important than the political repercussions that the reforms engendered. According to Hugh Roberts, Boumediene's commitment to agrarian reform carried with it a number of radical political implications. First, it politically disenfranchised the national bourgeoisie by directly attacking and undermining domestic private property. Second, the agrarian reform, by encouraging political mobilization of the rural masses, reactivated the vanguard role of national organizations like the FLN. Third, by creating parallel administrative structures, the reforms undercut the power of status quo interests in the bureaucracy. Fourth, it led to the founding in 1972 of the *Volontariat*, a student voluntary service organization aimed at mobilizing the countryside through education and propaganda (during vacation periods and intersessions of the university year). Fifth, the reforms introduced the army more directly into the political and social transformation of society. It was called upon to build socialist villages, construct the trans-Saharan highway, and plant the seedlings for the east-west reafforestation project.[13]

As potentially transforming as many of these measures may have been, their durability has come into question because Chadli's brand of "neoliberalism" effectively replaced Boumediene's "radical socialism." In the Chadli period the chronic problem of food production deficiency has overshadowed questions of populism and party-inspired mobilization. The reality is that the agrarian revolution or cooperative sector still only comprises 13 percent of the nation's arable land, contributing, in the 1977–1978 growing season, 14 percent of the production of winter cereals, 15 percent of industrial crops, 8 percent of vegetables, 4 percent of wine, and 5 percent of Mediterranean fruits (see Table 5.1).

The favoring of traditional crops by the production cooperatives and the increased mechanization of agrarian reform land, with much machinery remaining underutilized, have further weakened the agrarian revolution's potential. A heavy-handed bureaucracy, overcentralized decisionmaking, and widespread instances of corruption, mismanagement, price-fixing, black marketeering, and interventions of unregulated middlemen and commercial profiteers have all in combination revealed a fundamental problem with a strategy of the reforms, namely, the political mobilization of the peasantry from above. In the agrarian revolution, the central government rather than the peasantry itself determined those priorities of planning, production, and pricing that have the most direct impact on the peasants' lives. Purely political objectives were placed above agricultural ones—with essentially negative consequences for food production *and* social mobilization. The bureaucratization of one sector of agricultural life reduced peasants to the status of mere agricultural laborers, a kind of rural proletariat in which "farmer" and "peasant" had been stripped of their ecological and sociological meaning. Feeling alienated and isolated, the new rural worker could no longer identify with the land upon which he was working. In short, political mobilization from

TABLE 5.1

Cultivable Land and Crop Production, by Sector (percentages for 1977-1978 growing season)

	Area (hectares)	Total Production[a]	Socialist Sector		Cooperative Sector		Private Sector	
			Area	Production	Area	Production	Area	Production
Arable land	7,922,220	—	27	—	13	—	60	—
Irrigated land	313,340	—	44	—	13	—	43	—
Fallow land	3,660,450	—	16	—	11	—	73	—
Winter cereals	2,623,170	15,359,020	32	42	16	14	52	44
Artificial fodder	296,430	—	62	—	16	—	22	—
Industrial crops	34,070	1,493,960	73	67	9	15	18	18
Vegetable crops	141,030	10,339,860	35	32	10	8	55	60
Vines for wine making	190,260	1,840,000	83	88	4	4	13	8
Citrus fruits	49,850	4,475,060	83	86	7	5	10	9
Other fruits	49,660	934,980	49	50	8	6	43	44

Sources: Georges Mutin, "Agriculture et depéndance alimentaire en Algérie," Maghreb-Machrek, no. 90 (October-November-December 1980), p. 53, and La Documentation Photographique, "Algérie," no. 6054 (August 1981), p. 31. English-language reproduction, with some incomplete figures, found in Richard I. Lawless, "Algeria: The Contradictions of Rapid Industrialization," in North Africa: Contemporary Politics and Economic Development, edited by Richard Lawless and Allan Findlay (New York: St. Martin's Press, 1984), p. 174.

[a] hectoliters for the wine, quintals for the others

above may have been an appealing instrument to arouse popular support for the regime and to neutralize challenges from emerging bourgeois interests but, on balance, it failed both as an economic policy for improving agricultural production and as a social mechanism by which to raise rural living standards and thereby slow down outflow migration to the cities.

Despite the government's interventionist strategy via the socialist and cooperative sectors, 60 percent of the country's usable agricultural lands still remain under private ownership. There are today 800,000 privately owned farms, covering 5 million hectares of marginally productive land in the interior, on which 1.5 million farming families subsist. More than one-half of these farms are smaller than 5 hectares, and only 16,000 to 17,000 are medium-to-large–size farming units using modern agricultural techniques. Data from 1978 reveal the extent of undermechanization in the private sector. Private farmers possessed 23 percent of all tractors (10,053 out of a national total of 43,000), 22 percent of all agricultural machinery, and 34 percent of transport equipment. Earlier 1973 census-derived data are even more dramatic showing that nearly half such farms did not even use a metal plow, barely 10 percent purchased fertilizers, and only 26 percent were affected by mechanization.[14] More than 47 percent of the farms used animals as the prime source of power, and the rest used human labor. As backward as the private sector is, it still produces 60 percent of all vegetables, 95 percent of the livestock, 44 percent of the winter cereals, 18 percent of industrial crops, and 9 percent of citrus fruits.

Compared to the socialist and cooperative sectors, which have received government financial, technical, and marketing assistance, especially in the decade following the inauguration of the agrarian revolution in 1971, the private sector has been ignored and allowed to struggle on its own. Until recently it received little credit, few farm inputs and investment goods, and virtually no government services. The 1971 reforms saw a good portion of what constituted the private sector's modern component collectivized and integrated into the agrarian revolution sector. Deprived of state support, the private sector had to sell most of its produce on an unofficial market that, through the use of middlemen, effectively dominated the marketing of certain foodstuffs, including meat, many vegetables, and some fruits. This underground marketing and commercial network often worked at the expense of and in competition with the cooperative sector. Thus, despite the lack of direct governmental assistance it is in the private sector that most of the country's agricultural growth has occurred in the past ten years.

Some attempt at integrating the country's three competing agricultural structures has been made with the setting up of the service cooperatives or CAPCS. Located in virtually all rural communes—this objective was achieved by 1977 when 654 CAPCS were recorded—their goal is to "organize agricultural production" by providing a number of necessary services for working the land, including seeds, agricultural machinery, and storage facilities.

The Role of the Market

As indicated earlier, Chadli Benjedid had become disenchanted with his predecessor's state-centered strategy of development. Its excessive centralization had "stifled local initiative, reduced output, and, by rigidly applying national policies, failed to make the most of Algerian physical and human resources."[15] Toward a Better Life became the principal theme of the FLN extraordinary session in June 1980, which put forth the first Five-Year Development Plan (1980–1984), which was intended to overcome many of the problems of overcentralization. This theme was meant to signal the shifting from the previous emphasis on heavy industry to a greater concern for the social needs of the people and the development of food-related and consumer industries.

Despite repeated assertions that "change within continuity" remains the regime's overall objective, the truth is that Boumediene's form of socialist orthodoxy is being dismantled piece by piece. In its place has come a commitment to rehabilitation of the private sector in order to stimulate growth and increase productivity, especially in the critical areas of agriculture, food production, and rural development. At the third congress of the farmers' union (UNPA), held on January 14, 1982, for example, Chadli sounded the theme of Self-sufficiency, the Fundamental Objective of the Revolution. He stressed the "absolute necessity" of raising the level of agricultural production both as an economic imperative but also as a means of guaranteeing national independence inasmuch as the "food weapon" was being used by "great powers" to influence the options of developing countries such as Algeria. He noted that two-thirds of cereal production was currently being provided by the relatively backward private sector, mostly for self-consumption, while the modernized socialist sector remained in serious deficit. In 1981, for example, the government spent 1.5 million Algerian dinars in order to cover the financial shortfall that had occurred during the 1978–1979 growing season. Attacking the bureaucracy for its insensitivity to farmers' demands, Chadli stressed the need for greater personal initiative and promised that "not a

Local merchant selling vegetables in open-air market in central El Goléa.

single measure would be taken that was incompatible with the will of the farmers."[16]

This same theme of support for farmers was sounded at the fifth FLN congress in December 1983 which, as we noted earlier, had as its motto, Work and Discipline to Guarantee the Future. Agriculture was also the central concern of an important National Conference on Development that took place in February 1984 and brought together, under Chadli's chairmanship, government leaders, party representatives, heads of mass organizations (UNPA, UGTA, etc.), presidents of professional unions, national company directors, and local government authorities. Three themes dominated the deliberations: professional training, especially the need to establish more balance between students of law and medicine, of whom there are too many, and technicians and engineers, of whom there remain too few; better use of the country's natural resources, which are currently being abused and depleted; and achieving food self-sufficiency. In regard to the latter issue Chadli once again emphasized the role of the private agricultural sector and the importance of the small farmers whom he described as "allies of the Revolution" and not a threat to it.

Much of this rhetoric is not altogether new; party congresses and national conferences in the past have been replete with noble and high-sounding resolutions which often end up as political sermons intended more to mobilize popular support for the regime than to be serious blueprints for social or economic policy. Boumediene himself at the second UNPA congress in 1978 had criticized the heads of the farmers' union for ignoring the plight of the small farmer. The National Charter of 1976 as well points out that "the Agrarian Revolution's aim to improve rural society [is to] include the farmers in the private sector, now that the large exploiting landowning class in this sector has been eliminated."

Yet there is reason to believe that something more fundamental is at work in Algeria today, reminiscent of the radical changes that Sadat introduced in Egypt following the death of his mentor Nasser. Although it would be incorrect to describe Chadli as a "liberal reformer" à la Sadat, the Algerian president seems to be challenging many axioms of Third World development, especially the notion that comprehensive central planning is indispensable for the progress of poor countries. "Increasingly the most satisfactory criterion being put forth in differing circles concerning economic development has to do with the extension of the range of choice of people as consumers and producers," a well-known British economist has written. "Extension of the range of choice is most likely to be promoted by an economic order in which individuals and enterprises largely determine what is produced and consumed, where they will work, how much they will save and how they will invest their savings."[17]

To be sure, the Chadli regime has not gone this far in altering the economic priorities of the state. Yet the philosophy behind such a private initiative strategy does seem to be in evidence. Never before have questions about the advantages of centrally planned economies and of market-oriented economies been raised as they have been under the current government. Western-trained economists and efficiency-minded technocrats have argued, persuasively it would seem, that extensive state economic controls in the past have obstructed the movement of people between jobs and places, the establishment of enterprises, and the expansion of efficient producers. Such controls, it has been argued, have inhibited the emergence and spread of experimentation and new ideas, but they have not hastened the discarding of attitudes and customs harmful to material progress, especially as these apply to the backward rural areas. In the past, hostility to the market and contempt for ordinary people have often worked together to distance the people from their leaders.

Blair's description of the causes for the failure of the *autogestion* experiment applies just as well to current critiques being leveled at Boumediene's centralist policies.

> The mandarins of socialism were sophisticated urbanites who had little appreciation of rural folkways and no understanding of the peasant's desire to farm his own land—his attachment to a *lopin de terre* ("a little plot of land")—which is the foundation of traditional agriculture today. With no awareness of the specific problems retarding the peasants' [development], the militants shouted imprecations and waved ideological slogans at them, without lighting even one candle to drive away the demons of rural darkness.[18]

To be sure, nationally directed political mobilization, financial assistance, instruction in land use, and service cooperatives have all been important instruments in obtaining peasant consent and participation. But as past experience has repeatedly shown wherever compulsory state-controlled farm projects are initiated, difficult if not insurmountable problems of combining individual initiative with economies of scale arise.

Moves to decentralize and reform the state sector while stimulating private-sector activity during the past four years are beginning to show some preliminary results. A major restructuring effort of the self-management and cooperative farms is currently underway. In place of the old units there are now 3,389 "socialist agricultural estates," covering a total area of 2,766,201 hectares and employing some 2,000 agricultural engineers, 4,500 accountants, and 2,000 technicians with specialized training in the use of machinery. State financial aid to private-sector farmers reached a zenith in 1983 when US$522 million was made available to them. Additionally, extension services for this sector have been developed along with the creation of an agricultural bank, *Banque Agricole et du Développement Rural* (BADR), whose function is to help finance the agricultural projects of private-sector farmers. Headquartered in Blida with several hundred branch offices throughout the country, BADR has recently been instructed to simplify loan application procedures and to provide preferential rates of interest for loans made to private farmers. The latter have also been exempted from paying taxes. Finally, peasants in the traditional private-sector farms are being provided new housing and expanded social services in order to improve their living standards.

Expectations, based on a late 1983 draft of the second five-year plan (1985–1989), are that substantial improvements in agricultural output will take place during the rest of the decade. According to Ministry of Agriculture officials,

> the aim is for domestic production by 1989 to cover totally the national demand for fresh and dried vegetables, fruit and white meat and to reduce Algeria's dependence on imports such as cereals and milk. Since there is no scope for extending the total cultivated area, growth can only come from increased productivity, and to secure this much reliance will be placed on extending irrigation, improving techniques of irrigation, and increasing mechanization.[19]

The severe shortage of qualified personnel in the agricultural sector is being addressed with the training, both at home and abroad, of increased numbers of agricultural engineers and technicians. Additionally, more and more students are being sent to Europe and the United States for training in such specialties as meat processing, dairy technology, and soil science, which are not taught in Algeria. In 1977, for example, only 27 such students went abroad but this figure has increased steadily since: 62 in 1980, 143 in 1983, and 791 in 1984. Finally, for people already employed in agriculture, whether engineers, technicians, accountants, or mechanics, supplementary in-service courses are being made available. In a four-year period, 1980–1983, for example, 9,282 people took such courses, including 1,716 manager-engineers and 58 cooperative directors. Currently there are 7,175 agricultural workers taking specialty courses in areas such as poultry farming. These professional training courses are intended to improve the quality of agricultural personnel, which for many years was being sacrificed to quantity.

Probably nothing is so important to the creation of self-sustained agricultural growth as a market-sensitive pricing policy. For too long, in order to provide inexpensive food to urban customers, agricultural producer prices have been fixed well below world prices and prices that would be determined by a free market. Realizing as much, the Chadli government implemented on August 1, 1983, a 10 to 30 percent increase in the price of basic foodstuffs (including bread, cooking oil, and eggs). Additionally, to stimulate cereal production, authorities approved an increase of around 15 percent of the producer price of soft wheat. The government's argument was that such increases were necessary to "correct certain imbalances in the domestic market, reduce food imports by promoting national production, and improve the condition of small businessmen and merchants without reducing the purchasing power of the consumer."[20]

Agricultural growth will also depend on more intensive use of land. Because of natural resource constraints, however, other measures must be introduced including a continued shift in cropping patterns to high-value crops in line with changing demand. The kind of technologies and investments required to achieve a more rapid pattern of growth, as identified by the World Bank, include: the green revolution seed-chemical input-farm machinery technologies; new farm implements; numerous irrigation technologies; greenhouses; improved cultivation practices; new soil conservation and reforestation strategies; several livestock development activities including improved stock, animal shelters, and health facilities; marketing facilities; fruit tree investment, and rural infrastructure.

Summary and Conclusion

Algerian agriculture was very much neglected until the 1971 agrarian revolution, but even then this sector remained a stepchild to an industrialization that continues to take away valuable water resources, able-bodied young men, and finances. Fifty percent of the population remains involved in agriculture but contributes only 7 percent of the GNP. Increasingly this sector's weakness is having critical consequences for the nation's economic equilibrium. Although agricultural production continues to stagnate or decline, the population and its food needs continue to increase dramatically. Domestic food supplies of wheat as well as many other agricultural items are being provided from abroad. Serious food dependency is a reality in 1985.

Industry itself has been slow in providing the agricultural machinery necessary to modernize farming because of insufficient output, bureaucratic bottlenecks, poor quality, spare parts problems, poor maintenance and service. More problematic perhaps has been the whole notion of mechanizing agriculture, including the use of fertilizers and pesticides, on already fragile soil. What all of this raises is the appropriateness of the "industrializing industries" strategy as applied to agriculture. In fact, for agriculture a completely different approach needs to be developed that would make better use of labor, soil, and modern techniques, and a gradual, selective, and appropriate mechanization should be introduced. What needs to be reconsidered is the unplanned way Algerian bureaucrats apply national industrial machinery to agriculture to modernize it. Experiences in Iran, Libya, and the Sudan, for example, confirm the serious harm caused by uncritical application of chemicals and machinery to fragile and marginal agriculture. Techniques and methods that are successful elsewhere do not necessarily work in different settings.

Ultimately the successful application of new, indeed "radical" agricultural policies will depend on the government's willingness to liberate market forces from state control and thereby allow individual farmers to determine for themselves the most effective strategy for increasing yields and the levels of mechanization and technological application. In this regard a recommendation on ways to halt the desertification in the African Sahel is equally applicable to improving Algerian agricultural production: "Give local people responsibility for their pasture, water or firewood and they [rather than national government planners] can roll back the desert."[21]

Current government strategy is aimed at restoring the balance in favor of the private sector in agriculture and, to a lesser degree, industry. Whether the authorities feel secure enough in their power and prestige to maintain the kind of support needed to transform the agricultural sector into a viable force in the economy will very much depend on the political choices made at the top. Based on all the evidence so far, Chadli's agricultural policies seem to be guided by much more than rhetoric. Only time will tell whether a revitalized private sector operating in a more market-sensitive environment can achieve what government-controlled mechanization and mobilization policies in socialist and cooperative agricultural sectors have failed to achieve: greater agricultural productivity and a lessened dependence on imported food supplies. Reaching these goals will have implications for economic growth, social development, and political stability in the years ahead.

NOTES

1. Richard I. Lawless, "Algeria: The Contradictions of Rapid Industrialization," in Richard Lawless and Allan Findlay, eds., *North Africa: Contemporary Politics and Economic Development* (London: Croom Helm; New York: St. Martin's Press, 1984), pp. 161–163.

2. *El Moudjahid*, June 1980.

3. Richard F. Nyrop and others, *Area Handbook for Algeria* (Washington, D.C.: Government Printing Office, 1972), p. 291.

4. Lawless, "Algeria," p. 172.

5. Lawless, "Algeria," p. 177, as adapted from Georges Mutin, "Agriculture et dépendance alimentaire en Algérie," *Maghreb-Machrek*, no. 90 (October-November-December 1980), p. 56.

6. Kevin M. Cleaver, *The Agricultural Development Experience of Algeria, Morocco, and Tunisia: A Comparison of Strategies for Growth* (Washington, D.C.: The World Bank, 1982), p. 8.

7. Tahar Benhouria, *L'Economie de l'Algérie* (Paris: Maspero, 1980), p. 145.

8. Mutin, "Agriculture et dépendance," p. 59.

9. Thomas L. Blair, *"The Land to Those Who Work It"*: *Algeria's Experiment in Workers' Management* (Garden City, N.Y.: Anchor Books, 1970), p. 68.

10. Lawless, "Algeria," p. 173, as adapted from Mutin, "Agriculture et dépendance," p. 51.

11. Keith Sutton, "Algeria: Centre-Down Development, State Capitalism, and Emergent Decentralization," in W. B. Stöhr and D. R. Fraser Taylor, eds., *Development from Above or Below?* (London: John Wiley, 1981), p. 364.

12. Hugh Roberts, "The Politics of Algerian Socialism," in Lawless and Findlay, eds., *North Africa*, p. 12.

13. Ibid., pp. 13–15.

14. Mutin, "Agriculture et dépendance," p. 54.

15. John R. Nellis, "Decentralization in North Africa: Problems of Policy Implementation," in G. Shabbir Cheema and Dennis A. Rondinelli, eds., *Decentralization and Development: Policy Implementation in Developing Countries* (Beverly Hills, Calif.: Sage Publications, 1983), p. 140.

16. *Le Monde*, January 16, 1982.

17. P. T. Bauer, *Reality and Rhetoric: Studies in the Economics of Development* (Cambridge: Harvard University Press, 1984), p. 22.

18. Blair, *"The Land To Those Who Work It,"* p. 142.

19. Economist Intelligence Unit, *Algeria*, no. 1 (1984), p. 14.

20. *Le Monde*, July 31, 1983.

21. *The Economist*, May 26, 1984, p. 100.

6

The Dynamics of Political Life

The dynamics of Algerian political life can best be understood by looking at its four component parts: political culture, political structures, political processes, and political power.

POLITICAL CULTURE

The concept of political culture includes an analysis of the orientations and psychological predispositions of a population toward political life. For any society political culture involves the linking of those dimensions of an individual's thoughts, feelings, or behaviors to the creation and maintenance of a society's fundamental political order. Moreover, political culture provides an explanation of how such sentiments influence political action—the ways in which the people respond to authority, the political roles they play, and their degree of participation in political affairs. In other words, political culture guides the behavior of political actors and contains the catalysts as well as the constraints to political action. Regardless of ideological orientation or political intent, most regimes are captives of their own political culture.

As elsewhere in the Maghreb, elite political culture differs from mass political culture in Algeria. To the extent that the masses are cognizant of belief systems at all, they identify unswervingly with Islam and its religious symbols. It is only in the relatively small modernized sector and its even smaller elite component that one finds political culture and ideology as at all meaningful categories of analysis. As would be expected, therefore, those Algerians who must deal with power and have responsibilities for the decisions of government invariably develop outlooks on politics different from those in the society who remain simply observers or marginal activists.

Algerian political culture reflects the impact of both general cultural values and of recent historical experiences, especially the revolutionary war, on the people who have assumed leadership positions in the state. From both these environments has emerged a conflictual political culture where intra-elite hostility and mistrust predominate. Algerian politicians often behave and expect others to behave as if they are constantly maneuvering and scheming to acquire more power. The pejorative term *boulitique*—an Arabic dialectical borrowing and transformation of the French word *politique* (politics)—has come to describe this characteristic brand of elite political behavior in Algeria.

One immediate consequence of *boulitique* behavior is the personalization of political differences where personal rivalries and personal clashes substitute for legitimate political discourse. Another consequence is the distrust of any form of political opposition. In part because of the debilitating intra-elite conflicts that took place during and immediately after the war of independence, Algerian politicians tend to see any form of public political disagreement as illegitimate and harmful to the political process. Hence the persistent effort to create homogeneous ruling groups that can insure political stability.

Yet even this attitude may be changing, as over ten years of homogeneous rule under the late Houari Boumediene and his successor regime have led elites to encourage and even articulate the need for "legitimate" dissent and a free expression of opposing opinions. The animated debates in 1975 and 1976 over the National Charter, for example, were remarkably open and, in some cases, candidly harsh. Although this experience does not foreshadow the rise of liberal democracy, it may represent a modification in the previously conspiratorial and unitary mentality so characteristic of incumbent elites. It also may feed off another, paradoxical aspect of Algerian political culture, namely, the strong feeling that—widespread distrust of one's colleagues in politics notwithstanding—political relations must be based on equality and reciprocity. Despite the apparent contradictions and tensions inherent in such an inconsistent perspective, it continues to coexist in the minds of many Algerian leaders.

The most noteworthy expression of this demand for equality is found in the notion of collegial rule and support for consultation and in the rejection of the idea of a cult of personality. This latter trait was the most damning accusation made against Ahmed Ben Bella. Boumediene and now Chadli Benjedid, in contrast, have emphasized collegiality and consultation, albeit among a narrow group of political advisers, technocrats, and military men.

This mixture of distrust and egalitarianism in political life is often explained away by the so-called individualistic nature of Algerians, that is, the fact that Algerians both distrust those who have power and demand an equal share of influence for themselves is attributed to their individualism. Yet this individualism, manifest at times in a kind of public rebellion and sporadic violence, belies an underlying pressure to conform to rigorous norms that must be followed, to social codes that must be obeyed, and to a public opinion that must be paid due reverence. The compelling need to conform and the private docility that it engenders undermine the meaning of individualism (as it is understood at least in the West: innovative behavior, tolerance for deviance, willingness to break with tradition) in Algerian political life.

As intra-elite relations are marked by coexisting contradictory impulses, so too are the attitudes toward the proper role of government characterized by fundamentally inconsistent views. The colonial and war experiences have had particularly profound impact on the elite's perception of the proper role of government. Specifically, there is a general belief in the need for a strong centralized state, often referred to by critics as "state capitalism," or etatism, when applied to economic development and organization. Simultaneously, and in apparent contradiction, Algerian political culture places great stress on the role of the impoverished masses, reflecting a populist orientation. The principles and practices of autogestion in agriculture and industry, although significantly reduced since 1967, exemplify the meaning of populism in the economic sphere. In its essentials, populism consists of two fundamental principles: first, the supremacy of the will of the people, which is identified with justice and morality above all other norms; and secondly, the importance of a direct relationship between the people and their leaders in which intermediary institutions and mediating structures can play no meaningful role.

These unreconciled perceptions of the role of government originate from a strongly felt sense of nationalism and a less clearly defined attachment to the rhetoric and symbolism (much less the content) of socialism. Among the political elite the dual notions of nationalism and socialism have assumed sacrosanct status. The etatist policies of Algerian development elites are, in fact, justified in nationalist terms, wherein the state is viewed as having the "right" to intervene in many areas of national life. In particular, it is felt that the state must control its own resources and territory. Yet there remains a genuine commitment to the masses that transcends the excessive, revolutionary socialist rhetoric. This commitment is reflected in the areas of welfare, education, and social services where government policy has been progressive and enlightened. There is also a commitment to the idea of eventual mass political participation and administrative decentralization, as the National Charter debates, new constitution, and presidential and legislative elections since 1976 have demonstrated.

Other elements of political culture and ideology in Algeria include belief in a continuing revolution, Arab unity, and the resurrection of an Algerian Arab-Islamic culture through the means of Arabization and under the guidance of a mass mobilization political party. The Islamic component of socialism remains a salient feature of contemporary ideology. For Algerian ideologues, socialism can have no meaning outside the realm of Islamic belief; in the Algerian context, socialism refers to a belief system whereby a centralized governmental structure is concerned with the allocation of resources. The government's objective is the control and utilization of national economic wealth so as to prevent one class from monopolizing the products. Yet this takes place within the world of Islam, which constitutes the "heart, mind, and soul" of Algerian consciousness.

Thus, not only is there no admitted contradiction between scientific socialism and religious belief, but in theory the former has no meaning outside the Islamic context of Algerian national and cultural identity. This perspective is reaffirmed in both the National Charter and new constitution which explicitly extol Islamic socialism as the road to political, economic, social, and cultural salvation. Earlier political documents including the Tripoli Program, the 1963 constitution, and the Algiers Charter were attempts at institutionalizing this Islamic socialist concept.

In practical terms this has permitted incumbent leaders to sustain a conservative, indeed puritanical, policy in the areas of personal, religious, and moral affairs while simultaneously pursuing a radical modernization policy involving rapid and sweeping economic growth, the use of advanced technology and scientific know-how, and dependence on Western secularists for administrative, organizational, and financial expertise. Inevitably, the coexistence of socialist-revolutionary, French-republican, and Arab-Berber-Islamic traditional influences generate unexpected tensions and contradictions that the current rulers have not yet satisfactorily reconciled, notwithstanding the long step forward taken in the National Charter and constitution.

By way of summary, Algerian political culture can be described as containing several contradictory elements. Intra-elite relations, for example, are characterized on the one hand by a high level of mistrust and on the other by a naive-sounding expectation that reciprocity and equality will be respected. In addition, in terms of the elites' perception of the proper role of government, a strong statist orientation growing out of intense nationalism coexists with a populist orientation that emphasizes extensive mass participation and governmental decentralization. Finally, there is support for total Arabization and for the practice and perhaps imposition of ascetic, rigid, and austere Islamic orthodoxy coexisting with a nationalist ethic that seeks to implement rapid and sweeping economic and social modernization, that is, Westernization, at the expense of Arabization.

In terms of ideology, both empirical and affective socialism coexist under the rubric of Islamic socialism. Despite the current rhetorical emphasis on Algerian "nationalism," it appears that a broad consensus has emerged concerning an overall socialist orientation. This orientation has been provisionally institutionalized since the reactivation of parliamentary, constitutional, and party life. Socialist ideology thus enables the government not only to reject the West and to identify with other radical Arab states but also to reject certain aspects of local tradition found to be obstacles to social progress. Through numerous government-controlled propaganda organs and the communications media, the regime has continued to advance a socialist program aimed primarily at building up the economic strength of the state, raising the standards of living of its rural and urban population, and providing a framework for rapid industrialization and agrarian reform.

POLITICAL STRUCTURES

The 1965 coup d'état suspended the National Assembly and constitution that had been put in place under Ben Bella in 1962 and 1963, respectively. During the next ten years, Algerian political life was strongly centralized under the Council of the Revolution and the Council of Ministers, both headed by Col. Houari Boumediene. In the absence of a constitution, the Council of Ministers became responsible for the day-to-day administration of the government and thus became the effective executive and legislative body. For nearly a decade, the National Liberation Front (FLN), Algeria's only political party organization, and other national-level institutions were allowed to atrophy in order that Boumediene's vision of a strong, secure, centralized government could evolve free of the challenge that such organizations could present. Boumediene believed that institutional development could emerge only from the base upward via a systematic process of political education supervised from the top.

In accordance with this strategy, local APC (*Assemblée Populaire Communale*) elections first took place in 1967 and were renewed every four years (1971, 1975, 1979, 1983). Likewise, regional APW (*Assemblée Popularire de Wilaya*) elections were held in 1969 and every five years thereafter (1974, 1979, 1984). However, these local and regional assemblies (in 1984, 700 and 48 in number, respectively) remain largely administrative in nature and have no significant political authority. A congress of the presidents of these assemblies is held annually, and although there is no juridical basis for these meetings, they have attained quasi-institutional status.

Despite the regime's claim that the assemblies were created with the objective of instituting a greater measure of self-government at the local level, they actually strengthened national political control. For example, although the elections permit choice among candidates— there are, according to the electoral law passed in June 1981, three times as many candidates as seats to be filled—all of the candidates, until just recently, have been nominated by the FLN. There is neither party competition nor do candidates engage in an electoral context, as campaigning is the work of FLN notables and ministers. The result is politically lethargic and administratively marginal local-level associations that depend on the central authorities for guidance and animation.

With local representative bodies in place it was just a matter of time before a broader process of political legitimation was undertaken. Thus, in the middle 1970s, Boumediene began to call for greater politization of the masses by advocating renewed involvement in the FLN as the sole ideological and institutional organ of the socialist revolution. In mid-1976, he personally directed the revival of constitutional politics in the form of public debates that preceded the voting on the National Charter.

As a broad philosophical blueprint describing Algeria's future political, economic, social, and diplomatic goals, the National Charter was meant to provide a conceptual framework upon which the more specific legal instrument of a constitution could be based. The back-to-back nationwide referenda that approved the charter and a new constitution in June and November 1976, respectively, represented the formal reestablishment of constitutional government.

The 1976 constitution (with amendments introduced in 1979) states that the republican nature of the state cannot be altered and that the state religion is Islam. It reaffirms the socialist system and the territorial integrity of the country and guarantees freedom of expression and assembly. The document also reaffirms state control of the means of production, land reforms, free medical care, worker participation in industry, and campaigns against corruption and nepotism. It guarantees that so-called nonexploitative private property of artisans, small farmers, and traders who derive their income from their own work will be respected. The constitution also guarantees the "liberation of women and their full participation in the political, economic, social and cultural life of the nation."

Executive powers are vested in the president of the republic, who is elected for a five-year term by direct, adult suffrage and can be reelected for an unlimited number of terms. The day-to-day administration of government is the responsibility of the cabinet (Council of Ministers), and the president is empowered to enact laws by decree when the legislature is not in session.

In each of the three presidential elections that have taken place under the new constitution—Boumediene in 1976 and Chadli Benjedid in 1979 (following Boumediene's death in 1978) and 1984—the single FLN candidate has received over 95 percent of the popular vote. These overwhelming electoral endorsements have bathed the presidential office with populist legitimacy, enabling the incumbent to act decisively and authoritatively.

Constitutional prerogatives already concentrate virtually all important powers in the executive branch of government. Article 111 of the constitution, for example, identifies eighteen separate presidential powers and prerogatives. The president, for example, is the guarantor of the constitution, the commander in chief of the country's armed forces, and the head of the Supreme Court, presides over the Council of Ministers, makes appointments to high military and civilian positions, concludes and ratifies international treaties, and appoints and recalls the country's ambassadors. In brief, both the constitution and the National Charter confirm the president's power to determine Algeria's domestic and foreign policies. Additionally, the president holds the top leadership post in the FLN, that of secretary-general of the party, along with the defense ministry (see Figure 6.1) creating a highly centralized and powerful presidential system of government.

For many Algeria observers the constitutional and other statutory mechanisms ensconcing executive authority flow from a more profound compulsion toward "sultanic rule" that has historically characterized Algerian political culture. Jean Leca and Jean-Claude Vatin, for example, use the Weberian concept of "sultanism" to describe Algeria's form of political power in which the leader seeks, "with more or less success, to make himself independent of all groups having an autonomous base of power, whether these be institutional, political, administrative or social."[1] The dynamic of the Algerian political process "reproduces a tightly closed circle of power around a single leader."[2] In almost every instance the three postindependence Algerian regimes have evidenced "an obsession with organic unity."[3] Despite the

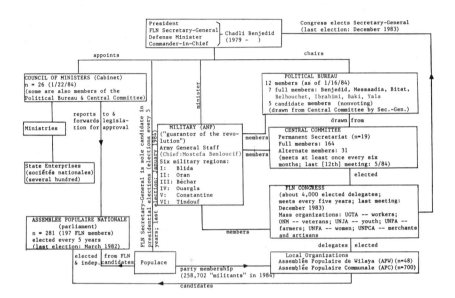

FIGURE 6.1 Algeria's political organization (1984): ANP: People's National Army (since 1962 official designation of the Algerian military establishment); APC: Popular Communal Assembly (popularly elected representative body at the communal or local level; over 700 in number); APW: Popular *Wilaya* Assembly (popularly elected representative body at the *wilaya* or provincial level; 48 in number); FLN: National Liberation Front (country's single party); ONM: National Organization of Guerrilla Fighters (national veteran's organization); UGTA: General Union of Algerian Workers (trade union organization under FLN sponsorship; formed in 1956); UNFA: National Union of Algerian Women (national women's group formed in 1962 under FLN auspices); UNJA: National Union of Algerian Youth (national organization of nonstudent youth; created in 1975); UNPA: National Union of Algerian Peasants (national farmers' organization under FLN sponsorship; created in 1973); UNPCA: National Union of Small Merchants and Craftsmen (national organization of Algerian small merchants and artisans formed in 1983 under FLN sponsorship).

existence of multilevel elected assemblies (APC, APW, APN) no political institution is allowed to escape the control of the central state. Both culture and structure thus combine to create a presidential position of unassailable primacy and power. Other systemic features further concentrate and centralize political power at the top—the centralization of the administrative and bureaucratic systems, the virtual absence of ways to oust the top man short of a palace coup, the secrecy surrounding his actions and decisions, the ban on effective debate or criticism outside the tiny elite at the top, the extensive security apparatus, and even the character of the Algerian people themselves: the national bent for order and authority.

Despite recent efforts by the Chadli regime to decentralize and deconcentrate authority in the political and economic spheres it is uncertain that power configurations at the top or the flowchart of executive authority have been much altered. Nonetheless, governmental and political bodies continue to be utilized in accordance with constitutional provisions and consistent with the regime's stated effort at broader political participation for the Algerian citizenry.

The Popular National Assembly (APN) is the country's unicameral legislature; members are elected by secret, direct, and universal suffrage for a period of five years. The first APN elections held in well over a decade took place in early 1977 with 783 FLN-sponsored candidates vying for the 261 available parliamentary seats. The next such elections occurred in 1982 under more liberalized conditions that allowed, for the first time, non-FLN candidates to compete for parliamentary seats in the expanded 281-seat body. The electoral results saw a major turnover in the incumbents, with nearly half the parliamentarians being newcomers and only 197 winning seats under the FLN banner. Earlier local elections in December 1979 for approximately 700 communal assemblies saw newcomers win more than 80 percent of the seats. It is still too early in the young history of Algeria's political institutions to determine whether the revitalized APN will be permitted to act as a forum for serious political debate or whether it will simply serve as the regime's bureaucratic rubber stamp.

Technically, the state's principal policymaking organ is the National Liberation Front (FLN), Algeria's sole legal political party as designated by Article 95 of the constitution. Through its Political Bureau and Central Committee, the FLN draws up policy, which is then put before the National Assembly in the form of bills for enactment into law. The Council of Ministers is given the responsibility of putting policies and laws into effect. To coordinate better the policymaking (FLN) and executive (cabinet) functions the president of the republic is automatically secretary-general of the FLN (see Figure 6.1).

According to Part 2 of the National Charter, the FLN is officially given a vanguard role in Algerian politics and society. Organized along recognizably Leninist lines, the FLN is, in theory, "the supreme mobilizer of the masses, guardian of ideological standards, watchdog over bureaucratic excesses and deviations, and arbiter of policy. In reality, it is of very limited practical importance."[4]

The FLN has experienced a great deal of institutional activity beginning in the mid-1970s and continuing through the current period. Although it has remained the institutional symbol of the revolution, the FLN is being eclipsed in power by the military, the government bureaucracy, and the state enterprises. Despite increased involvement in local affairs allowing the FLN a greater role in relaying local opinion to the center of power, the party "is being utilized as an instrument of mobilization in the hands of the state rather than as the controlling organ over the state that official doctrine [like the Charter] declares it to be."[5]

The party's chief policymaking body, the Political Bureau, has undergone several major reshuffles and purges since Chadli's election to the presidency in February 1979. Composed of many strong personalities and independent figures who were for many years members of the Council of Revolution, the politburo posed both a threat to and an opportunity for the politically untested Chadli Benjedid. In calculated phases the Algerian president first increased the membership to seventeen (March 1979), then dramatically reduced that number to seven in June 1980, increased it by three in December 1981, and during the most recent reshuffle (January 1984), divided the membership into two categories: seven full members and five candidate or nonvoting members. As a result of these shifts Chadli has eliminated virtually all potential contenders for power along with any personalities associated with the Boumediene clientelist network. By staffing the bureau with loyalists the president has reduced the Political Bureau to an advisory council rather than the decisionmaking body that its planners intended it to be.

Directly below the Political Bureau is the party's Central Committee, a broadly inclusive body representing diverse functional, professional, and regional interests. It is organized into numerous functional commissions, some paralleling governmental ministries, responsible for formulating party policy on such matters as foreign, financial, economic, and social affairs, military and judicial matters, education, Arabization, and political orientation. The committee is also responsible for establishing the various party organs, managing party finances, executing congressional decisions, and, most importantly, providing the pool of candidates whom the secretary-general of the party selects for membership into the Political Bureau.

Like the Political Bureau, the Central Committee has also experienced a major turnover of personnel since Chadli's incumbency. The most recent housecleaning has involved a virtual elimination of the last vestiges of the Boumediene era. At the fifth party congress held in December 1983 the total membership of the Central Committee was reduced from 200 to the current 164 (with 31 alternates). Several key figures of the Boumediene period were ousted from the committee, including Mohamed Salah Yahiaoui, once a serious contender for the presidency (in 1979); Ahmed Draia, the former police chief and member of the Council of the Revolution; Slimane Hoffman, formerly head of the FLN's International Affairs Committee and a high-ranking presidential aide; Mustapha Lacheraf, one of Algeria's most distinguished intellectuals, education minister in 1977–1978, and noted for his opposition to the policy of rapid Arabization; and Mouloud Oumeziane, general secretary of the labor union (UGTA) in 1965–1969 and minister of labor since 1979. Earlier, influential ex-ministers and foreign policy figures such as Redha Malek, Layachi Yaker, and Mohamed Zerguini had been removed from the Central Committee. In combination these purges have constituted a veritable "de-Boumedienization" of the FLN's central political organs. Capping this process has been the new composition of the Permanent Secretariat of the Central Committee with Mohamed Cherif Messaadia at its head. In effect, the elevation of this lackluster party hack to the number two position in the FLN signals the backseat status the party has assumed under Chadli.

Technically, the FLN congress, with its 4,000 or so elected delegates, constitutes the highest organ of the party. It is given responsibility for establishing general party policy, adopting and modifying FLN statutes, and electing both the party secretary-general and the Central Committee. Between party congresses the Central Committee functions as the country's "supreme political body."

Other national organizations within the party hierarchy are the labor (UGTA), farmers' (UNPA), women's (UNFA), youth (UNJA), and small merchants and artisans' (UNPCA) unions as well as the veterans' association (ONM). The presidents and to a lesser extent the executive councils of these bodies constitute separate, but not autonomous, elite groups.

Despite the gradual "civilianization" of the regime since 1968, the role of the military has remained decisive in Algeria's political organization. The Army General Staff (currently headed by Major

General Mostefa Benloucif), Ministry of Defense (controlled by Benjedid—as it was by Boumediene during his incumbency), the Gendarmerie (national police), and the commanders of the country's six military regions all constitute critical sources of power and political influence. The army's political role was clearly demonstrated in the manner in which it acted during the uncertain period following Boumediene's death and the election of a new president. Not only did the Ministry of Defense assume full powers during Boumediene's illness—notwithstanding the constitutional provision that designates the president of the National Assembly (Rabah Bitat) as interim president for forty-five days—but it was a thoroughly professional military man, indeed the highest-ranking military officer with impeccable revolutionary credentials—the forty-nine year old Col. Chadli Benjedid—who was eventually chosen to succeed his former commander in chief.

The army has always been represented in the key civilian decisionmaking bodies such as the now defunct Council of the Revolution and the Council of Ministers. Although the army has never ruled directly, it has continued to expand its presence and influence. This was even the case when the FLN was given new political life following the approval of the National Charter, for it was a high-level officer and a former director of the prestigious military academy in Cherchell, Mohamed Salah Yahiaoui, who was appointed the party's coordinator from October 1977 to July 1980. This trend has been maintained and, in some instances, expanded under Chadli, with high-level officers appointed to all key civilian decisionmaking structures of society (see Figure 6.1). Consistently, military elites have emphasized their national, professional, and technical attributes, thus making them available for political involvement. This has resulted in a thorough integration of the military into the policymaking organs of government, administration, and the party, notwithstanding the change in "uniforms."

That the army has been able to initiate and maintain such a noticeable presence is due in part to the historical circumstances of and the army's role in the revolutionary struggle and in part to the army's internal composition, guiding principles, and practical policies, which in combination have resulted in a legitimizing and noncoercive framework for participation in the political process. Although in the early years of Boumediene's regime (1965–1967) power was maintained by the use of coercive force or the threat of it, ten years later the military's integral role in the technocratic system was an accomplished fact.

The army's several guiding principles, which have dictated the military's posture since 1965, work to maintain cohesion and continuity, both within the military and the society at large: (1) the army identifies with the people; (2) the revolution to them that made it; (3) political unity is "natural," but division is an artificial "counterrevolutionary trick"; (4) a strong state structure must be built; (5) the army, as the "guardian of the revolution," has the primary task of safeguarding its own group interests; (6) the army's primary military task is to build itself into a modern professional armed force; (7) as a military organization the army must have control over its own forces; and (8) the most important precondition of an effective army is its military unity.[6] The army's direct involvement in rural and developmental projects has gained it wide, popular appeal that has further enhanced its legitimacy as the authentic instrument for organizing, directing, and implementing the socioeconomic goals of the revolution.

Unlike the situation in mid-1965 when the country's political institutions were reduced to insignificance or eliminated altogether, Algeria today is governed by a complex network of interactive structures that provide institutional stability, direction, and predictability to the political system. No understanding of the political process, to which we turn next, can be had without first appreciating the structural configurations now in place.

POLITICAL PROCESSES

Politics in postindependence Algeria has been characterized by a stable system of rule with power concentrated among relatively few individuals who are situated within select institutions. Although incumbent elites remained relatively unchanged during the Boumediene years (1965–1978), significant changes in top political elites and within the state's political institutions have taken place since the middle 1970s. The turnover of personnel in upper leadership positions has been particularly pronounced in the early 1980s.

As we have seen, the series of nationwide participatory efforts (National Charter and constitution in particular) were preceded by a number of carefully prepared local and regional assembly elections and followed by a systematic series of conventions of the various national organizations (such as UGTA, UNJA). A party congress of the National Liberation Front was convened in January 1979, following Boumediene's death, and a single presidential candidate was selected (Chadli Benjedid) and confirmed a month later by the electorate in a national election. Local (1983), regional (1984), party (1983), legislative (1982), and presidential (1984) elections have been renewed since the 1979 FLN convention, all according to specific constitutional and statutory provisions.

The accelerated pace of political activity after nearly a decade of authoritarian one-man rule at the national level reflects the growing importance of institutional life and the concurrent de-emphasis of informal, patron-client, and personalized politics at the highest levels of power. This does not mean, however, that the historically pervasive influence of informal politics or the importance of clientelist, personal, and other face-to-face ties have been completely eradicated from Algerian political life. Indeed, some have suggested that despite removal of high-visibility individuals on corruption charges (Abdesselam, Bouteflika, Ahmed Bencherif, Tayebi Larbi, Mohamed Liassine, to name a few), the "system of patron-client relations and its roots in the wider relationship between the bureaucracy and the public remain undisturbed."[7] Nonetheless, such behavior has now been incorporated into more formal and regularized settings under closer public scrutiny.

The peaceful transfer of power from Boumediene to Benjedid attests in part to the credibility and effectiveness of these various institutional arrangements put into place by Boumediene and his colleagues during the last decade of his life. Particularly significant has been the emergence of a powerful and interlocking technocratic system with its tripartite mobilizational, managerial, and military components working collectively to ensure a relatively effective and unchallenged operation of the state.

Effective power is concentrated in the hands of a technocratic elite whose claim to authority is based on the modern skills that they possess and for which there is a high value in the society. Algeria's technocratic system consists of three major units—the military, the party, and the government-administration. They have very different internal characteristics, but they are united in an overriding new allegiance to the state and its developmental objectives. Most of them share a common background in the National Liberation Army (ALN) and its experience in the revolutionary war. In the decade following his consolidation of power in 1968, Boumediene depended on this triad to maintain and aggrandize power as well as to erect his socialist state by using the crucial technical skills that this group possesses. For the better part of this 1968–1978 period, however, these elements were unevenly aligned, with the FLN reduced to a minor, functionary role while the military and the administrative elite were elevated to predominant positions.

Initially, with the elimination of the past political elite and the establishment of an internal cohesion within the army's structure of

City hall in central El Biar.

authority, the new Boumediene regime sought to strengthen its hold on the economy and administration by recruiting civil servants and technicians in such a way that the congruence between military and managerial elites was maximized. Yet to a certain extent this was achieved at the expense of the single party, which was left in the hands of faithful party hacks like Ahmed Kaid who, although they did not lack enthusiasm, loyalty, and personality, were clearly second-rate by the educational and technical standards used to recruit and maintain the military and administrative elites.

The balancing of forces began to take place in the mid-1970s when Boumediene, at the time of the tenth anniversary of his 1965 coup d'état, or, as he was to label the event, the "corrective revolution" (*redressement révolutionnarie*), launched a campaign to revitalize political life at the national level through the formulation and implementation of a national charter and a new constitution, followed by presidential and legislative elections—all organized under the political guidance of the FLN. The acid test came rather suddenly with Boumediene's death, leaving the single party (in formal structure and statutory language at least) significantly enhanced in power and prestige. The Political Bureau and Central Committee of the FLN replaced the dissolved Council of the Revolution as the country's supreme political body.

The Military

Until such time as the party tests and sustains its theoretically defined political clout, however, the military remains the most decisive elite group in Algerian politics today. This has been the case since the old dissensions between the conventional nationalist army (ALN) and the *moujahidines* or *wilayists* (the latter, those who fought in the interior of the country during the revolutionary war) were resolved in favor of the former, renamed the People's National Army (ANP) in 1963.

The army's claim to privileged status is not limited to the obvious fact that it monopolizes the nation's coercive instruments of force. Nor is it based entirely on the fact that Boumediene was the wartime chief of staff and later defense minister who provided the critical support that brought Ben Bella to power and later engineered his overthrow in a military coup. Equally important has been the following: the military continues to possess a revolutionary mystique; it was instrumental in establishing law and order from the chaos that followed independence; it possesses the special skills of organization and management that have enabled society to stabilize and develop; it has become directly involved in local rural affairs, thus gaining popular support at the mass level; and finally, it has continued to adhere firmly to the notion that it alone is the guardian of the revolution. In fact, the military has so far played a guardian role, directly involving itself in politics only when the situation required, as it did in 1962 and 1965. In each instance of direct army intervention, the military followed a policy of "returning to the barracks" to observe the political process carefully, with a discrete but always present eye.

In addition to its explicitly military functions, the army is also heavily involved in a variety of civic-action and educational projects. Its involvement in the state-building process further enhances its already wide appeal among the rural masses. Its representation in all elite political institutions, including the Council of Ministers, the National Assembly, and the FLN, permits the military to monitor all political activities directly. Military elites are also active participants at the local and regional levels. At the local level, for example, army officers collaborate with the communal administration, often providing goods and services and dispensing favors that the party is unable or unwilling to provide. At the intermediate level, the heads of the country's military districts function in capacities as regional governors with more influence than the heads of the forty-eight APWs.

Finally, the qualitative and quantitative improvement in manpower and equipment since the 1967 Arab-Israeli War, when Soviet

military assistance and training accelerated noticeably, has made
Algeria a power in regional Arab and North African affairs, further
enhancing the military's domestic standing among elites and masses
alike. In the 1980s the diversification of arms purchases, including
obtaining advanced U.S. transport aircraft and British missiles, along
with the further professionalization of the army through military
training agreements with the United States and other Western powers,
have added power, prestige, and pride to the Algerian officer corps,
which have carried over into the society at large.

The Administrative Elite

The administrative elite constitutes a second important component of the Algerian political system. In fact, with the increasing
industrialization and complexity of Algerian society, the administrative
elite may eventually replace the military as the paramount voice in
policymaking.

This category includes the civil service, whose activities extend
beyond the actual administration of the country into the substantive
functions of various other ministries and their local networks, as well
as a more narrowly defined new class of technocrats who have the
authority and responsibility for the planning, development, operation,
and expansion of the nation's industrial complex, particularly petro-
chemicals. The largest and most prestigious of all the state-owned
industries is SONATRACH, the huge Algerian state petroleum enterprise, which has recently been broken up into several constituent
parts without, however, diminishing its importance in the national
economy.

The administrative elite has expanded so rapidly since the
Boumediene takeover that it has tended to divide into component
groups. In fact, ever since the technocratic revolution began in the
late 1960s, bureaucratic politics within the ministerial and presidential
councils have been conducted primarily among the competing administrators. This administrative group constitutes an important subelite within the larger ruling elite and has been the most noticeable
recipient of new class status, including conspicuous wealth and other
tangible signs of social advantage. Furthermore, unlike the military
and party elites, the administrators manage programs that exert a
major influence on the country's development and its political dynamics.

The Party

Although the role of the FLN in achieving national independence
was a decisive one, the party was not able to maintain its power

and prestige after independence. Factionalism that had been suppressed in the name of national unity during the revolution quickly reappeared when the party leaders vied with one another for positions of power. The quality of FLN leadership at the local level declined, and individual party officials in many cases seemed more intent on personal advancement than in building up the party as an effective peacetime organization.

For their part, the state and the army have not allowed the party any independent political activity. Party work is unattractive to young people with an educated and intelligent interest in politics because they are required, as party members, to be more conformist than nonmembers. Most debilitating has been the virtual powerlessness of the party as a dispenser of even the most minor favors and services. For the better part of Boumediene's thirteen-year rule, the FLN was anything but a vanguard party; indeed its role was simply to propagate others' policies or defend others' candidates. Consequently, the influence and role of the FLN has been negligible.

Despite its shortcomings, the party remains the predominant institutional medium for the expression of popular will. It remains subordinate, however, to the military and administrative elites. At one time it was thought that this inferior status might have undergone a transformation in the aftermath of the fourth party congress (held in early 1979) to select a new presidential candidate. The authority and prestige of the FLN had grown because of Boumediene's prodigious effort to revitalize it. He had initiated campaigns to gain support and legitimacy for the charter and constitution, both of which institutionalized the FLN as an integral force in national politics. Clearly it was Boumediene's intention to create a viable national political organization that would permit popular participation in the political life of the state, thereby maintaining the populist quality of the regime. As he told an assembly of mayors in early 1973 when he initiated his campaign to reactivate party life: "A revolution needs revolutionaries and the socialist revolution socialist militants. Whoever has faith in the revolution and its objectives must join the party. Otherwise he can have no place at any level of responsibility."[8]

With new responsibilities, power, and resources, the party elites in 1979 firmly believed that Algeria would soon be transformed into an effective single-party system. As we have already seen, however, by 1984 Chadli's manipulation of the critical party organs, the Political Bureau and Central Committee, had reduced the FLN into a passive bureaucracy: a receptacle of dead ideas headed by a "oui-oui" functionary.

Various other national organizations remain subordinate to the FLN: the workers' union (UGTA), the farmers' organization (UNPA), the youth association (UNJA), the organization of former resistance fighers (OMN), the women's association (UNFA), and the newly formed (May 1983) union of small merchants and artisans (UNPCA). None have any significant power or authority. The student union is the only group that has sought to challenge centralized authority and assert its own view; and it was finally suppressed in 1971 after a series of student boycotts, strikes, and demonstrations. It has not been revived and is conspicuously absent from the list of national organizations included in the party section of the National Charter. Its activities have been incorporated into the more docile and politically ineffective UNJA.

At the UNJA youth congress held in January 1979, however, more radicalized elements known as *"Pagsistes"* managed to achieve several positions of leadership with the potential of transforming the UNJA into a meaningful representative of independent student interests. *Pagsistes* were also elected in March 1979 to the executive commission and national secretariat of the UGTA. The *Pagsistes*, referring to members of the *Parti de l'Avant-Garde Socialiste* (PAGS), is an opposition party devoid of legal standing and heir to the principles of the defunct (1962) *Parti Communiste Algérien* (PCA). PAGS is as constant and continuous in its criticism of the current regime as it was of the former one, especially after the onset of the agrarian revolution in 1971. It has also been active in the various committees of the *Volontariat*, a national service organization for youth and students.

Chadli Benjedid's regime has been much less tolerant of the *Pagsiste* presence in these and other national organizations. At the most recent congresses of both the UNJA (May 1982) and the UGTA (April 1982), for example, the curtailment of left-wing influence was demonstrated by the election of a new secretary-general of the labor union and the reelection of a noncontroversial incumbent as the secretary-general of the youth movement. As in virtually all aspects of the party apparatus, the militantly socialist and leftist tendencies associated with former FLN coordinator Yahiaoui have been permanently displaced.

POLITICAL POWER

What are the sources of power availabe to each of these three major elite groups as they seek to maintain and expand their positions of political influence in the state? The principal sources of power in

Algeria's technocratic system are organizational in nature. Colonialism and the revolution severely disrupted and undermined the impact of traditional and religious bases of power on national decisionmaking processes. Power predicated on class consciousness and other forms of socially inspired group association may emerge in the future but do not yet exist, notwithstanding arguments to the contrary put forth by class-oriented and Marxist scholars. Personal power tied to some exceptional or charismatic qualities of a leader with only incidental or marginal institutional ties has most likely diminished, but not disappeared, with the death of Boumediene, whose regime was characterized at its apex by strong, one-man rule. Clientelist relations constitute important sources of power, but in their modernist (that is, bureaucratic) rather than traditional form. In sum, the technocratic character of the system put into place by Boumediene and perpetuated by Benjedid has elevated organizational sources of power above traditional-religious, class, personal, and clientelist sources. Since the 1960s, technical competence rather than political orientation or prior wartime record have become the distinguishing criteria for elite incumbency and the powers associated with it. Boumediene was unambiguous in this regard when he told a French interviewer in 1975: "The generation of Algerian leaders who participated in the war of independence played a particular role during a specific period. For me this era is definitely over."[9]

The term *technician* has often meant not being identified with any specific clan, nor commanding a fief anywhere in the country, nor possessing an independent political power base of one's own. It is in this respect that the new managerial, military, and party elites can be defined as technicians. Even though the wartime ALN experience has remained an important heritage for them, it has become secondary to their membership in one of the new technical groups— army, administration, party. Furthermore, most members of these elites have been without strong antecedent ties and obligations and are therefore ready to identify with their particular groups, which have their own natures and demands. One consequence of all this has been the technical elites' strong identification with the new organizations. "Unlike scions of old families who take their place in institutions . . . as 'delegates' from their social groups, the new elites of Algeria became organization men with the particular imprint of their organization. Because both were new, the elites and the organizations grew together, the elites using the organizational power to defend and promote the organization's interests."[10]

Organizational power is manifest in all three principal ruling hierarchies with the power imbalance so evident in the 1960s having

given way to an "institutional rectification" (*redressement institu-*
tionnel). Now all three institutions—party, administration, and army,
the latter two more than the party—possess legitimacy and influence
at each of the national, regional, and local decisionmaking levels, can
and do dispense political favors and patronage, recruit and retain
ambitious and qualified cadres, have adequate mobilizational, managerial, and military resources to assure the noncoercive application
of popular and not-so-popular socioeconomic programs and policies,
and, in general, command response and respect from a populace that
increasingly is being socialized to accept rational-legalistic rather than
traditional or charismatic forms of authority and power. This institutionalization process is still in its infancy, but a decade of stable
rule (1968–1978) and gradual institution building from the bottom
up has resulted in one of the few instances where a nonviolent,
constitutional transfer of power has taken place in the Third World.

Obviously the power resources available to the military, however
discreetly used, are superior to those held by the party and administration but only if a narrow definition—military hardware—is employed. Since technical skill increasingly is a resource unto itself, once
attached to legitimate organization it becomes a power equalizer.
Hence, in the current scheme of things, a regional military commander
is no more or less powerful than a director-general of a major
nationalized industry, a *wali* of an administrative district, a Central
Committee member of the FLN, or a president of one of the National
Assembly's eight permanent commissions. Indeed, that same military
figure is eligible to fill any one of these managerial, administrative,
party, or governmental posts, a situation that reflects the inter-
changeability of incumbents in a technocratic system.

Revealingly, however, civilian technocrats are *not* available for
military appointments. Therefore, in the final analysis, authoritative
decisionmaking in transitional societies remains in the hands of the
armed forces, whose strong sense of group identity and cohesion
leads them to jealously guard their rights and protect their interests
against the incursions of outsiders. The implicit or explicit threat of
intervention constitutes the military's "bottom line" of available power,
one permanently denied to other groups in the society. Yet, if the
Iranian case is at all instructive, the threat of military intervention
can be neutralized under conditions of imperfect or incomplete
institutionalization. Such a realization is important in understanding
the integrative nature of the Algerian elite system, with its inter-
changeability of technocratic parts designed to insure that no decisionmaking component of the political system becomes disengaged
from its popular base.

In a sense, the Algerian experiment is an empirical working out of the "crises of development" fundamental to the building of state and society; indeed, the nature and sources of power available to the national-level elite and their ruling structures are aimed at resolving the crises of identity, legitimacy, participation, penetration, and distribution in a harmonious, nonconflictual manner. The military's commitment of its diverse power resources to this functional enterprise, coupled with its participatory but noninterventionist posture in civilian politics, has been central to the system's stability and relatively effective political performance in the past decade and a half.

The power resources possessed by the administrative elite are the most expansive and politically significant in the state inasmuch as its ministerial, bureaucratic, and technological-economic activities are under the control and jurisdiction of the administrative elite. The party's once modest human, material, organizational, and symbolic resources have been improved in recent years, especially at the national level. Yet only time will tell whether the party elites, as FLN leaders in their own right rather than as the president's men or transplanted military officers, can command the kind of authority and power now possessed by the army and administration. Yahiaoui's removal in July 1980 as party coordinator and replacement by the aging functionary, Mohamed Cherif Messaadia, designated permanent secretary of the Central Committee, have compromised the party's incipient power and prestige. The FLN returned to its more modest role as the country's principal "ministry of mobilization" to be used at ad hoc moments such as elections and discussions of selective government initiatives.

Nonorganizational sources of power become relevant only within existing institutional arrangements. For example, despite the importance accorded religion, Algerian elites have not permitted religious authorities or leaders to establish an independent power base, at least not one that has an impact on national politics. Boumediene, himself a devout Muslim and a strong advocate of a religiously based traditional culture, made certain to attach directly the minister in charge of religious affairs to the presidency. He thus ensured official Islam's cooperation in the cultural revolution, the third component (along with industry and agriculture) of Boumediene's tripartite revolution. It was shown in Chapter 4 that Chadli has been even more determined than his predecessor was to contain and control the religious idiom. Similarly, in the secular sphere, single individuals, whether as power brokers themselves or as clients to more influential patrons, assert their authority and flex their political muscle as people of the organization, rarely as independent spokesmen or popular heroes.

Although much remains speculative regarding future configurations of power in the state, it is clear that the resources and tactics
that enable the elites to remain in power are and will continue to
be organizational in nature. To the extent that patron-client relations
and horizontal coteries maintain themselves and that other forms of
traditional and personal power develop, they will interact within a
highly regularized technocratic system, leaving little room for the
kinds of personal intrigues, elite conflicts, clashes, and dissensions
that so paralyzed the Ben Bella regime and the early governments
of Boumediene.

What has also become highly regularized is the manner in which
elites have been "circulated"; that is, the recruitment and retirement
of incumbent elites have become institutionalized, particularly but
not exclusively at the secondary level. Even among the national
decision makers, neither earlier involvement in the revolutionary
struggle nor previous association with Boumediene is a sufficient
criterion for access to or retention in top elite positions. Indeed, events
of the past half decade seem to have proven otherwise, as clients of
the former president have been systematically dislodged from high
positions of power and influence. Similarly, the arbitrariness of one-
man rule seems to have diminished with the death of Boumediene
and the dispersal of formal political authority among various high-
level institutions. Based on the manner in which the president and
cabinets have been selected in recent years, the consultative process
has become an intrinsic feature of elite circulation. What has not
been completely eliminated, however, is the "wheeling and dealing"
and backdoor personal power struggles that seem to be inherent in
all interelite relations and may possibly be intrinsic to the whole
Algerian political process.

Regular elections to the various local, regional, and national
assemblies constitute one important and direct device for elite recruitment at both the top and the secondary levels. This applies as
well to the congress, Central Committee, and Political Bureau elections
of the FLN. Every unit of the party has procedures for regular
mandatory elections legitimized under the National Charter's banner
of "democratic centralism."

For all top-level technical and civil service positions, expertise
and political loyalty continue to be determinative criteria for elite
entrance. Additionally, at all levels of bureaucracy and administration,
the patronage system, which, as one example, entails the obligation
to find jobs for war veterans still prevails. In fact, most ministries
continue to adhere to an earlier policy that required each government

agency to recruit at least 10 percent of its total staff from veterans' groups.

The relatively regularized system of elite circulation currently in effect is in marked contrast to the pattern of constant turnover in top political leadership evident in the decade prior to Boumediene's consolidation of power. In comparison, the 1968–1978 decade was a period of remarkable stability among top elites—in the Council of Ministers alone, for example, there was an uninterrupted seven-year stretch (1970–1977) before a personnel reshuffle of any consequence took place—with changes occurring because of resignation, promotion, retirement, rebellion, or death, natural or otherwise. The Chadli incumbency has witnessed the creation of three new governments and the reshuffling of two cabinets in the five-year period beginning with the first Chadli government of March 1979. The fact that only two men (Mohamed Benahmed Abdelghani and Abdelhamid Brahimi) have assumed the premiership during this period reflects the continuation of a relatively stable system of rule on the pattern established by Boumediene.

It has been difficult to determine exactly what causes an incumbent leader to lose favor with the "powers" and be promoted out (to embassies or the National Assembly), forced to resign, or, once in exile, assassinated (Mohamed Khider in 1967 and Belkacem Krim in 1970, for example). Even so-called natural and accidental deaths of those fallen from favor—Kaid of a heart attack in 1978 and Ahmed Medeghri of injuries resulting from a car accident in 1974—are rarely accepted at face value, especially in an environment where even a mild political deviation from the narrowly defined norm is reprimanded.

Such suspicions are reinforced by the fact that, under Boumediene at least, the game of political musical chairs, so finely developed by Habib Bourguiba in Tunisia and King Hassan II in Morocco, was rarely played in Algeria. That is, there was none of the "exile-and-reintegration" phenomenon that has always kept incumbent and oppositional elites in Tunisia and Morocco on their feet. For those who so disagreed with Boumediene by reason of temperament, policy, or ideology that they could no longer play by the rules of the game, the alternatives were few and virtually irreversible. Throughout the Boumediene years, there was "elite circulation up and circulation out, but not circulation back in."[11]

There is some preliminary evidence that Chadli's system of elite circulation may differ from its predecessor in providing opportunity for previous outcasts to return to the political process, once they have been appropriately chastened. The experience of Ahmed Ghozali is instructive in this regard. A bright star of the Algerian technocracy, Ghozali headed SONATRACH for over a decade (1966–1977) and then became minister of energy and petrochemical industries for two years during the heyday of Boumediene's industrialization-first developmental strategy. He took a political nosedive, however, after Chadli was elected. Chadli had decided to replace powerful clients of the former patron, Boumediene; to shift developmental priorities from industry to the social and agricultural sectors; and in response to widespread social discontent, to confront directly instances of public corruption and bureaucratic mismanagement at the highest levels of government. Under Boumediene it would have been highly unlikely that someone as well situated as Ghozali would have had an opportunity for political resurrection. In mid-1984, however, Chadli appointed Ghozali as Algeria's ambassador to Belgium, a not insignificant diplomatic post in a country with which Algeria has had close economic ties, however minor the overt political importance of this gesture may have been. Nonetheless, it remains uncertain whether this particular case constitutes a rare exception or foreshadows the application of the exile and reintegration principle.

Whether representative or not, the above example does not apply to the basic pattern established by Boumediene and continued by Chadli Benjedid of handling dissent. To date elite opposition has been successfully suppressed at home and made politically insignificant abroad due in part to the government's close and continuous supervision of people and ideas within and across its borders. Where potentially disruptive oppositional tendencies have manifested themselves, as among university students and urban workers, the government has employed a combination carrot-and-stick approach to bring them into line. This has meant that once public disorders have been terminated, students have been granted increased rights in the determination of university-level policies, and the promise of future employment opportunities within the public sector. As for the workers, impressive pay increases have been awarded. When dock and railroad workers went on several wildcat strikes in fall 1977, one result was a whopping 30 percent pay raise announced several months later in a presidential address to the fifth annual UGTA congress.

The system's expanding economy, with its productive industrial and manufacturing sectors, provides the regime—in the short run at least—with sufficient resources to co-opt or buy off potential opposition. Moreover, unlike the situations in Morocco and Tunisia, upward mobility to subordinate elite status within the various components of the technocratic system is still possible for qualified and ambitious university-trained Algerians. Such a situation makes it all the more difficult for oppositional forces at home and abroad to gain credibility and widespread support.

Yet clandestine and occasional public challenges to elite incumbents do take place in Algeria and in France, where it is more pronounced. One well-known case of "above ground" domestic opposition took place during the heady days of public debate and discussion preceding the approval of the National Charter and consitution in 1976. At that time a group of former leaders of the revolution issued a series of manifestos in Algiers and elsewhere beginning with a March 6, 1976, "New Appeal to the Algerian People." The appeal condemned the absence of democratic institutions in Algeria and deplored the foreign policy that had led to a split in North Africa and had increased the danger of war with Morocco over the issue of the Western Sahara. The four men who took the initiative in demanding genuine constitutional democracy included two ex-presidents of the Algerian government-in-exile (GPRA) (Benyoussef Ben Khedda and Ferhat Abbas), a former secretary-general of the MTLD (Hocine Lahouel), and a member of the former National Council of the Algerian Revolution (Mohamed Kheiriddine). All four had criticized Boumediene for totalitarian rule and the cult of personality. For his part, the Algerian president rejected these criticisms of his rule as the work of "bourgeois reactionaries" and declared that the revolution had reached the point of no return.

Despite the legitimation of certain democratic liberties implied in the formal approval of the charter and constitution, the manifesto signatories were placed under house arrest, where they remained until early 1980. Ben Khedda's pharmacy in Algiers was nationalized, and Kheiriddine, who owned a plastics factory just outside the capital, was confronted with a strike by his employees, who denounced him as an "exploiter." The factory was also nationalized. As part of Chadli Benjedid's liberalization decrees, these properties were later returned back to their owners and their pensions (provided to all former GPRA presidents and ministers) were reactivated. The Ben Khedda-Abbas experience marked the beginning, but not the end, of public declarations of opposition by those who criticize not only policies and their execution—a "lawful" exercise—but policymakers and their legitimacy as well—a subversive act.

It has not been possible to determine with any accuracy whether other sources of organized opposition exist within the country among current or disaffected elites. It is, however, known that Algeria's economic and military support for the POLISARIO Front in its guerrilla war against Morocco in the former Spanish Sahara has on occasion divided, but not fractured, the core elite. In addition, there is diffuse dissatisfaction among certain categories of nonelites, especially university students and urban laborers, as indicated above. In the middle 1980s several configurations of domestic political opposition have emerged to challenge the regime. The largest and most threatening have been the Muslim fundamentalists and their brand of populist Islam, discussed in Chapter 4. Other groups include followers of former president Ahmed Ben Bella ("Ben Bellists") of which more below, radical left-wing militants of the Workers' Socialist Organization (OST), and militant feminists of the "women's collective," who have opposed the government's support of the conservative Family Code and the Muslim clergy's growing influence on Algerian family and social life. Less organized but no less threatening are the "Berberists," consisting principally of Berbers from Kabylia who have become unhappy with Algeria's Arabization program and overall Arabic-oriented cultural policies.

In 1982 following large-scale disturbances on Algerian university campuses the regime began a systematic process of imprisoning, often without cause or legal justification, hundreds of leaders and supporters of these various opposition movements. Most were released prior to the celebration of the thirtieth anniversary of the beginning of the Algerian revolution (November 1, 1954), except for a hundred or so of the fundamentalists. The presidential amnesty of political prisoners served several purposes: It satisfied the appeals of international organizations and human rights groups, thereby enhancing the regime's worldwide reputation; it demonstrated the government's sense of political security vis-à-vis groups that are universally regarded as unrepresentative of the large majority of Algerians; and it reaffirmed the applicability of the carrot-and-stick approach for those who respond favorably to the regime's rules of the game.

Chadli has also continued a policy of "historical rectification," involving not only the release of famous (Ben Bella) and not-so-famous (Mohamed Seghir Nekkache) political prisoners but also rehabilitating the political reputations of revolutionary figures who are dead, living in exile abroad, or in internal exile at home. A national commission for just such purposes was announced by Chadli during a speech on May 8, 1984, commemorating the French massacre of 45,000 Algerians in the Sétif area in 1945.

Despite the regularity and intensity of social protest at home, some of it extremely violent and bloody, it has not taken concrete or sustained political form. One impediment to such a development has been the virtual absence of any respected or popular opposition leader. Ahmed Ben Bella comes closest to fulfilling this role, yet there appears to be no grass-roots support for the man or his ideas among

Algerians. He has remained abroad ever since his release from house arrest in 1980 by Chadli. From bases in France and later Switzerland, Ben Bella has attempted to create a movement of opposition, the most recent being the *Mouvement pour la Démocratie en Algérie* (MDA), which was announced on May 20, 1984, by his supporters situated in Paris. The founding congress of this new movement met in a Paris suburb on May 26 and 27, 1984, with 265 delegates in attendance. Unable to attend the meeting himself (because of charges against him by French authorities related to arms smuggling and transportation of illegal explosives), Ben Bella's recorded message was played before the movement's delegates. In it he called for all opposition groups to form a "democratic front" to work for the establishment of a multiparty democratic system in place of what he labeled the current "fascist" regime in Algiers. Ben Bella also reaffirmed that the MDA would constitute no more than the "Algerian section" of an "Arab-Islamic International." As with the many public statements made by the former Algerian president since his release, no one is certain about what exactly he stands for, inasmuch as he has spanned the ideological spectrum from Islamic fundamentalism to liberal democracy, along with everything in between. As such he constitutes more of an oddity on the Algerian political landscape than a serious force to contend with.

There exist a number of other exiled Algerian political leaders who have formed miniscule opposition parties that to date have gained very little support among the thousands of Algerian students and workers living in France and elsewhere in Europe. For example, Mohamed Boudiaf, who left the FLN at the time of independence, founded the *Parti de la Révolution Socialiste* (PRS), which, through its Paris-based newsletter, *PRS Information,* continues its attack on Algeria's "confiscated" revolution, state capitalism, and burgeoning class of nouveaux riches. Hocine Ait Ahmed (b. 1926) was one of the nine historic chiefs and minister of state under Ben Bella but later broke with him. Ait Ahmed organized a rebellion in Kabylia in 1963–1964 under the banner of his new opposition party, *Front des Forces Socialistes* (FFS). He was caught and condemned to death but escaped prison in 1966. Although his movement is centered in Paris, Ait Ahmed lives in exile in Switzerland. Ben Kedda's *Union Nationale pour la Liberté et la Démocratie* (UNLD) is little more than a paper organization that reflects the views of the four signatories of the March 1976 manifesto. *Le Rassemblement National pour la Démocratie* (RND) was created in Paris by Ali Mahsas, a former minister of agriculture under both Ben Bella and Boumediene. It represents another feeble attempt to put forth a democratic alternative to Algeria's current socialist path. The alternative would be legitimized under the personal leadership of such unanimously respected individuals as Abbas, Ben Khedda, and Ben Bella. Mohamed Lebjaoui, former head of the FLN federation in France, fled in 1966 to Switzerland, where he formed the *Mouvement Algérien des Forces Populaires et de l'Armée pour la Démocratie et l'Union Maghrebine* as a means of continuing his support for Ben Bellist principles.

In August 1975 a group calling itself "Soldiers of the Algerian Opposition" bombed Algerian embassies in three European capitals and issued a communiqué demanding free democratic elections and an end to "dictatorship." Among the leaders of the group was thought to be Col. Tahar Zbiri who, following his unsuccessful attempt to overthrow Boumediene by military coup in December 1967, had sought refuge in Tunisia and later moved to Morocco. Chadli has granted him executive pardon and invited him to return to Algeria a free man.

Other exiled leaders, such as Hocine Zahouane, Mohamed Harbi, Mohamed el Hadi Hadj-Smaine, and Bachir Boumaaza, who were either loyal Ben Bellists or early supporters of Boumediene, quickly became disenchanted. They continued to oppose socialist Algeria more as separate individuals, however, than as representatives of specific political organizations or ideological groups. None have made their peace with the Chadli regime although the regime has extended a hand of reconciliation to all of them.

The significant features of all these groups and individuals are that they: (1) represent the past more than the future; (2) have little political support among current elites or subelites; (3) reflect the political points of view of single individuals with personal gripes more than that of ideologically based movements with wide appeal; and (4) possess insufficient resources to confront adequately or challenge seriously the power and authority of the incumbent regime. Despite the numerous differences that divide the ruling elite, they are firmly united against the subversive claims of discredited former elites.

The most volatile and potentially disruptive category of oppositional forces is the partially educated, inadequately trained, monolingual Arabists with strong traditional and religious ties who are rapidly swelling the ranks of the urban unemployed. Because it will take at least one or more decades for the country's program of capital-intensive selective industrialization to affect the national employment picture meaningfully, especially its minimally skilled and unskilled sectors, the potential for excessive, if not revolutionary, demands seem great. The fact that nearly 65 percent of the country's population is under eighteen years of age (along with an over 3 percent net annual birthrate) aggravates an already precarious situation.

Moreover, these groups seem most vulnerable to psychologically inspired and culturally motivated religious appeals. Their bleak economic futures are ensconced within an anomic sociopsychological environment in which family ties are disintegrating, sexual frustrations are increasing, crime and other expressive forms of personal disaffection are mounting. In fact, a general social malaise is imposing itself on all of Algeria's burgeoning urban conglomerations. Inasmuch as a socialist revolution is theoretically already in place, and both communism and capitalism in their "pure" forms remain unacceptable, only a religious Islamic revolution can successfully alleviate the growing sense of social isolation and personal alienation so evident among this current generation of youth and young adults. Much more so than the ineffectual political opposition abroad, these "disruptive dropouts" constitute a direct threat to the system's social stability and an ominous, indirect threat to its political viability.

NOTES

1. Jean Leca and Jean-Claude Vatin, "Le Système Politique Algérien (1976–1978): Idéologie, Institutions et Changement Social," in *Développements Politiques au Maghreb: Aménagements Institutionnels et Processus Electoraux*, ed. Jean Leca and others (Paris: Editions du Centre National de la Recherche Scientifique, 1979), p. 27.

2. Robert A. Mortimer, "Algeria's New Sultan," *Current History* 80, no. 470 (December 1981), p. 434.

3. Leca and Vatin, "Le Système Politique Algérien," p. 20. See also John R. Nellis, "A Comparative Assessment of the Development Performances of Algeria and Tunisia," *The Middle East Journal* 37, no. 3 (Summer 1983), p. 375.

4. Nellis, "A Comparative Assessment," p. 372.

5. Mortimer, "Algeria's New Sultan," p. 420.

6. I. William Zartman, "The Algerian Army in Politics," in *Man, State, and Society in the Contemporary Maghrib*, ed. I. William Zartman (New York: Praeger, 1973), pp. 217–221.

7. Hugh Roberts, "The Politics of Algerian Socialism," in *North Africa: Contemporary Politics and Economic Development*, ed. Richard Lawless and Allan Findlay (London: Croom Helm; New York: St. Martin's, 1984), p. 41.

8. *El Moudjahid*, February 1973.

9. *Jeune Afrique*, no. 912 (June 28, 1978), p. 33.

10. I. William Zartman, "Algeria: A Post-Revolutionary Elite," in *Political Elites and Political Development in the Middle East*, ed. Frank Tachau (New York: Schenkman Publishing Co., 1975), p. 273.

11. I. William Zartman, "The Rise and Passing of the Algerian Radical Military Regime," unpublished paper (1978), p. 15.

7
Worldview

INTRODUCTION

More than is the case with any other Arab country, Algeria's foreign relations must be analyzed in the global context. In the Maghreb as in the Machriq (eastern Arab world) Algeria has been the most active state in the politics of the Third World, North-South relations, and efforts at creating a "new international economic order" (NIEO). The country's relatively broad-based national capabilities push it far above Morocco, Tunisia, and even Libya in the North African region and beyond Egypt, Iraq, and Saudi Arabia in the Middle East area. Algeria stands at the top of the less-developed countries—in Africa alone in 1982, for example, Algeria ranked fourth in GNP per capita (US$2,350), behind South Africa ($2,670), Gabon ($3,860), and Libya ($8,510)—and can even be considered a global middle power not unlike Brazil's similar designation in the Latin American context.

Algeria is also involved in a wider range of issues and with a greater number of partners beyond the Middle East and North Africa than any other Arab country. Although many of these interactions are low key and businesslike, there is also the widely publicized impact of Algeria in Third World political-economic affairs and in petroleum matters through its membership, since 1969, in the Organization of Petroleum Exporting Countries (OPEC).

Algeria has one of the more developed foreign policies in the Arab world in that its interests—ideological posturing notwithstanding—are flexibly framed on operational case-by-case terms that are then backed up with sophisticated diplomatic and organizational skill. Within the Arab arena, for example, Algeria has successfully built a reputation for seriousness and neutrality in disputes among Arabs themselves as well as between Arabs and Iranians. In addition, without excessive moralizing, Algeria has moved other Arab states that are in and out of OPEC to an appreciation and understanding of the major issues in the debate over a new world economic order. Unlike other actors of the Middle East and North Africa, Algeria has also demonstrated remarkable continuity in its postindependence foreign policy under three very different political leaders—Ahmed Ben Bella (1962–1965), Houari Boumediene (1965–1978), and Chadli Benjedid (1979–   ).

By the early 1980s Algeria, by virtue of its hydrocarbon-based economic development and the variety of its foreign undertakings, had clearly confirmed itself as a nation of the first rank in the Middle East and North Africa and as one claiming greater significance in the world arena as an incipient middle power.

ORIENTATION

Since independence, Algerian leaders have promoted and advanced their country's revolutionay war of independence as the example to be emulated by other Third World states in the struggle against colonial repression. Boumediene and his successor, Chadli Benjedid, have repeatedly cited Algeria's control over its national economy for the sake of economic development as the example the Third World should follow in its relations with developed countries. This in turn has led to Algerian advocacy—in diverse international forums, UN-sponsored conferences, and Third World groupings—of a new world economic order based on equality between developed and underdeveloped countries.

The intimate relationship between Algeria's internal development and external orientation, especially its Third World connection, was summarized by one specialist on Algerian foreign policy:

> More than many other countries, Algeria has perceived its national development as integrally linked to international politics. During its prolonged struggle for national independence (1954–1962), Algeria developed a radical outlook in which Third World solidarity and militant anti-imperialism were closely allied. For the Algerians, political independence was but a first victory in a longer term struggle against the prevailing international economic structures that reproduced much the same dependence that the Third World has known under colonial rule. Algeria has needed the diplomatic solidarity of others to achieve independence, and saw Third World political solidarity as equally necessary to break the post-colonial system of structural dependence.[1]

Despite the many divisions that characterize Third World politics, Algeria has remained constant in its demand for a fundamental reallocation of the world's wealth. Algeria's agenda includes more and easier credit terms, better access to northern markets for goods manufactured in the Third World, higher and more stable prices for the primary goods the Third World exports, and easier terms for the purchase of oil. From the Algerian perspective, these demands do not constitute "massive transfers of wealth" but instead clearly negotiable and not unreasonable goals.

Algeria believes that time, morality, and worldwide public opinion will eventually work in its favor and allow a basic restructuring of the existing international political economy. The current global economic division of power is regarded as the result of four forces: (1) the structure of the world market economy through which the industrial nations dominate most major markets; (2) the framework of rules designed to maintain order and stability in world markets; (3) national rules geared to promote and protect domestic markets, industry, and trade, rules that affect the Third World by the sheer size of the rich economies in comparison with the weaker ones; and (4) at the operational level, the buying and selling in which the largest countries and their firms have numerous advantages. The General Agreement on Tariffs and Trade (GATT) and the International Monetary Fund (IMF), according to the Algerian viewpoint, are considered structures of the second category, in which, by design and definition, the economically strong are favored. In short, the international monetary and multilateral trading systems that evolved during the postwar decades served the interests and objectives of the Western industrialized nations. Developing nations have largely been outside this privileged circle, with many coming to view the existing economic structure as inimical to their interests and perpetuating their underdog status.

As to Algeria's particular experience, the country's underdevelopment is viewed as the result of but one force—imperialism. The Algerians consider the nearly one hundred and fifty years of colonial domination, economic exploitation, deculturalization, and physical destruction rather than the land's unproductivity or the innate backwardness of its people as the cause of Algeria's underdevelopment. In this context the notion of class conflict is more appropriate to global imbalances than to internal conditions. Underdeveloped Algeria, to the extent that it represents the general condition of all Third World states, constitutes the proletariat of the periphery. Thus the country's nationalization decrees of 1971 were meant as a political act of independence, an act of economic necessity, and as a concrete demonstration of the link between domestic and international politics. Subsequent measures of economic militancy were meant to have a demonstration effect (or to employ Bruno Etienne's apt French expression, "le montreur de conduite")[2] on others of the Third World and thus to show how they could become "masters of their own house." According to Algeria's frame of reference, in order to break out of the condition of economic dependency several drastic but necessary policies have to be followed: Sell as much as you can at the highest price possible to overcome the continuing unequal terms of exchange and diversify your trading partners so as to minimize the risks of increasing dependence. Only by taking the management of one's resources into one's own hands, the Algerians have reasoned, can the underprivileged states of the Third World gain power and thus begin to bargain effectively with the West on the many other issues that affect the structure and process of the global economic system.

Based on its own direct political and economic experiences, Algeria perceives the existing division of global political power into two hostile ideological camps as the source of the capitalist-dominated international political economy. The country views itself as playing three interrelated roles on the world stage: identification, mediation, and leadership.[3]

Identification

Algeria, remembering its own complex and tortuous revolutionary experience, identifies with worldwide national liberation movements. The country's two national statutes—its constitution and the National Charter—both proudly proclaim Algeria's "solidarity with the countries of the Third World in their struggle for political and economic liberation," which draws its origins "from the high ideals of liberty, independence, and the anti-imperialist struggle of the Algerian revolution." The identification "with the peoples of Africa, Asia and Latin America constitutes an essential component of Algeria's foreign policy." This empathy has now reached mythological proportions and constitutes one of the country's ideological pillars as it seeks to buttress its radical image in world affairs. Despite subtle and obvious changes undertaken at home by Chadli Benjedid since his election to the presidency in February 1979, Algeria's support for liberation movements and the right of people for national self-determination remains as much a prominent foreign-policy issue under Benjedid as it was under his immediate predecessor.

Once referred to as the "Mecca of the revolutionaries," Algiers was the most visible center of anticolonial politics in the 1960s and 1970s and gave substantial diplomatic, financial, and logistical aid to a variety of African national liberation movements bent on overthrowing colonial rule. Such support was intended just as much to eliminate the vestiges of Western imperialism as it was to insure the establishment of progressive regimes that at independence would share Algeria's militant orientation toward world affairs.

During the heyday of its support for revolutionary and radical groups, Algeria often became involved in numerous terrorist activities, including serving as the asylum for hijacked international aircraft and providing terrorist training for guerrilla organizations. For a while Algiers became the home of Eldridge Cleaver and the headquarters of the militant Black Panther party, which he led.

By the middle of 1970s, however, these actions were significantly reduced because they had begun to compromise Aleria's more serious image as a responsible, albeit activist, articulator of Third World causes. Yet, as recently as mid-1980, Algeria was directly linked with a U.S. suspect involved in the Washington, D.C., assassination of Ali Akbar Tabatabai, an outspoken critic of Iran's Ayatollah Khomeini, whom the Algerians support. This may indicate that although overt terroristlike activities have been officially disavowed, there still exists a willingness to support such actions, under more clandestine conditions, when political circumstances so justify.

This amalgam of political, paramilitary, and terrorist backing for liberation movements is nowhere better demonstrated than in the case of the Palestinian struggle against Israel. The Algerians have consistently identified with this struggle through their strong support for the Palestine Liberation Organization. Algeria has steadfastly taken a militant anti-Israel position, and the 1967 Six Day Arab-Israeli War (Algeria calls it "the November First of the Arab revolution"—referring to the start of its own revolutionary struggle against the French on November 1, 1954) further hardened this position, which has remained virtually unchanged in the nearly two decades since that war. As one observer has commented: "The struggle with Israel . . . [has] always [been] important in the Algerian consciousness. It [has] involved all of those issues about which Algerians [have] felt most intensely: Algeria's definition of her personality as Arab, the practical problems she [has] faced in fulfilling this identity, the attitude towards Third World independence movements and full acceptance of violence as a means to political ends."[4]

Given Algeria's official tendency to form analogies between the various Third World liberation movements and its own struggle for independence, the cease-fire ending the 1967 hostilities was considered an "outrage" by Algerians. They viewed the Arab "revolution" as stillborn with the occupation of mere "territories" (the Sinai Peninsula, Golan Heights, West Bank, and the Gaza Strip) as insufficient cause to accept a "dishonorable" cease-fire. Had not Algeria—all of Algeria—been occupied for over a century and yet the struggle continued? As the Algerians had lost thousands of lives over the years so too must Arabs be prepared to sacrifice many "heroes" and "heroines" in order to insure an ultimate victory. At the time of the cease-fire this sentiment was held widely and sincerely, however impractical it remained in operational terms. To this day the residue of this attitude is found in official and unofficial Algerian thinking. Calls for death and sacrifice are now more circumspect, but the Algerians are not supporting a Sadat-like gesture leading to a "humiliating" negotiation, recognition, and peace. Through a combination of direct experience, national mythmaking, and historical education the Algerian revolution has come to touch "the lives of all Algerians and [has given] them a particular world view. The Arab-Israeli conflict [has brought] that world view into focus and [continues to revitalize] Algeria's revolutionary self-conception."[5]

Until this very day the image of Algeria's revolutionary purity remains an object of respect and admiration within Arab revolutionary circles. One illustration, among many that could be cited, involves the decision to choose Algiers as the site for the 1983 meeting of the Palestinian "legislative" body.

The Palestinian National Council (PNC)—the so-called parliament of the PLO—had met in the past in Jerusalem, Amman, Cairo, and then in Damascus in 1981. Each choice had its political significance. Following the Israeli invasion of Lebanon in summer 1982 and the expulsion of the PLO from Beirut, the political situation in the Arab East had changed. Syria was now viewed as hostile both to the PLO and to Yasir Arafat in particular. Thus the idea of convening the next PNC meeting in Damascus was rejected as was Tunis, the logical next choice, given the move of PLO headquarters there and its being the location of the Arab League. Yet it was Algiers that was finally chosen by the Palestinian leadership. The choice was meant to convey a number of political messages to the Arabs and to the world. First, and perhaps most important, Algeria

> continues to symbolize a successful militant liberation struggle against settler-colonialism, and remains firmly ensconced in the anti-imperialist camp. Algeria has nurtured the Palestinian movement since its inception, but unlike many Arab states, has refrained from intervening in the internal affairs of the movement. In his welcoming remarks to the Council, Algerian President Chadli Benjedid warned the Palestinians that they, like others before them, will be subjected to enormous pressures to accept less than their legitimate rights; but he assured them that Algeria respects the integrity of Palestinian decision-making. Finally, it would have been virtually impossible for any Arab state to

comment either adversely or derisively on holding the Council in
Algiers, as there is an Arab national consensus on Algeria, which
protected the gathering [of February 14–22, 1983] from the fickle opinions
of competing Arab states.[6]

Once an activist member of the now-defunct Arab Steadfastness
and Rejectionist Front, which, along with Libya, Syria, South Yemen,
and the PLO, opposed an accommodation with Israel, Algeria has
been preoccupied in recent years with attempting to mediate the
numerous internal political and personality splits that have divided
the Palestinians and the Arab world in general. This important aspect
of Algeria's foreign policy orientation will be discussed below.

As crucial as the Palestinian issue and the Arab world remain
for Algeria's policy environment, they are subordinate to the Maghrebin
region itself. It is within the constellation of the immediate states of
North Africa (Morocco, Tunisia, and Libya—which constitute the
primary theatre of foreign policy action) and the emerging trans-
Saharan subsystem (Mauritania, Mali, and Niger) that Algeria believes
it has an important role to play. Central to this role is the effort at
creating a unified bloc of Afro-Arab states that share Algeria's goals
of eradicating all vestiges of colonialism and imperialism. Foremost
among these goals is the support for the POLISARIO guerrilla
movement and its objective of establishing a progressive and independent Sahrawi Arab Democratic Republic (SADR) in the Western
Sahara (ex-Spanish Sahara), which is currently being claimed and
administered by Morocco.

Intra-Maghrebin relations have alternated between periods of
relative détente and periods of tension, hostility, and occasional armed
conflict. Ideological differences, territorial disputes, direct and indirect
acts of state subversion, and the rivalry between Algeria and Morocco
for regional supremacy have all worked to inhibit the development
of a political consensus in postindependence North Africa. Recently,
the concept of a Greater Maghreb has been reactivated—with 1983
a particularly active year in this regard. However, following the unity
scheme concluded in August 1984 between Libya and Morocco, the
pendulum has swung back once again toward tension and discord.

Algiers has been at the center of much political and diplomatic
activity aimed at enhancing regional stability and economic cooperation
among governments in the Maghreb. Of immediate importance has
been the desire to formalize colonially determined boundary arrangements in order to forestall annexationist designs. The current conflicts
in Chad and the Western Sahara, for example, have been made
possible by people like Colonel Muammar Qaddafi of Libya. Treaty

Central mosque in El Biar, a residential suburb of Algiers and the site of many embassies and diplomatic missions.

agreements providing for definite demarcations of common frontiers were signed by Algiers with Niger (January 1983), Tunisia (March 1983), Mali (May 1983), and Mauritania (August 1983).

For years Algerian-Tunisian relations had been reluctantly negative as Algerian domestic and foreign policies under Boumediene were tending far to the left of Tunisia's careful middle way. This did not mean that normal interstate relations were absent, however. During the 1960s, for example, Tunisia and Algeria maintained close economic relations, particularly in the energy field. In January 1970 a border treaty between the two countries was concluded, and two years later Boumediene and Bourguiba made official state visits to each other's countries. The disputes arising from the 1974 Djerba agreement, which called for a political union between Tunisia and Libya that was never implemented, and from the 1980 Gafsa and 1982 Kasserine attacks, which involved the use of Algerian territory as a zone of transit for Tunisian dissident forces trained and supported by Libya, have characteristically not been allowed to disrupt the normal conduct of state-to-state relations.

In recent years important trade agreements have been concluded and customs formalities have been eased. The simultaneous lifting of a Tunisian travel ban on Algerian tourists and Algeria's elimination of exit visa requirements for its own citizens led to a record 350,000 Algerians visiting Tunisia in the summer of 1980. Prime Minister Mohammed Mzali's trip to Algiers in September 1981, followed by the creation of a binational high commission that met in Tunis the following month, marked a rapid and noticeable improvement in relations. The improvement was maintained as high-level delegations went to each country's capital; this was capped by the highly publicized and emotionally charged visits of Benjedid to Tunis and Bourguiba to Algiers in 1983 (March 18–20 and May 29–31). The March visit concluded with the signing of a twenty-year Treaty of Friendship and Harmony between Algeria and Tunisia. This document formalized the harmonious relationship that had been evolving since Chadli's accession to power. It provided for small adjustments of the common frontier and pledged both parties not to permit violent acts directed against each other's regimes nor to allow hostile groups to utilize each other's territories as bases for attack. These stipulations were supposed to prevent the repetition of attacks like those directed at Gafsa and Kasserine. The treaty also emphasized the historic "community of destiny" of the Maghrebin world and invited other states to membership in an eventual political union—an invitation quickly and formally taken up by Mauritania in December 1983.

The most concrete form of cooperation has occurred in the energy field: the building of a natural gas pipeline from Algeria through Tunisia, passing under the Mediterranean Sea to Sicily, and finally reaching the Italian mainland. On May 18, 1983, the presidents of Tunisia, Algeria, and Italy met at El Haouraria, near Cap Bon, Tunisia, to inaugurate the Transmed pipeline. This project is a major technological and political achievement, given past difficulties in overcoming diverse economic, nationalistic, and bureaucratic interests existing on all sides. The forty-eight-inch pipeline stretches nearly 1,600 miles, begining at the Hassi R'Mel gas field in Algeria. The pipeline represents a substantial commitment by the Algerians to stabilize currently friendly relations with the Tunisians on a long-term basis. The economic benefits accruing to both North African states reflect the confluence of reformist policies currently being pursued by both governments.

Ever since Qaddafi's assumption of power in 1969, Libyan-Algerian relations have been tense and uneasy (despite the apparent concurrence of both regimes on a number of Afro-Arab and Third World issues). Boumediene's more ideological orientation found favor in Tripoli and enabled Libya and Algeria to cooperate within OPEC, to form a steadfastness alliance against Israel, and to coordinate their efforts in supporting the POLISARIO in its struggle against Morocco in the Western Sahara. Libya supplied much of the military equipment and Algeria provided logistical support, territorial bases, and diplomatic headquarters. Despite occasional frustrations with Qaddafi's unpredictable behavior, the Boumediene government felt closer to Libya than to either Tunisia or Morocco. Chadli's government, however, has been much less patient with and less tolerant of Qaddafi's rhetorical excesses and military adventurism.

A number of issues with respect to Libyan foreign-policy behavior have annoyed and angered the Algerian leadership. Libya's military support for the attacks against Gafsa and Kasserine, Tunisia, infuriated Algiers. Unconfirmed reports indicate that one reason that former FLN party coordinator Yahiaoui was removed from the Political Bureau and the Central Committee was that he was in some way involved in the Libyan operations but had failed to notify Benjedid. Whether accurate or not, there is no doubt that Libyan-Algerian relations took a serious turn for the worse following those events.

Algeria has also disagreed with Libya on the latter's direct involvement in the Chad civil war, Libya's support for anti-Arafat forces within the PLO, and Libya's consistent pricecutting in the international oil market, thereby undermining Algeria's attempt to maintain OPEC solidarity in negotiations with Western customers. The unilateral and previously unannounced resumption of Libyan-Moroccan diplomatic relations undercut Algeria's support for a resolution sponsored by the Organization of African Unity (OAU) for resolving the Saharan dispute. The general effort by Colonel Qaddafi to forge some kind of vague trans-Saharan republic from Chad to Mauritania, which could arouse irredentist aspirations among some of Algeria's already independent-minded Berber tribes in the south, has aroused consternation and dismay in Algeria. These concerns have been sharply aggravated following announcement of the 1984 Libyan-Moroccan merger. Rather than confronting Qaddafi directly or publicly on these many issues, however, the Algerians have sought to negotiate their differences or apply behind-the-scenes pressure so as to achieve the kind of regional stability they feel is essential if Algeria's development is to proceed in its more reformist direction.

It is in this context that one must understand the significance of Qaddafi's visit to Algiers on July 24 and 25, 1983. Despite the inflated rhetoric in support of creating a Greater Arab Maghreb contained in the joint communiqué made public at the end of the visit, it was clear that Algeria's participation was but another way of disarming and neutralizing Libya so that Algerian efforts to create a more temperate political climate within which the business of economic and social development could take place would not be inhibited. Two months earlier Algiers had sent Mohamed Cherif Messaadia, the lackluster FLN coordinator and Political Bureau member, to Tripoli for discussions on Algerian-Libyan relations. It is expected that formal and proper relations will be maintained as much as is diplomatically possible. There is no assurance, however, that the next outrage committed by Qaddafi will not once again cause dismay and create anxiety among the leadership in Algiers, as was the case with the Libyan-Moroccan union.

The key bilateral conflict in the Maghreb has been and still is between Morocco and Algeria. More than anything else, the fighting in the Western Sahara between Morocco and the Algerian-supported POLISARIO guerrilla movement highlights the pressures and contradictions in North African relations. Yet, even if there were no Saharan problem, Algeria and Morocco would still be very much at odds. Both countries remain in a competitive struggle to achieve political and economic dominance in the Maghreb, a struggle that reflects the "natural" pattern of internal development being pursued by each state—industrialization, bureaucratization, militarization, etc. This desire for supremacy is reinforced in Algeria by its extensive links to and integration within the global capitalist system via its large-scale oil- and gas-based development plans, which have opened up large markets for Western equipment, technology, expertise, and turnkey operations. For the intermediate future, natural gas exports to Europe and the United States (despite the cessation of most gas deliveries to the latter since April 1980) will be the backbone of Algeria's developmental schemes, including its efforts to expand its petrochemical and heavy industries. From Algeria's perspective, therefore, Morocco's annexation of the former Spanish Sahara—with its large phosphate deposits—threatens to make Morocco Algeria's economic equal.

As early as 1962, at the time of Algeria's independence, Morocco and Algeria had already developed mutually incompatible nationalistic objectives. Morocco had provided important diplomatic and logistical assistance to Algeria's preindependence provisional government (GPRA) and the FLN guerrillas, yet in retrospect it was inevitable, given the revolutionary pretensions of the Algerian leadership and the traditionalism of the authoritarian Moroccan monarchy, that relations between independent Algeria and Morocco would not be cordial.

The inconclusive three-week border war—the "War of the Sands"—that erupted in the fall of 1963 between Algeria and Morocco in the Tindouf area went beyond a dispute about the mere ownership of vast stretches of sand. More fundamentally, it involved questions of ideology, regional power, national prestige, and economic advantage resulting from the development of potentially sizable iron ore deposits in the area. In many ways, that brief and indecisive war proved to be a precursor for the far longer and more violent conflict that was to break out twelve years later between the same adversaries. In addition, then as now, the attempt by each country to utilize for its own ends the domestic opponents of the other regime backfired, inasmuch as the conflicts increased the nationalist fervor in both countries, thereby consolidating support for the existing regimes.

Algeria has always been the key to any discussion of North African unity. Until recently the Algerians have regarded their own national strength, defined in terms of rapid and massive industrialization, as more important than regional development or cooperation. This was especially the case when Morocco was perceived as a noncompetitor, a situation that altered with King Hassan's annexation of the Western Sahara by stages in 1975 and 1979, with all the economic, geopolitical, military, and diplomatic advantages such an act was perceived as giving Morocco. This helps explain why Boumediene, following agreement on the Tindouf border dispute in Algeria's favor, reneged on the earlier verbal promises he had made to Hassan. Boumediene had initially expressed reticent approval of the idea of a Moroccan takeover of part of the Western Sahara; this stance was later replaced by one of silent disinterest. By 1976, he came out publicly in favor of the area's political self-determination, granted political and diplomatic recognition to its government-in-exile (SADR), and provided logistical and military support to its guerrilla movement, which operated from bases in Algeria and, later, in Mauritania. In so doing, Boumediene entered into a confrontation with Morocco that put both his global standing and his socioeconomic strategy in jeopardy; it involved, among other things, a direct, albeit short-lived, armed conflict and the severance of diplomatic relations, which have yet to be reestablished, although land and air communcations and transportation have recently been normalized.

Initially, Chadli Benjedid was less willing to pursue his predecessor's cause célèbre. The policy shift was aided by Libya's aggressive trans-Saharan policies and, later, the reestablishment of diplomatic relations between Libya and Morocco. Other signs of diplomatic moderation were evident in the Algerian president's December 20, 1981, state-of-the-nation address to the country's National Assembly, in which he set out a "good neighbor policy" and implicitly extended a hand of reconciliation to Morocco. A series of diplomatic encounters between high Moroccan and Algerian officials in each other's capitals during and following the aborted twelfth Arab Summit meeting in Fez in late November 1981 were another indication that Algeria's hitherto hard-line attitude toward Morocco might be softening.

These diplomatic initiatives continued through 1982 despite the apparent setback suffered by Morocco when SADR was admitted into the Organization of African Unity at a foreign ministers' meeting in Addis Ababa in February 1982. A year later Hassan and Chadli met at a historic summit at a Moroccan border point. Many issues were discussed, but no agreement was reached on the Saharan question nor were diplomatic relations reestablished. According to Chadli himself, as revealed in an interview he gave to *Le Monde* during his November 1983 official visit to France, his willingness to meet Hassan was meant to demonstrate Algeria's conciliatory approach toward Morocco, which had pressed for the meeting in the first place. Within six months after the summit, however, basic differences still remained, with increased criticisms of each country's Saharan policies appearing in the government news media of Algeria and Morocco.

The Arab-African Federation between Morocco and Libya, signed in Oujda, Morocco, on August 14, 1984, was interpreted by the Algerians as a significant shift in the regional balance of power. It would work to Morocco's advantage particularly with respect to the Western Sahara conflict, in which Libya had once been a principal financial and military supplier for the guerrillas. For the Algerians, the Oujda treaty was reviled as a potential cause of "destruction and discord" and as a completely wrong approach to the stated goal of uniting the whole of the Maghreb. Indeed, it was under strong Algerian pressure that the OAU, meeting at its twentieth summit on November 12, 1984, in Addis Ababa, seated the SADR as the fifty-first member of the all-African organization. The year before the POLISARIO delegation, although legally entitled to be seated since its formal admission to that body in 1982, had been advised not to force the issue and had unilaterally absented itself from the OAU gathering. The POLISARIO delegates feared that a threatened Moroccan pull-out would seriously fractionalize an already divided regional body. The Oujda accord, however, so infuriated Algiers that it threw caution to the wind and lobbied actively among OAU members to allow the SADR its legal representation. Days earlier the Algerians had succeeded in obtaining Nigerian recognition for SADR, placing additional diplomatic pressure on the Moroccans, who predictably withdrew from the OAU on November 13, 1984—the first such member-state to do so since the founding of the organization in 1963.

For two countries as well balanced as Morocco and Algeria in human and natural resources, and sharing many sociopolitical goals, a common colonial heritage, and similarities in language, culture, and religion, a more cooperative, if not united, Maghreb would seem to be the obvious framework in which they could achieve agreement and settle their disputes. Yet, since the early 1960s their governments have responded aggressively to territorial and ideological imperatives, often making provocative, predatory moves. As a consequence, the Western Sahara conflict has come to dominate, indeed overshadow all regional politics. Distrust, bitterness, and discord have characterized Moroccan-Algerian relations as a result of this conflict. Yet this dispute reflects more fundamental differences that will not quickly disappear if and when the Saharan war is satisfactorily resolved.

Mediation

Algeria, given its nonaligned status and activist orientation in world affairs, considers itself ideally suited for the role of mediator. This mediating role is consistent with Algeria's efforts to forge an effective Third World coalition capable of challenging the economic and political might of global capitalist power. To the extent that intra–Third World disputes divert efforts at achieving political solidarity and collective self-reliance among the nonaligned, Algeria believes that mediation is an essential process worthy of serious pursuit.

It is for this reason that Algeria has become directly involved in several Third World mediation efforts, including: resolution of the 1977 border conflict between Libya and Egypt; negotiation of what became known as the Algiers Accords, which resolved the territorial dispute along the Shatt-al-Arab estuary between Iran and Iraq in 1975 and led, indirectly, to a cessation of the Kurdish struggle in Iraq; and, most spectacularly, the successful negotiation for the release of fifty-two U.S. hostages from Iran in early 1981. The latter effort was undertaken by Algeria less to ingratiate itself with a hostile superpower than to release Iran from the calumny of world public opinion that had isolated a country that had successfully overthrown a Western puppet regime and could now be expected to proceed into the progressive camp. As a militant ally within OPEC and potential regional influence, Iran's fundamentalist regime gained the prompt support of the Algerians. The Third World character of this mediation effort was reaffirmed in October 1982 with Algeria's temporary unwillingness to release funds to U.S. companies that had been awarded millions of dollars in claims against the Iranian government by an international tribunal. Because of its pivotal role in the hostage negotiations, Algeria had been designated as the intermediary that had to approve payments. Prior to this snag Algeria had routinely approved similar payments to other U.S. companies, but it was clear that Algeria's current position was related to charges by Iran that the United States had violated aspects of the Algiers Declaration—the agreement under which the hostages were released on January 20, 1981.

Similarly, Algeria's attempt to terminate hostilities between Iran and Iraq and negotiate a peaceful settlement of the war begun in September 1980 flows from the perspective that any conflict within the Third World only impedes the process of collective self-reliance and global solidarity by which the South can effectively stand up to the North. It was in one such negotiating venture that Algeria's respected foreign minister, Mohamed Seddik Benyahia, and twelve of his top advisers lost their lives when their chartered executive jet was mysteriously shot down near the Iranian-Turkish border. They were on a flight from Iraq to Teheran as part of one more effort at "shuttle diplomacy" undertaken by the Algerians. Within OPEC in late 1982, Saudi Arabia began pressing Algeria to try to mediate the serious pricing disagreements that pitted the Gulf Arab group, composed of the Saudis, Kuwait, and the United Arab Emirates, against the African producers, notably Nigeria, Libya, and, to a lesser extent, even Algeria itself. Iran and Venezuela have aligned themselves with the Africans, refusing to comply with Saudi demands that they boost their oil prices to ease pressures on Gulf producers, who have seen their share of the world market shrink since 1982. Finally, the Algerian foreign minister, Ahmed Taleb Ibrahimi, has been involved since June 1983 in attempting to mediate the serious dispute between Yasir Arafat, chairman of the Palestine Liberation Organization, and President Hafez al-Assad of Syria.

The rift within the PLO and between the PLO and Syria has reached crisis proportions, especially since a Syrian-backed faction of Al-Fatah forced out the last of Arafat's troops from Tripoli, Lebanon, in December 1983. For some of the reasons stated earlier Algeria has come to assume a key mediating role in this dispute—with Arafat making regular visits to the Algerian capital to consult with President Chadli Benjedid and Foreign Minister Ibrahimi in an effort to convene the long-delayed meeting of the Palestine National Council (PNC) as a means of reestablishing Arafat's political prominence in the PLO. His visits have also been intended to give moral support to the eight hundred or so Palestinian fighters still based in Algeria. The deep divisions, personal rivalries, and political mistrust besetting the Palestinian movement have made mediation extremely difficult even for so adroit a diplomatic negotiator as Algeria; this situation was made no easier by the convening of a rump PNC under Arafat's leadership on November 22, 1984, for a five-day gathering in Amman, Jordan.

These several representative examples illustrate Algeria's continued commitment to a leading mediating role in disputes involving Third World states, although not every outcome or negotiating posture has proven successful or advantageous. The conflict in the Western Sahara, the civil war in Chad, the continuing battle in the Horn of Africa between Ethiopia and Somalia and dissident movements within both countries, and the Namibia dispute are but a few examples on the African continent where Algerian mediation efforts—whether direct or indirect—have either been rebuffed or proven unsuccessful.

Leadership

The role that Algeria believes it is best qualified to assume is that of leadership. It considers itself a natural leader of the Third World, especially its more progressive component. Algeria bases its claim on its impeccable anti-imperialist credentials, its activist posture in North-South encounters, and its relatively hard-line position within OPEC, where it argues that it is motivated by concerns for the worldwide struggle against capitalist exploitation. Algeria's self-assigned role as the spearhead of the Third World assumes two interrelated political and economic components: nonalignment and a new international economic order (NIEO).

Nonalignment

Nonalignment remains the centerpiece of Algeria's foreign-policy orientation and is guided by three principles: a vigilant anticolonialism that finds unswerving Algerian support for movements of national liberation; the organization of the struggle against imperialism, which assumes a simultaneous struggle for the creation of a new global economic order involving the solidarity of all "exploited" states; and determined action in favor of maintaining world peace.

The country's constitution and National Charter both make explicit commitments to the principle of nonalignment. Article 90 of the 1976 constitution, for example, states that Algeria, "faithful to the principles and objectives of nonalignment," is working for "peace, peaceful coexistence, and noninterference in the internal affairs of other states." For its part, Section 5 of the National Charter speaks of nonalignment as

> the expression of Algeria's total independence from all foreign powers. It is a concretization of the Revolution's determination to be free of all outside influence and to determine its domestic and foreign policies in terms of the interests of its people. . . . The policy of nonalignment constitutes a solid base for collective action of all Third World countries

who are struggling to achieve their total freedom, political independence, and a defense of their economic interests against all foreign seizure.

The nonalignment espoused by the Algerian leadership differs somewhat from the ideas originally put forth by Gamal Abdel Nasser, Jawaharlel Nehru, and Marshall Tito in Bandung in 1955. Similarly, the concept of nonalignment pursued by Benjedid is at variance with the policy articulated and applied by Boumediene. In its simplest sense, positive neutralism or nonalignment of the 1950s and 1960s referred to the Third World's refusal to align itself automatically with the Soviet bloc or the United States on issues affecting the underdeveloped states or to become directly involved in the quarrels between the superpowers themselves. This particular formulation was never fully accepted by the Algerians because of their revolutionary heritage and violent, anti-imperialist struggle for independence. Indeed, by the early 1970s, Algeria had come to espouse militant anti-imperialism as a substitute for nonalignment as an organizational principle. This was consistent with Boumediene's sympathy for and association with Soviet anti-imperialist objectives worldwide. From his perspective, the struggle against imperialism—which the Algerians define as "the system of vast economic disparities bequeathed by the colonial era and now defended by American economic and military power"—was paramount with the Soviet Union's being viewed as the natural ally of Third World countries. In the Middle East the Soviet Union was the only power capable of providing the arms and support for the Arabs to combat Zionism and the U.S.-supported Israeli "menace." As the guarantor of the Cuban and Vietnamese revolutions, the Soviet Union, without a colonial past, could not be placed on the same level as the West. In any case, for Boumediene nonalignment had less to do with superpower entanglements and quarrels than with the need to fight off what Algerians believe was the emerging transideological industrial power complex that controls and inhibits Third World development. For the Algerians of that time and today nonalignment is a corollary of assertive national independence in the political and economic spheres.

Even though continuity best characterizes Algeria's foreign policy orientation under Chadli, there have been nuanced changes that the current president has initiated in regard to the nonalignment principle. The sense of righteousness that has permeated Algerian foreign policy ever since independence still remains. Despite a world filled with nationalism and pragmatism, Algeria continues to believe that its diplomacy gains strength from noble purpose and high moral authority. Algerians still are confident that the fundamental tenets of anticolonialism, anti-imperialism, and nonalignment give the country a loftiness of outlook.

For the current Algerian leadership nonalignment remains a substantive and serious concept. It is now being interpreted, however, in a more classic fashion reminiscent of the early Nasser period. It means Algeria refuses to align itself automatically with either the USSR or the United States and remains free to criticize both. From Algiers, nonalignment is not passivity, nor neutrality, nor fence sitting; it is a positive policy reflecting the country's determination to decide issues on their merits. A policy of "equidistance" seems the best way to describe Chadli's current orientation toward the superpowers. In the critical area of arms purchases, however, a visit in early October 1984 to Algiers by a high-level U.S. military delegation caused anxiety in Moscow and concern among pro-Soviet elements in the Algerian leadership, who fear that equidistance is being carried too far. Algeria's shift, however, relates less to ideological than to pragmatic considerations, particularly the country's perceived need to diversify arms suppliers so as not to become overly dependent on any single source. This position is consistent with Algeria's broader objective of diversifying economic relations and trading partners within the Eastern and Western camps.

Increasingly dissatisfied with the quality of Soviet military equipment, Algeria has for several years been actively looking into the purchase of advanced military equipment from the West, especially France, Britain, and the United States. Morocco's military modernization involving the purchase of U.S. and French equipment has also forced a serious rethinking about Algeria's virtual dependency on the Soviets for heavy equipment. Earlier purchases of U.S. Lockheed C-130 Hercules transport planes were followed up in October 1983 by another sale of more advanced C-130Hs to Algeria's air force; the inventory of such aircraft totals fourteen. In addition, a large purchase involving two rapid patrol boats and two warships from Britain's Brooke Marine company in 1983 has been concluded. Also thirty or so military training centers are being set up by the British engineering firm, Pauling. Other equipment being considered for purchase from the British include: twenty to thirty Hawk training aircraft, several helicopters, trucks, armored vehicles, and equipment to modernize Soviet-made tanks. The French-German company, Alpha Jet, is also being considered to supply aircraft to Algeria.

Chadli's redefinition of the nonalignment principle was given concrete diplomatic expression in April 1982 when the Algerian president made important visits to Yugoslavia, China, and India. From the perspective of the current Algerian leadership the "natural ally" thesis propounded by Boumediene had gone too far in favor of one side to the overall detriment of Algeria and the Third World in general. In traveling to these three countries Chadli was delivering a clear message: He wants to reestablish a more balanced nonaligned posture that may ultimately replace the Boumediene-forged Algiers-Hanoi-Havana axis with Chadli's own Algiers-Belgrade-New Delhi axis. These visits to China, Yugoslavia, and India represented more publicly important and ideologically valuable shifts in Algeria's non-alignment orientation than the earlier steps taken in the area of arms purchases. In his speech in Belgrade, for example, Benjedid attacked the current world situation in which all Third World problems were being defined in terms of the conflict between the global superpowers. He called for the reactivation of the nonaligned movement as a means by which to reduce East-West conflict and thereby facilitate the resolution of intra–Third World differences. Chadli's visit to China lasted nearly a week and involved trips to the countryside (in contrast to the thirty-six-hour visit to Moscow a year earlier). This could be interpreted as a rebuff to Moscow and a further signal to the outside world that Algiers was seeking to draw back from its too close association with Moscow.

Playing the "China card" is of additional significance inasmuch as Peking has pursued foreign policy goals that Algiers has found inimical such as supporting Sese Seko Mobutu of Zaire, giving aid to insurgent forces in Angola, and recognizing the government of General Augusto Pinochet in Chile. Overall, these recent diplomatic moves and similar reconciliation efforts elsewhere have demonstrated the current regime's belief that only in reestablishing the primacy of the nonalignment principle can Algeria transcend its regional and continental concerns and refocus its priorities where it feels they have always belonged and should always remain—on the world stage.

Chadli Benjedid would concur with one observer's prescription for maintaining the nonalignment principle as an effective foreign policy instrument for the Third World: "Try to maintain a moral and political presence in the world that would make it difficult for superpowers to go on a rampage; raise the moral and political costs of interventions by powerful states; and don't barter away your autonomy, for it is much tougher to recover it once you get used to depending upon others for essential needs."[7]

New International Economic Order

The leadership role Algeria has assumed in confronting the existing global structure and its call for the creation of a new international economic order are probably the most distinctive and striking attributes of its foreign policy orientation. Algeria's global approach to understanding the international division of labor begins by identifying the imperial state system—the contemporary version of international capitalism—as that which controls the internal politics of weaker states. Through this system the industrialized nations, led by the United States, dominate most of the Third World. Dominance requires a monopoly of economic, military, and ideological resources. After World War II, the United States financed and benefited from imperialism, but since the middle 1960s it has had to share the power with other capitalist nations, especially Japan and Germany. Through the years, the tools and patterns of imperialist power have shifted to accommodate changes in resources, finances, and production. From this historical condition conflict has emerged between the developed and developing states, between the North and the South. According to Algerian analysts, the North and South are divided by a structural inequality that has political, economic, and social dimensions, but this structural inequality is also reflected in the incapacity of the South to participate in the NIEO. Needed are a reform of the economic system, guaranteed access of the poor countries to development, and their participation in the process of international decisionmaking. Until these obtain, interference and intervention by some countries in the affairs of others will continue.

The Algerian view on the need for a fundamental restructuring of the international political economy can be summarized as follows:

> The Third World was poor because it had been economically ransacked by others who continued to use their economic power to frustrate the aspirations of the developing countries. Previous international development strategies were an acknowledged failure because of the lack of political will in developed countries to implement them. Therefore, individual and collective self-reliance within the developing world was the necessary precondition for bringing about a new system of world economic relations based on equality.[8]

By basically changing principles, norms, rules, and procedures that affect the movement of goods and factors in the world economy, Algeria, as a self-proclaimed leader in the Third World, could enhance not only its economic well-being but also its political control.

Procedurally Algeria utilizes three methods designed to achieve a new global political economy: (1) a North-South dialogue principally within United Nations organizations; (2) promoting and practicing a policy of "cartelization" or "indexation" among Third World raw-materials producers that ties the prices developing nations receive for the goods they export to the capital goods they import from the North; and (3) utilizing an array of South-South exchanges and arrangements in the economic, political, diplomatic, and cultural fields to confront the North more effectively.

Algeria's NIEO orientation calls for more rapid economic development, increased transfer of resources and technology from industrialized to developing nations, and a more favorable distribution of global economic benefits. Other issues raised by the Algerians have to do with aid, trade, foreign investment, foreign ownership of property, activities of multinational corporations, debt relief for developing nations through cancellation or rescheduling, commodity price stabilization, and compensatory financing mechanisms to stabilize export earnings.

Conclusion

Algeria has consistently taken seriously its dual leadership roles in the nonaligned movement and the Group of 77, the informal body of developing states representing the Third World's call for a new international economic order. Yet in the three roles of identification, mediation, and leadership that it has carved out for itself, Algeria's overriding concern remains that of building a "powerful, prosperous and influential Algeria." Algeria's leaders pursue global interests not as a means of expanding territorially or fostering a particular ideology but in order to buttress an intensely nationalistic state system. Foreign-policy statements as recorded by Algerian leaders in their official documents and texts are all aimed at improving the national sphere and having Algerians gain mastery of their own destiny. The same leaders, however, continue to stress the principled character of their foreign policy, reflecting the fundamental dualities of Algeria's global orientation—an admixture of reality and idealism, flexibility and intransigence, pragmatism and ideology.

NOTES

1. Robert A. Mortimer, "Global Economy and African Foreign Policy: The Algerian Model," *African Studies Review* 27, no. 1 (March 1984), p. 19.

2. Bruno Etienne, *L'Algérie, Cultures et Révolution* (Paris: Seuil, 1977).

3. See Bernard Cubertafond, "L'Algérie du President Chadli," *Politique Etrangère*, no. 1 (March 1981), pp. 160–162.

4. Richard A. Roughton, "Algeria and the June 1967 Arab-Israel War," *The Middle East Journal* 23, no. 4 (Autumn 1969), p. 437.

5. Ibid., p. 444.

6. Ibrahim Abu-Lughod, "Flexible Militancy: A Report on the Sixteenth Session of the Palestine National Council, Algiers, February 14–22, 1983," *Journal of Palestine Studies* 12, no. 4 (Summer 1983), p. 27.

7. Fouad Ajami, "The Fate of Nonalignment," *Foreign Affairs* 59, no. 2 (Winter 1981/82), p. 384.

8. Robert A. Mortimer, "Algeria and the Politics of International Economic Reform," *Orbis* 21, no. 3 (Fall 1977), p. 687.

8

Conclusion

Contemporary Algeria has evolved into a bureaucratic polity—a political system in which power and national decisionmaking are shaped almost exclusively by the employees of the state, and especially by the topmost levels of the officer corps, single-party organization, and civilian bureaucracy, including the significant socioeconomic class of managers and technicians. It is this complex political legacy that Boumediene bequeathed to his successor, Chadli Benjedid.

In the half dozen or so years since his first election to the presidency in February 1979, Chadli has pursued a cautious, middle-of-the-road policy consistent with his strong military identification and institutional loyalty. These attributes made him, during the critical five-day FLN congress convened to select a new president following the unexpected death of Boumediene, a perfect symbol of the army as guarantor and arbiter of the national interest. "His personal image reinforced his claim—Arabo-Muslim in cultural orientation, a nationalist unsullied by intrigue."[1] Chadli's nomination reflected the army's determination to protect its own place at the very center of Algerian politics by preventing a marked shift of power to either the party or the civilian administration.

Chadli's uncertain status and his initial hesitancy to tamper with Boumediene's political legacy have given way to a more pronounced political design that reflects both the continuity and change that have been the hallmarks of postindependence Algeria. Within the narrow circle of the ruling elite, the anticipated power struggle was virtually completed by early 1983 when Chadli's power and influence were consolidated at the expense of both his immediate rivals (Yahiaoui on the left and Bouteflika on the right) and of some other individuals and groups newly seeking entry into the core elite.

Institutionally and at the outset of Chadli's first presidency, power and authority were more effectively redistributed among army, party, and government, eliminating in the process the single-man concentration of power that for so long had characterized Boumediene's system of rule. In theory at least, in the first full year of the Chadli era, the premiership and the party leadership constituted alternative bases of power. Yet, all three men had common military origins and associations—indeed, that Chadli (president), Abdelghani (premier), and Yahiaoui (party coordinator) all held the rank of colonel, which at that time was the highest military grade, was ample reminder that the ANP had not surrendered its influence—and shared in the belief of the supremacy of a strong and secure state.

Despite common military roots, however, Algeria's "obsession with organic unity" could not long tolerate real or potential contenders for power especially at the apex of the political pyramid. Therefore, once Boumediene's appointees and clients were displaced from decisionmaking positions, the balance of political forces began to shift in favor of the presidency, whose incumbent had the full backing of the army. Whatever autonomy and independent authority the party, nationalized enterprises, and governmental administration had developed over the years were now significantly diminished as each structure was either demobilized, deconcentrated, or decentralized in a manner intended to diffuse political power everywhere but at the very top. In the process, Chadli recreated the structure of power—sultanism—that Boumediene had fashioned for himself. The presidentially directed purge of the political right and left was additional testimony to this effort at maintaining a narrow political consensus. Challenges at the mass level, as we have seen, were also effectively neutralized through a carrot-and-stick policy, enabling the Chadli team to formulate and implement its own vision of how state and society should evolve.

In the domestic sphere, for example, Chadli began giving greater attention to the pressing social and economic problems besetting his country. The abolishment of the notorious exit visa (a bureaucratic nightmare required of citizens and foreign residents alike for any travels abroad) was enthusiastically received. This important decision reflected Benjedid's determination to loosen up the overly bureaucratized and enormously inefficient socioeconomic system without, however, undermining the centralized nature of political life at the national level.

From their perspective the current Algerian leaders want the institutionalization process begun by Boumediene to continue, while they respond more effectively to the myriad demands of an ever increasingly dissatisfied mass public. It is uncertain, however, to what extent social and economic demands may be satisfied without simultaneously raising political expectations that already go far beyond the relatively limited framework for independent political expression established by the regime. Yet most of this is a problem for the future; for now, attention is being directed at untangling the complex maze of redundant bureaucratization that is currently suffocating the country's productive capacities.

For some observers, however, this narrow preoccupation with state-sponsored bureaucratic "tinkering" is being pursued at the expense of society and the majority of its underprivileged masses. One critic, for example, has noted the loss of socialist élan and populist enthusiasm that Boumediene had generated with his threefold cultural, agricultural, and industrial revolution beginning in 1971 and the national-level political mobilization begun a few years later. According to Hugh Roberts, Boumediene's "audacious strategy of popular mobilization around an extremely ambitious program of radical socialist policies" has given way to bureaucratic routinization. The course being pursued by Chadli and his colleagues, according to Roberts, is one of "utilizing the impatience of the younger generation of technically qualified Algerians to bring about a rejuvenation of the administrative apparatus without thereby substantially altering the manner in which it functions."[2]

Few would disagree with the fact that the relationship of state and society in Algeria today have undergone noticeable changes under Chadli.

> [Specifically,] the state has lost the capacity it possessed under Boumediene to capture and canalize the political reflexes of the underprivileged sections of the population and, with the loss of élan in the regime's economic development strategy, popular discontent has tended increasingly to surface in the form of competing claims to representation in the state apparatus expressed in terms of cultural identity and legitimacy, and a growing disposition to contest the prerogatives and legitimacy of the state apparatus when these claims are frustrated. To the claims of the Berberists are counterposed those of the *arabisants* and the Islamic radicals. Both the first and the last of these groups comprise elements disposed to contest the entire basis of the political system, the former inspired by Western democratic and pluralist models, the latter by the message from the East. It remains to be seen whether the Chadli regime will be able to contain this ferment, or whether it will develop into a coherent and sustained challenge to the state.[3]

It was inevitable that socially generated protest movements of the type described above would emerge under Chadli, given his determination to "liberalize" society through a broadly based program of decentralization, deconcentration, and (limited) democratization to rectify the many abuses of government and instances of gross mis-management that so stifled Algeria's development, despite the avail-ability of impressive human and natural resources. In the meantime the regime continues to pursue a predominantly nationalist, Algeria-first orientation, one consequence of which is the relative decline in the country's Third Worldism and in its preoccupation with the "big issues" in foreign affairs. The only issue that remains a principal agenda item is the conflict with Morocco over the Sahara, a conflict that seems no closer to resolution under Chadli than it was under Boumediene. Even the so-called steadfastness and confrontation front of Arab militants opposed to Egypt's peace treaty with Israel is not drawing Chadli's attention the way it did for Boumediene, who was a prime factor in originally forging this front.

At home and abroad, President Chadli Benjedid has managed to consolidate his authority in a nonauthoritarian manner, gaining the respect of his colleagues without simultaneously arousing enmity of important individuals or cliques. He has "displayed an ability to listen and respond selectively to the demands and criticisms put forward by the public. The government has also managed to reorient policy in a number of areas while preserving a good deal of continuity with earlier strategic options, and to organize a far-reaching renewal of the regime's personnel with a minimum of political instability."[4]

Supported by a strong state-centered apparatus with the military at its core, Chadli is pursuing cautious and pragmatic policies intended to make the Algerian system work more effectively for the people themselves. In this effort he has the apparent support of the system's key people and institutions. That Chadli is unprepared to transform Algeria into another Egypt is shown clearly enough by the regime's determination to maintain Algeria's basic socialist configuration. Yet Algeria is not Syria and is far from being another Libya, rhetoric and selective ideological posturing notwithstanding. What Boumediene started, Chadli is simply pursuing to its logical conclusion—political institutionalization leading to political stability and development; mixed socialist-state capitalism-modified liberalism, based on exploi-tation of oil and gas resources, leading to economic growth and prosperity; and military strength and preparedness, insuring regional security.

NOTES

1. Robert Mortimer, "Algeria: Which Way Ahead?" *Africa Report* (May-June 1979), p. 11.

2. Hugh Roberts, "The Politics of Algerian Socialism," in *North Africa: Contemporary Politics and Economic Development*, ed. Richard Lawless and Allan Findlay (London: Croom Helm; New York: St. Martin's, 1984), p. 41.

3. Ibid.

4. Hugh Roberts, "Algeria: Thirty Years After the Revolution," *Africa Report* 29, no. 6 (November-December 1984), p. 7.

Acronyms

ALN	*Armée de Libération Nationale* (National Liberation Army)
AML	*Amis du Manifeste et de la Liberté* (Friends of the Manifesto and Liberty)
ANP	*Armée Nationale Populaire* (People's National Army)
APC	*Assemblée Populaire Communale* (Popular Communal Assembly)
APN	*Assemblée Populaire Nationale* (Popular National Assembly)
APW	*Assemblée Populaire de Wilaya* (Popular *Wilaya* Assembly)
BADR	*Banque Agricole et du Développement Rural* (Agricultural and Rural Development Bank)
CAPCS	*Coopérative Agricole Polyvalente Communale de Service* (Communal Service Multipurpose Agricultural Cooperative [service cooperative])
CRUA	*Comité Révolutionnaire d'Unité et d'Action* (Revolutionary Committee for Unity and Action)
DA	*Dinar Algérien* (Algerian Dinar)
ENA	*Etoile Nord Africaine* (North African Star)
ENAGAS	*Empress Nacional de Gas* (Spain's national gas company)
ESDNC	*Entreprise Socialiste pour le Développement National de la Construction* (Socialist Company for the National Development of Construction)

213

FFS	*Front des Forces Socialistes* (Socialist Forces Front)
FLN	*Front de Libération Nationale* (National Liberation Front)
GATT	General Agreement on Tariffs and Trade
GPRA	*Gouvernement Provisoire de la République Algérienne* (Provisional Government of the Algerian Republic)
IMF	International Monetary Fund
LNG	liquified natural gas
LPG	liquified petroleum gas
MDA	*Mouvement pour la Démocratie en Algérie* (Movement for Democracy in Algeria)
MNA	*Mouvement National Algérien* (Algerian National Movement)
MTLD	*Mouvement pour le Triomphe des Libertés Démocratiques* (Movement for the Triumph of Democratic Liberties)
NIEO	new international economic order
OAS	*Organisation Armée Secrète* (Secret Army Organization)
OAU	Organization of African Unity
ONM	*Organisation Nationale des Moudjahidine* (National Organization of Guerrilla Fighters)
OPEC	Organization of Petroleum Exporting Countries
OS	*Organisation Spéciale* (Special Organization)
OST	*Organisation Socialiste des Travailleurs* (Workers' Socialist Organization)
PAGS	*Parti de l'Avant-Garde Socialiste* (Progressive Socialist Party)
PCA	*Parti Communiste Algérien* (Algerian Communist Party)
PLO	Palestine Liberation Organization
PNC	Palestine National Council
POLISARIO Front	*Front Populaire pour la Libération de la Saguiat el Hamra et du Rio de Oro* (Popular Front for the Liberation of Saguiat el Hamra and Rio de Oro)
PPA	*Parti du Peuple Algérien* (Algerian People's Party)

PRS   *Parti de la Révolution Socialiste* (Party of the Socialist Revolution)

RND   *Le Rassemblement National pour la Démocratie* (National Assemblage for Democracy)

RTA   *Radio-Télévision Algérienne* (Algerian Radio-Television)

SAA   *Société Algérienne d'Assurance* (Algerian Insurance Company)

SADR   Sahrawi Arab Democratic Republic

SNS   *Société Nationale de Sidérurgie* (National Iron and Steel Company)

SONACOME   *Société Nationale de Constructions Mécaniques* (National Company for Mechanical Construction)

SONATIBA   *Société Nationale des Travaux d'Infrastructure et du Bâtiment* (National Company for Building Construction)

SONATRACH   *Société Nationale pour la Recherche, la Production, le Transport, la Transformation et la Commercialisation des Hydrocarbures* (National Society for Research, Production, Transport, Transformation, and Commercialization of Hydrocarbons [national oil and gas company])

SONELEC   *Société Nationale d'Electricité et d'Electronique* (National Company for Electricity and Electronic Equipment)

SONITEX   *Société Nationale des Industries Textiles* (National Company for Textile Industries)

UDMA   *Union Démocratique du Manifeste Algérien* (Democratic Union of the Algerian Manifesto)

UGTA   *Union Générale des Travailleurs Algériens* (General Union of Algerian Workers)

UNFA   *Union Nationale des Femmes Algériennes* (National Union of Algerian Women)

UNJA   *Union Nationale de la Jeunesse Algérienne* (National Union of Algerian Youth)

UNLD	*Union Nationale pour la Liberté et la Démocratie* (National Union for Liberty and Democracy)
UNPA	*Union Nationale des Paysans Algériens* (National Union of Algerian Peasants)
UNPCA	*Union Nationale des Petits Commerçants et Artisans* (National Union of Small Merchants and Craftsmen)

Suggested Readings

BOOKS AND ARTICLES IN ENGLISH

Abun-Nasr, Jamil M. *A History of the Maghrib.* 2d ed. Cambridge: Cambridge University Press, 1975.

Bennoune, Mahfoud. "Algerian Peasants and National Politics." *MERIP Reports,* no. 48 (June 1976), pp. 3–24.

———. "The Industrialization of Algeria: An Overview," in Halim Barakat, ed., *Contemporary North Africa: Issues of Development and Integration.* Washington, D.C.: Center for Contemporary Arab Studies, 1985, pp. 178–213.

Berque, Jacques. *French North Africa: The Maghrib Between Two World Wars.* London: Faber and Faber, 1967.

Blair, Thomas L. *"The Land to Those Who Work It": Algeria's Experiment in Workers' Management.* Garden City, N.Y.: Anchor Books, 1970.

Bourdieu, Pierre. "The Algerian Subproletariat," in I. William Zartman, ed., *Man, State, and Society in the Contemporary Maghrib.* New York: Praeger, 1973, pp. 83–92.

———. *The Algerians.* Boston: Beacon Press, 1962.

Danziger, Raphael. *Abd Al-Qadir and the Algerians: Resistance to the French and Internal Consolidation.* New York: Holmes and Meier, 1977.

Descloitres, R. and C., and J. C. Reverdy. "Urban Organization and Social Structure in Algeria," in I. William Zartman, ed., *Man, State, and Society in the Contemporary Maghrib.* New York: Praeger, 1973, pp. 424–438.

Entelis, John P. "Algeria: Technocratic Rule, Military Power," in I. William Zartman and others, *Political Elites in Arab North Africa.* New York: Longman, 1982, pp. 92–143.

———. "Algeria in World Politics: Foreign Policy Orientation and the New International Economic Order." *American-Arab Affairs,* no. 6 (Fall 1983), pp. 70–78.

———. *Comparative Politics of North Africa: Algeria, Morocco, and Tunisia.* Syracuse, N.Y.: Syracuse University Press, 1980.

――――. "Democratic and Popular Republic of Algeria," in David E. Long and Bernard Reich, eds., *The Government and Politics of the Middle East and North Africa.* Boulder, Colo.: Westview Press, 1980, pp. 415–436.

――――. "Elite Political Culture and Socialization in Algeria: Tensions and Discontinuities." *The Middle East Journal* 35, no. 2 (Spring 1981), pp. 191–208.

Etienne, Bruno. "Clientelism in Algeria," in Ernest Gellner and John Waterbury, eds., *Patrons and Clients in Mediterranean Societies.* London: Duckworth, 1977, pp. 291–307.

Fanon, Frantz. *A Dying Colonialism.* New York: Grove Press, 1967.

――――. *The Wretched of the Earth.* New York: Grove Press, 1968.

Farsoun, Karen. "State Capitalism in Algeria." *MERIP Reports,* no. 35 (February 1975), pp. 3–30.

Gallagher, Charles F. *The United States and North Africa: Morocco, Algeria, and Tunisia.* Cambridge: Harvard University Press, 1963.

Gellner, Ernest. "The Unknown Apollo of Biskra: The Social Base of Algerian Puritanism." *Government and Opposition* 9, no. 3 (Summer 1974), pp. 277–310.

Gordon, David. *The Passing of French Algeria.* London: Oxford University Press, 1966.

Griffin, Keith B. "Algerian Agriculture in Transition," in I. William Zartman, ed., *Man, State, and Society in the Contemporary Maghrib.* New York: Praeger, 1973, pp. 395–414.

Heggoy, Alf Andrew. *Historical Dictionary of Algeria.* Metuchen, N.J.: The Scarecrow Press, 1981.

――――. *Insurgency and Counterinsurgency in Algeria.* Bloomington: Indiana University Press, 1972.

Helie, Damien. "Industrial Self-Management in Algeria," in I. William Zartman, ed., *Man, State, and Society in the Contemporary Maghrib.* New York: Praeger, 1973, pp. 465–474.

Hermassi, Elbaki. *Leadership and National Development in North Africa: A Comparative Study.* Berkeley: University of California Press, 1972.

Horne, Alistair. *A Savage War of Peace: Algeria, 1954–1962.* Middlesex, England: Penguin Books, 1977.

Humbaraci, Arslan. *Algeria: A Revolution that Failed—A Political History since 1954.* New York: Praeger, 1966.

Hutchinson, Martha Crenshaw. *Revolutionary Terrorism: The FLN in Algeria, 1954–1962.* Stanford, Calif.: Hoover Institution Press, 1978.

Jackson, Henry F. *The FLN in Algeria: Party Development in a Revolutionary Society.* Westport, Conn.: Greenwood Press, 1977.

Knapp, Wilfrid. *North West Africa: A Political and Economic Survey.* 3d ed. Oxford: Oxford University Press, 1977 ("Algeria," pp. 51–173).

Knauss, Peter R. "Algeria Under Boumedienne: The Mythical Revolution 1965 to 1978," in Isaac J. Mowoe, ed., *The Performance of Soldiers as Governors: African Politics and the African Military.* Washington, D.C.: University Press of America, 1980, pp. 27–100.

———. "Algeria's 'Agrarian Revolution': Peasant Control or Control of Peasants?" *African Studies Review* 20, no. 3 (December 1977), pp. 65–78.

Korany, Bahgat. "Third Worldism and Pragmatic Radicalism: The Foreign Policy of Algeria" in Bahgat Korany and Ali E. Hillal Dessouki, eds., *The Foreign Policies of Arab States*. Boulder, Colo.: Westview Press, 1984, pp. 79–118.

Laroui, Abdallah. *The History of the Maghrib: An Interpretative Essay*. Princeton, N.J.: Princeton University Press, 1977.

Lawless, Richard I. "Algeria: The Contradictions of Rapid Industrialization" in Richard Lawless and Allan Findlay, eds., *North Africa: Contemporary Politics and Economic Development*. London: Croom Helm, 1984, pp. 153–190.

———. *Algerian Bibliography: English Language Publications 1830–1973*. London and New York: Bowker, in association with the Centre of Middle Eastern and Islamic Studies of the University of Durham, 1976.

Lawless, Richard I., comp. *Algeria*. Santa Barbara, Calif.: CLIO Press, 1980.

Lawless, Richard I., and Gerald H. Blake. *Tlemcen: Continuity and Change in an Algerian and Islamic Town*. Boulder, Colo.: Westview Press, 1976.

Lazreg, Marnia. *The Emergence of Classes in Algeria: Colonialism and Socio-Political Change*. Boulder, Colo.: Westview Press, 1976.

Leca, Jean. "Algerian Socialism: Nationalism, Industrialization, and State-Building" in Helen Desfosses and Jacques Levesque, eds., *Socialism in the Third World*. New York: Praeger, 1975, pp. 121–160.

Lewis, William H. "The Decline of Algeria's FLN." *The Middle East Journal* 20, no. 2 (Spring 1966), pp. 161–172.

MacKendrick, Paul. *The North African Stones Speak*. Chapel Hill: The University of North Carolina Press, 1980.

Marshall, Susan E., and Randall G. Stokes. "Tradition and the Veil: Female Status in Tunisia and Algeria." *Journal of Modern African Studies* 19, no. 4 (December 1981), pp. 625–646.

Minces, Juliette. *The House of Obedience: Women in Arab Society*. London: Zed Press, 1982.

Miner, Horace, and George De Vos. *Oasis and Casbah: Algerian Culture and Personality in Change*. Ann Arbor: University of Michigan Press, 1960.

Montagne, Robert. *The Berbers: Their Social and Political Organisation*. London: Frank Cass, 1973.

Moore, Clement Henry. *Politics in North Africa: Algeria, Morocco, and Tunisia*. Boston: Little, Brown, 1970.

Mortimer, Robert A. "Algeria and the Politics of International Economic Reform." *Orbis* 21, no. 3 (Fall 1977), pp. 671–700.

———. "Algeria's New Sultan." *Current History* 80, no. 470 (December 1982), pp. 418–421, 433–434.

———. "The Algerian Revolution in Search of the African Revolution." *The Journal of Modern African Studies* 8, no. 3 (October 1970), pp. 363–387.

———. "Global Economy and African Foreign Policy: The Algerian Model." *African Studies Review* 27, no. 1 (March 1984), pp. 1–22.

————. *The Third World Coalition in International Politics.* 2d, updated ed. New York: Praeger, 1984.

Nellis, John R. *The Algerian National Charter of 1976: Content, Public Reaction, and Significance.* Washington, D.C.: Georgetown University Center for Contemporary Arab Studies, 1980.

————. "Algerian Socialism and its Critics." *Canadian Journal of Political Science* 13, no. 3 (September 1980), pp. 481–587.

————. "A Comparative Assessment of the Development Performances of Algeria and Tunisia." *The Middle East Journal* 37, no. 3 (Summer 1983), pp. 370–393.

————. "Decentralization in North Africa: Problems of Policy Implementation" in G. Shabbir Cheema and Dennis A. Rondinelli, eds., *Decentralization and Development: Policy Implementation in Developing Countries.* Beverly Hills, Calif.: Sage Publications, 1983, pp. 127–182.

————. "Maladministration: Causes or Result of Underdevelopment? The Algeria Example." *Canadian Journal of African Studies* 13, no. 3 (1980), pp. 407–422.

————. "Socialist Management in Algeria." *Journal of Modern African Studies* 15, no. 4 (December 1977), pp. 529–554.

Nelson, Harold D., ed. *Algeria: A Country Study.* 3d ed. Washington, D.C.: Government Printing Office, 1979.

Ottaway, David B. "Algeria" in Donald K. Emmerson, ed., *Students and Politics in Developing Nations.* New York: Praeger, 1968, pp. 3–36.

Ottaway, David and Marina. *Algeria: The Politics of a Socialist Revolution.* Berkeley: University of California Press, 1970.

Pfeifer, Karen. *Agrarian Reform Under State Capitalism in Algeria.* Boulder, Colo.: Westview Press, 1985.

Quandt, William B. "The Berbers in the Algerian Political Elite" in Ernest Gellner and Charles Micaud, eds., *Arabs and Berbers: From Tribe to Nation in North Africa.* Lexington, Mass.: Lexington Books, 1972, pp. 285–303.

————. *Revolution and Political Leadership: Algeria, 1954–1968.* Cambridge: MIT Press, 1969.

Roberts, Hugh. "Algeria: Thirty Years after the Revolution." *Africa Report* 29, no. 6 (November-December 1984), pp. 4–9.

————. "The Politics of Algerian Socialism" in Richard Lawless and Allan Findlay, ed., *North Africa: Contemporary Politics and Economic Development.* London: Croom Helm, 1984, pp. 5–49.

Roughton, Richard A. "Algeria and the June 1967 Arab-Israeli War." *The Middle East Journal* 23, no. 4 (Autumn 1969), pp. 433–444.

Saivetz, Carol R. "Algerian Socialism under Ben Bella and Boumediene: The Soviet Assessment." *The Maghreb Review* 7, nos. 3–4 (May-August 1982), pp. 87–93.

Smith, Tony. "The Political and Economic Ambitions of Algerian Land Reform, 1962–1974." *The Middle East Journal* 29, no. 3 (Summer 1975), pp. 259–278.

Spencer, William. *Algiers in the Age of the Corsairs*. Norman: University of Oklahoma Press, 1976.

Sutton, Keith. "Algeria: Centre-Down Development, State Capitalism, and Emergent Decentralization" in W. B. Stohr and D. R. Fraser Taylor, eds., *Development from Above or Below?* London: John Wiley, 1981, pp. 351–375.

―――. "Population Resettlement—Traumatic Upheavals and the Algerian Experience." *The Journal of Modern African Studies* 15, no. 2 (June 1977), pp. 279–300.

Tlemcani, Rachid. *State and Revolution in Algeria*. London: The Zed Press, forthcoming.

Valensi, Lucette. *On the Eve of Colonialism: North Africa Before the French Conquest*. New York: Africana Publishing Co. 1977.

Vallin, Raymond. "Muslim Socialism in Algeria" in I. William Zartman, ed., *Man, State, and Society in the Contemporary Maghrib*. New York: Praeger, 1973, pp. 50–64.

Vatin, Jean-Claude. "Popular Puritanism versus State Reformism: Islam in Algeria" in James P. Piscatori, ed., *Islam in the Political Process*. Cambridge: Cambridge University Press, 1983, pp. 98–121.

―――. "Religious Resistance and State Power in Algeria" in Alex Cudsi and Ali E. Hillal Dessouki, eds., *Islam and Power in the Contemporary Muslim World*. Baltimore, MD: The Johns Hopkins Press, 1981.

Wolf, Eric. *Peasant Wars of the Twentieth Century*. New York: Harper and Row, 1969 ("Algeria," pp. 209–247).

Wolf, John B. *The Barbary Coast: Algiers under the Turks, 1500–1830*. New York: W. W. Norton, 1979.

Zartman, I. William. "Algeria: A Post-Revolutionary Elite" in Frank Tachau, ed., *Political Elites and Political Development in the Middle East*. New York: Schenkman Publishing Co., 1975, pp. 255–292.

―――. "The Algerian Army in Politics" in I. William Zartman, ed., *Man, State, and Society in the Contemporary Maghrib*. New York: Praeger, 1973, pp. 211–227.

BOOKS AND ARTICLES IN FRENCH

Ageron, Charles-Robert. *Histoire de l'Algérie Contemporaine. Tome 2: De l'Insurrection de 1871 au Déclenchement de la Guerre de Libération (1954)*. Paris: Presses Universitaires de France, 1979.

Balta, Paul, and Claudine Rulleau. *L'Algérie des Algériens: Vingt Ans Après*. Paris: Les Editions Ouvrières, 1981.

Benhouria, Tahar. *L'Economie de l'Algérie*. Paris: Maspero, 1980.

Benissad, M. E. *Economie du Développement de l'Algérie: Sous-Développement et Socialisme*. 2d ed. Paris: Economica, 1982.

Bourdieu, Pierre, and Abdelmalek Sayad. *Le Déracinement: La Crise de l'Agriculture Traditionnelle en Algérie*. Paris: Les Editions de Minuit, 1964.

Bouzar, Wadi. *La Mouvance et la Pause: Regards sur la Société Algérienne.* 2 vols. Algiers: SNED, 1983.

Burgat, François, and Michel Nancy. *Les Villages Socialistes de la Révolution Agraire Algérienne, 1972–1982.* Paris: Editions du CNRS, 1984.

Camau, Michel. *La Notion de Démocratie dans la Pensée des Dirigeants Maghrébins.* Paris: Editions du CNRS, 1971.

Chaliand, Gerard, and Juliette Minces. *L'Algérie Indépendante: Bilan d'une Révolution Nationale.* Paris: Maspero, 1972.

Chevaldonne, François. *La Communication Inégal: L'Accès aux Medias dans les Campagnes Algériennes.* Paris: Editions du CNRS, 1981.

Chikh, Slimane. *L'Algérie en Armes ou le Temps des Certitudes.* Paris: Economica, 1981.

Cubertafond, Bernard. *La République Algérienne Démocratique et Populaire.* Paris: Presses Universitaires de France, 1979.

Dahmani, Mohamed. *L'Algérie: Légitimité Historique et Continuité Politique.* Paris: Editions Le Sycomore, 1980.

Déjeux, Jean. *La Littérature Algérienne Contemporaine.* Paris: Presses Universitaires de France, 1975.

Dersa [pseud.]. *L'Algérie en Débat: Luttes et Développement.* Paris: Maspero, 1981.

Dufour, Dany. "L'Enseignement en Algérie," *Maghreb-Machrek,* no. 80 (April-May-June 1978), pp. 33–53.

Durand, Jean-Pierre. "Exacerbation des Contradictions Sociales et Resserrement des Alliances Politiques en Algérie" in Jean Leca and others, *Développements Politiques au Maghreb: Aménagements Institutionnels et Processus Electoraux.* Paris: Editions du CNRS, 1979, pp. 123–140.

Etienne, Bruno. *L'Algérie, Cultures et Révolution.* Paris: Seuil, 1977.

Gauthier, Yves, and Joël Kernarec. *Naissance et Croissance de la République Algérienne Démocratique et Populaire.* Paris: Editions Marketing, 1978.

Gourdon, Hubert. "Citoyen, Travailleur, Frère: La Deuxième Constitutionnalisation du Système Politique Algérien" in Jean Leca and others, *Développements et Politiques au Maghreb: Aménagements Institutionnels et Processus Electoraux.* Paris: Editions du CNRS, 1979, pp. 99–122.

Grimaud, Nicole. *La Charte Nationale Algérienne (27 Juin 1976).* Paris: La Documentation Française, 1976.

————. *La Politique Extérieure de l'Algérie.* Paris: Edition Karthala, 1984.

Ibrahimi, Ahmed Taleb. *De la Décolonisation à la Révolution Culturelle (1962–1972).* 2d ed. Algiers: SNED, 1976.

Julien, Charles-André. *Histoire de l'Algérie Contemporaine. Tome 1: La Conquête et les Débuts de la Colonisation (1827–1871).* Paris: Presses Universitaires de France, 1979.

Lacheraf, Mostefa. *L'Algérie: Nation et Société.* Paris: Maspero, 1976.

Leca, Jean, and Jean-Claude Vatin. *L'Algérie Politique: Institutions et Régime.* Paris: Presses de la Fondation Nationale des Sciences Politiques, 1975.

Lucas, Philippe, and Jean-Claude Vatin. *L'Algérie des Anthropologues.* New ed. Paris: Maspero, 1982.

Minces, Juliette. *L'Algérie de Boumediène.* Paris: Presses de la Cité, 1979.

Mutin, Georges. "Agriculture et Dépendance Alimentaire en Algérie." *Maghreb-Machrek,* no. 90 (October-November-December 1980), pp. 40–64.

Ourabah, Mahmoud. *Les Transformations Economiques de l'Algérie.* Paris: Publisud, 1983.

Sanson, Henri. *Laïcité Islamique en Algérie.* Paris: Editions du CNRS, 1983.

Schnetzler, Jacques. *Le Développement Algérien.* Paris: Masson, 1981.

Vatin, Jean-Claude. *L'Algérie Politique: Histoire et Société.* 2d ed. Paris: Presses de la Fondation Nationale des Sciences Politiques, 1983.

Zartman, William. "L'Elite Algérienne sous la Présidence de Chadli Benjedid." *Maghreb-Machrek,* no. 106 (October-November-December 1984), pp. 37–53.

Index